The Theory of
Equilibrium Growth

The Theory of Equilibrium Growth

A. K. DIXIT

OXFORD UNIVERSITY PRESS

1976

Oxford University Press, Ely House, London W.1

OXFORD LONDON GLASGOW NEW YORK
TORONTO MELBOURNE WELLINGTON CAPE TOWN
IBADAN NAIROBI DAR ES SALAAM LUSAKA ADDIS ABABA
KUALA LUMPUR SINGAPORE JAKARTA HONG KONG TOKYO
DELHI BOMBAY CALCUTTA MADRAS KARACHI

British Library Cataloguing in Publication Data

Dixit, A K
    The theory of equilibrium growth.
    Bibl. — Index.
    ISBN 0–19–877080–4
    ISBN 0–19–877081–2 PBK.
    1. Title
    339.5   HD82
    Economic development
    Equilibrium (Economics)

Printed in Great Britain
by Fletcher & Son Ltd., Norwich

Preface

This book has two major objectives. The first is to bridge the wide gap that exists between the elementary textbooks on growth theory, such as Solow's *Growth Theory: An Exposition*, and the advanced ones like Wan's *Economic Growth* and Burmeister and Dobell's *Mathematical Theories of Economic Growth.* I have tried to explain to the general economic theorist several of the methods and results of recent research, without developing in full detail the associated mathematical machinery. In each case, I have cited several references for those readers whose idea of this middle ground does not quite coincide with mine.

The second objective is to highlight and clarify the framework of intertemporal equilibrium that underlies much of growth theory. This approach allows only certain and foreseen change, and therefore could not hope to provide a complete theory of growth. However, it yields several very important insights, and provides a systematic and usable framework for economic analysis of growth. Moreover, many economists who deny the relevance of such a method usually use some equilibrium notions without realizing it. Therefore it is vital to achieve a proper understanding of the approach from the outset, and to be aware of its strengths and weaknesses, uses and abuses. This is the philosophy behind this book, and this is the reason why the first chapter contains a critical discussion of a kind that is commonly concealed from undergraduates and even beginning postgraduates. It is also my justification for a seemingly excessive emphasis on the relations between the prices of assets and other prices and rents. It will be found that this greatly clarifies and unifies the treatment of such diverse topics as depreciation, technological progress, optimum saving, and the depletion of natural resources.

In this sense, my approach is firmly neo-classical. However, it is an important part of my purpose to show that there is a great deal more to neo-classical growth theory than the one-sector Solow-Swan model. With the exception of Meade's *A Neo-Classical Theory of Economic Growth*, models which prove this point are largely confined to very advanced books and articles. Also, the years that have passed since the appearance of Meade's book have seen many new developments.

Theories of growth with many assets, of optimum saving and resource depletion, and of technological progress, have all advanced a great deal. Notable advances in techniques have included the use of 'dual' methods, using cost and revenue functions instead of production functions. I have attempted to make these developments more accessible to the average student of economic theory.

My methodological discussion owes a great deal to the influence of Bliss' *Capital Theory and the Distribution of Income,* and I often refer to it for support and detailed analyses of some of my assertions. I hope my book will prepare students for reading his substantive arguments with greater ease. With this in mind, I have left almost all of capital theory to his superior treatment. Similarly, I have not developed the general theory of multi-sector models, and have chosen instead to illustrate many of the relevant points through simpler expository constructs.

Some knowledge of elementary differential calculus is indispensable for a proper study of growth theory, and I use it freely. Integral calculus is used much more sparingly, and alternative expressions using sums are often provided. Whenever readers find some mathematical details difficult, they should omit them at least at the first reading, and confine themselves to the associated verbal rationalizations or explanations. Models of embodied technological progress are probably the most likely instance where this will be necessary.

I have used a notational innovation that should be clarified. I use symbols consisting of pairs of letters for names of variables. For example, sp denotes the propensity to save out of profit income, and is not a product of s and p. This is like the usage in computer programming, and I have adopted it for the same reason, namely to allow a greater range and flexibility in naming variables without requiring subscripts or superscripts. It also enables me to avoid the clumsy notation of double subscripts altogether. Of course, since juxtaposition of letters now makes them into one symbol, I have to show products explicitly by dots.

I have accumulated several debts to colleagues in the course of thinking about this book and writing it. I am particularly grateful to Robert Solow for detailed and useful comments on an earlier draft, to James Mirrlees for giving me access to some of his work in progress that greatly improved my treatment of two-sector models, and to Norman

Ireland for his careful reading of the manuscript. I am also grateful to Peter Diamond, Walter Eltis, Geoffrey Heal, Peter Law, Nicholas Stern, Paul Stoneman and John Williamson for their comments on individual chapters. I am, of course, solely responsible for errors and hasty judgements that may have remained or been introduced into later versions. Finally, I thank Jenny Johnson, Shirley Hail, Joy Gardner and Yvonne Slater for their splendid co-operative typing effort amidst many other duties.

August 1975   A.K.D.

Contents

1. THE METHOD OF EQUILIBRIUM GROWTH THEORY   1
   1. Identities and theories   1
   2. Steady states   7
   3. Equilibrium growth   10
   Notes   14

2. PRODUCTION, COSTS, AND PRICES   16
   1. Fixed coefficients   17
   2. Factor substitution   19
   3. Production functions   25
   4. Technological change   30
   5. Several goods and factors   33
   6. Asset prices and rents   37
   Notes   42

3. ONE-SECTOR MODELS   44
   1. The Harrod-Domar model   46
   2. The Solow-Swan model   49
   3. Comparisons between steady states   55
   4. The Cambridge model   60
   5. Comments on saving behaviour   65
   6. Depreciation   66
   Notes   72

4. TECHNOLOGICAL PROGRESS   73
   1. Factor augmentation and bias   73
   2. Returns to scale   79
   3. Measurement   83
   4. Embodied technological progress   85
   5. Embodiment: fixed coefficients   88
   6. Embodiment with substitution   91
   7. Embodiment: putty-clay   94
   Notes   97

5. OPTIMUM SAVING   99
   1. The Keynes-Ramsey formula   99
   2. Optimum growth   103
   3. Generalizations and comments   112
   4. Life-cycle saving   116
   Notes   122

6. TWO-SECTOR MODELS   124
   1. Momentary equilibrium   124
   2. Equilibrium growth   130
   3. Comparisons between steady states   133
   4. Some generalizations   137
   5. Models with two assets   142
   6. Multi-sector models   146
   Notes   146

7. NATURAL RESOURCES   148
   1. Land   149
   2. Depletion plans   152
   3. Capital accumulation   156
   4. Steady states   160
   5. Equilibrium growth   163
   6. Optimum saving and resource use   166
   7. Further extensions   171
   Notes   172

8. DISEQUILIBRIUM MODELS   173
   1. Income-expenditure models   175
   2. Monetary models   179
   3. Temporary equilibrium   183
   4. Scale economies and monopoly   186
   5. Managerial and behavioural theories   188
   6. Concluding comments   191
   Notes   191

Bibliography   194

Index   203

1. The Method of Equilibrium Growth Theory

1. Identities and theories

Growth theory is full of pitfalls that await those who neglect some important conceptual distinctions. These pitfalls can be illustrated using a very simple identity and some equally simple consequences of it. Consider the ex post accounting equality between net investment and net saving in the economy at any time t:

$$I_a(t) = S_a(t) \qquad (1.1)$$

where the subscript a indicates actual or realized values. This can be transformed into other identities that appear more interesting and useful. First, let Y denote a measure of national product and K a measure of the stock of capital in the economy. Then we have

$$I_a(t)/K_a(t) = \{S_a(t)/Y_a(t)\}/\{K_a(t)/Y_a(t)\}, \quad \text{or}$$
$$g_a(t) = s_a(t)/v_a(t) \qquad (1.2)$$

where g stands for the rate of growth of capital, s for the proportion of saving in national income, and v for the capital/output ratio. Next, let P denote profits (in absence of uncertainty these will generally consist of the interest on capital), and write

$$I_a(t)/K_a(t) = \{S_a(t)/P_a(t)\} \cdot \{P_a(t)/K_a(t)\}, \quad \text{or}$$
$$g_a(t) = sp_a(t) \cdot r_a(t) \qquad (1.3)$$

where r denotes the rate of profit (here equal to the rate of interest) and sp the ratio of saving to profits. Finally, let πp stand for the proportion of profits in national income, and note that

$$S_a(t)/Y_a(t) = \{S_a(t)/P_a(t)\} \cdot \{P_a(t)/Y_a(t)\}, \quad \text{or}$$
$$s_a(t) = sp_a(t) \cdot \pi p_a(t) \qquad (1.4)$$

We can then combine equations (1.2) – (1.4) to write

$$\pi p_a(t) = r_a(t) \cdot v_a(t) \qquad (1.5)$$

As a matter of fact, even such mechanical manipulations of identities are not free from conceptual and practical problems. National income and wealth aggregates are scalar measures of lists of heterogeneous commodities, where the quantities are multiplied by market prices and the values added. Even if we leave aside all the practical problems that arise from market failures, we cannot avoid the conceptual problems associated with index numbers, and in particular the distinction between 'real' and 'value' measures.[1] While the choice of a measure can depend on the question being asked, it is essential to maintain consistency in the treatment of all the variables under consideration. All these issues are a vital part of the theory, but there are other questions that are at least as important, for they concern the whole approach to the theory, and I think they ought to be considered first.

We often find a superficial resemblance between accounting identities like the ones above, and equilibrium conditions which give real content to much of economic theory. The important difference is that the identities hold for actual magnitudes and the equilibrium conditions pertain to the planned ones. Economic analysis can become hopelessly confused if this distinction is blurred, and elementary textbooks try to hammer it home by using well-known 'paradoxes' and 'trick questions'.

The simplest example of this occurs in the theory of price determination in a competitive industry. Anything bought by someone is sold by someone else, so the actual quantity bought is always equal to the actual quantity sold. But the condition of equality of planned demand and planned supply is the basis of the theory of market equilibrium. It serves to determine the equilibrium value of the variable on which the planned demand and supply are supposed to depend, namely the price. We need knowledge of both functional relations – the demand and supply curves – in order to find the equilibrium price, and the common value of the planned quantities of demand and supply at this price.

The process is simpler for some forms of such functional dependence than for others. For example, if the supply curve is horizontal at the level of the minimum unit cost of production, we have a purely cost-determined price. An inspection of the relevant identities often suggests such simple cases, and their simple and attractive solutions are a great temptation. Unlike most temptations, however, this one should be resisted. Not only will the functional forms usually prove to be very poor approximations, but also the mode of thought will draw attention away from some crucial economic aspects of the problem.

For example, if the planned demand and supply in one market are significantly affected by prices in other markets, then the condition of equality of planned demand and supply in any one market will not suffice to determine the equilibrium price in it, no matter how complex the functional forms we allow. We must consider similar conditions in the related markets to determine the equilibrium prices in all of them together, either by an explicit solution of the equations simultaneously, or if that is not possible, by some substitute process of iteration.[2] Finally, even such a general equilibrium theory may at times prove a poor approximation to reality, and the common value of actual demand and supply may remain very far from the planned value of one or both. Investigation of this question is the study of stability, of the manner in which plans and prices are modified when earlier plans are not realized, and of the consequences. Some 'stories' of such adjustment processes in a single market are told in elementary textbooks. With many interrelated markets, the stories quickly run into some formidable technical and conceptual difficulties.[3]

All these points can be equally well illustrated by the other main topic of elementary textbooks, namely the determination of national income in the short run, using the Keynesian cross and the IS and LM curves. This will be a useful exercise for the reader.

A similar situation arises in growth theory. The identities (1.2) − (1.5) suggest assumptions which neglect several important economic influences and impose restrictions on various functional relationships, thereby producing quick but poor theories of determination of equilibrium values of some of the variables. Two examples will illustrate my argument.

Confine attention to situations of equilibrium. Assume that $g_a(t)$ is equal to an exogenously specified number g at all times. Assume also that wage-earners plan to consume all of their wages, while profit-earners plan to save a constant and exogenously specified fraction sp of profits. Thus $sp_a(t)$ will equal sp for all t. From (1.3), we see that

$r_a(t) = g/sp$ for all t, and we have a theory of the rate of profit: it is constant and equal to r, which is defined in terms of the assumed data by

$$r = g/sp \qquad (1.6)$$

Now suppose further that $v_a(t)$ is also constant and exogenously fixed at the value v. Then (1.5) says that the proportion of national income going to profits is constant and equal to πp, which is defined in terms of the data by the relation

$$\pi p = r \cdot v \qquad (1.7)$$

where r is to be found from (1.6). This gives us a theory of distribution.

On a different line of reasoning, suppose we assume instead that an exogenous and constant proportion s of all income is saved, while retaining the assumptions about the constancy of g and v. Then (1.2) becomes $g = s/v$, and with all three magnitudes fixed exogenously, there is no reason why this equality should hold. Thus we have posed a theoretical inconsistency in the idea of equilibrium growth, which is even more exciting.

These are not meant to be caricatures. The first type of theory, with some generalizations, has long been advocated by the 'Cambridge School'. The second is an interpretation placed by some writers on the work of Harrod. Both strands of thought are common in the literature, and I shall return to discuss them in detail in later sections. It will be more useful to examine some of their grossest shortcomings at this stage.

Consider first the assumption of a constant capital/output ratio. This is often claimed to be a fixed feature of the technology. But that is rarely an adequate explanation. When both Y and K are indices of diverse collections of commodities, relative prices can play a role in determining v. Even if fixed coefficients rule in each production process, aggregate factor use will depend on the composition of output so long as different commodities require different factor proportions. For commodities which can be produced in alternative ways using different proportions of inputs, the most economical production process will depend on the relative prices of all factors.

Further, output and factor markets are connected by the income and expenditure decisions of various agents. It is only in very special cases that are tantamount to assuming that all commodities in the economy can be aggregated into one, that we can even conceive of a purely technological determination of v. In any case, the question of whether we can cut through the general complex interactions of demand and supply in all markets should itself be a subject of economic inquiry. It is clearly not a question that a growth theorist could conceivably claim to be outside his scope of research.

If we are granted the circumstances that make v constant, we can analyze the constancy of the growth rate slightly further. In the absence of cumulative tendencies towards unemployment of labour or excess capacity, the rate of growth of labour must equal that of capital. It is this former rate that is then taken to be exogenous. Even this is not very satisfactory. There may be some little justification for leaving the theory of population growth largely outside the domain of economic analysis. But if there is any technological progress going on in the economy, the rate of growth of labour has to be measured in units of its economic effectiveness, and we cannot leave the process of advance of technology outside our scope for very long. Besides, as soon as we readmit the earlier complexities of a multiplicity of commodities, we must face the questions of whether all capital goods must grow at this common rate, and of what forces might operate to achieve this.

Such strictures apply even more strongly to the treatment of saving, whether out of profits or out of all of income. The decision to save is a choice made by economic agents in recognition of the time dimension of economic activity. Growth theorists would be overlooking a potentially vital part of the process they examine if, instead of analyzing the motives behind such a choice and including its operation in their theories, they assume it to be outside their domain and given in the form of simple rules that relate saving only to profits or to national income, neglecting a host of other economic factors that could influence the choice, and in turn be influenced by it.

All these critical comments involve two common themes. First, certain variables are assumed to be exogenous when they should be made subjects of economic analysis. Secondly, these are also taken to be constant over time. Both features are undesirable and unrealistic, but the first is by far the more serious shortcoming. For example, if it were

agreed that the capital/output ratio could be taken to be an exogenous
datum, then the possibility that it could vary over time would matter
less from the point of view of exposition of the theory. In so far as such
expositions are designed to help us comprehend the complex economic
forces at work by some simplification and selection, the use of some
exogenous function $v(t)$ could only be an unnecessary complication. In
applying the theory to a specific situation given a particular function
$v(t)$, we could always carry out the necessary numerical calculation.
Thus, if exogeneity is granted, then constancy is a mere expository
convenience without serious loss. It is exogeneity that is the really
serious and undesirable restriction. When variation over time in one
economic variable interacts with others, this feature should be an
integral part of the theory, and its neglect can produce very misleading
ideas.

I must admit that all this is really a matter of degree. Analysis can
always be pushed further back, even beyond what is conventionally
regarded as the boundary of economics, but each such step involves
increasing effort. Thus there can be a net gain from delimiting areas
which exclude outside considerations. After all, solid state physics
would gain nothing, and lose a great deal, if it insisted on accounting for
the electro-magnetic interactions between all particles in the universe and
and a particular piece of semiconductor material. All growth theorists
have found it useful to discuss models involving drastic aggregation, or
exogenous technological progress, or constant saving propensities, or all
three together. Some of this work will be discussed in the following
sections. Ultimately, the readers must form their own judgement as to
whether the various theories have been too narrow in their scope,
bearing in mind the pitfalls indicated above.

In so doing, it is unfortunately necessary to accept something of a
double standard. On one hand, there is always much room for
improvement beyond the existing state of the theory. There must be an
element of permanent dissatisfaction with the current state of any living
science if progress is to be made. On the other hand, the world does not
wait upon such advances, and we must often form judgements based on
the existing knowledge. This puts a premium on applicability, and on a
willingness to accept imperfect theories temporarily on faith. It is
difficult to achieve a balance between these two widely different
demands of exactitude and practicality, but it is worth a try.

2. Steady states

Growth theory finds it very useful to have 'benchmark' situations with some simple features like constant growth rates, saving ratios, income distribution, economic life of machines, or relative magnitudes of prices and quantities of all goods. Such situations are called steady states. Intelligent use of steady states differs from the earlier naive use in that the magnitudes in whose constancy we are interested are not imposed as exogenous assumptions, but derived from the workings of the theory. Different models attain this ideal in different degrees.

I shall devote the rest of this chapter to a general discussion of the way in which growth theory is built around the concept of steady states, and some comments on the resulting structure. The two go naturally together, but the first is a useful prelude to a study of various growth models, while the second is based on experience of them. Students will therefore find it profitable to return to these pages after reading some of the later chapters.

I shall take as my point of departure the fact that most of economic theory is tied together by, and revolves around, some concept of equilibrium. This poses a problem in the context of growth, where the main new feature of interest is the role of time. Inputs at one date can produce outputs at a later date, and consumers attempt to use income at one date to purchase commodities at another. Such demands for, and supplies of, various shifts of resources across time are an essential feature of growth. An essential aspect of equilibrium theory, on the other hand, is its decentralization of information. No agent in the economy needs to know anything about the rest of it except the conditions in the markets in which he deals; equilibrium prices are sufficient information in competitive conditions. All this is problematic if the markets pertain to commodities at later dates. There is a formal dodge around the problem: we simply label commodities by dates of availability, and assume that the equilibrium prices in all such dated commodities are known to all agents and that there is full freedom to use proceeds of sales in any one of these markets for making purchases in any other. For example, the supply of saving at date t is regarded as demand for commodities to be delivered at dates $(t + 1), (t + 2), \ldots,$ and the demand for investment at date t is the derived demand for intermediate inputs for the production process which will make such commodities available at these later dates. This is the basis for the treatment of capital following Irving Fisher that can be found in price theory texts.[4] There are two ways in which we could view the process. The first is to suppose that all the markets are held and cleared at the beginning of time. The objects bought and sold are contracts for delivery of stated commodities at stated dates, and the subsequent economic activity consists solely of the fulfilment of such contracts. The second is to suppose that equilibrium prices of commodities at later dates are confidently and correctly forecast by all agents, and they act on the basis fo such forecasts. Both these stories, 'perfect futures market' and 'perfect foresight', are quite hypothetical, and are meant to be no more than useful starting points for further analysis. They indicate what would happen in an economy in which the future was fully foreseen and reflected in the present actions, and enable us to use this as a starting point for further study of the consequences of the lack of such perfect information. This division of the problem is often fruitful.

If all prices and quantities are either constant or changing at constant rates through time, we at least have a logically credible setting in which agents can form confident and correct forecasts. This is why steady states are such a convenience. There are two other considerations which make steady states an interesting subject. First, they provide a simple setting that is consistent with Kaldor's stylized facts about growth, notably constant rates of growth, rates of profit, and capital/output ratios. Second, they provide a convenient method, and in some cases of multiplicity of goods the only available method, of getting a conceptual handle on the difficult problems of dynamic economics. This is to be understood as one stage of a research strategy, and experience in similar contexts seems to suggest that it is a useful one.

So analysis of growth using steady states as benchmarks consists of two broad areas. One is the characterization of steady states, and the essentially comparative static examination of how these characteristics depend on the behavioural assumptions and the exogenous parameters. The second is the examination of more general patterns of growth, and of whether they have a steady state as a limiting outcome. Both parts are important, and steady states can be securely established as a useful central concept of growth theory only on the basis of the two taken together. It goes without saying that the second question is generally far more difficult, and it is only in very special cases of highly aggregative models that a reasonably satisfactory analysis of both questions has been possible. When we have a characterization of steady states without an analysis of stability, we must regard it as only one step in the development of the theory. It may be a useful step, and a promising line of research, but it is incomplete as a theory, and at the very least needs careful supplements of other reasoning before even moderately reliable practical conclusions can be drawn from it.

As steady states are the simplest example of dynamic equilibria, we can classify various approaches to the analysis of stability according to the extent of their departure from a setting of equilibrium. The minimal relaxation of steady state conditions would be to remove the constancy of relative quantities and prices over time, but to retain the conditions of equilibrium. Such a study of equilibrium dynamics follows the development of the economy assuming perfect foresight and market clearing. This means that only a selection from possible non-steady state growth paths is being examined to see if it converges to a steady state. This particular class has a rather important role in the analysis of stability, and I shall turn to discuss it in more detail in a moment.

At the extreme of generality and difficulty, we might try to allow every foreseeable feature of disequilibrium, and the consequent effects on the expectations and actions of agents. It is fair to say that no such analysis exists, nor is any prospect of it at all realistic. I think that an attempt to theorize at this level of generality would confuse the issue instead of illuminating it. The literature on the subject is now full of models of isolated features of disequilibrium, each coming to its own conclusions that do not relate to any of the other models. What is needed is a system for classifying different issues raised by the study of disequilibrium growth.

This is an area of very active research. Although much remains to be done, some broad trends can be recognized. One line of approach has been to consider 'temporary' equilibria, where the assumption of perfect foresight is abandoned and the markets which are open at the prevailing date are cleared with individual's actions based only on their expectations about the future. Such temporary equilibria can be ones where prices are flexible in the short run, or Keynesian ones where expectations lead to sticky prices and some markets must be cleared by quantity adjustments. Another line is to consider the causes of market failure. This can involve transaction costs, increasing returns generally, or informational uncertainty. Finally, we can look at the consequences of having an incomplete set of markets. This can involve a study of monopolistic situations, or ones where individuals follow 'behavioural' rules of thumb and learn as the economy evolves.

3. Equilibrium growth

A great deal of growth economics is, however, confined to analyses of equilibrium paths, with some minor generalizations. This is commonly called the neo-classical approach. Its strongest supporters claim that it is a good approximation, that the only important aspect of disequilibrium in any economy is the deficiency or excess of aggregate effective demand, and that once monetary and fiscal policies are chosen to eliminate such discrepancies (deflationary and inflationary gaps), equilibrium growth paths will provide a reasonable description of the dynamic economy.[5]

I do not have faith in this strong version of the 'neo-classical synthesis', for I think there are several important features of disequilibrium that have to do with the micro-economic aspects of the economy and not merely with aggregate demand. Issues of imperfect information are often at the heart of the matter. However, I would claim that study of equilibrium growth has an important role to play as a first approximation, or as a first step in a chain of reasoning. This is because the method of neo-classical growth theory distills several important common features and forces that operate in all problems of growth, and gives a unified treatment of them. Further factors to be taken into account are very often specific to each situation, and are therefore best incorporated at the next stage. The alternative would be to treat each problem on its own from the outset. This would make us lose sight of all the common features, and would therefore be wasteful of effort and liable to error.

Used carefully, equilibrium analysis of growth can be invaluable in several ways. First, it generalizes the usual static interrelations between equilibria and Pareto-efficient allocations. Thus, allocations that are efficient in an intertemporal sense, where it is not possible to increase the amount of any net output at any date without decreasing that of some other good at some other date, can be realized as paths of equilibrium growth. This is why there turns out to be a close connection between the study of stability of equilibrium paths and that of optimum growth. This provides an independent reason for being interested in equilibrium growth. Even if we have no interest in markets per se, we will find that an efficient intertemporal allocation of resources could be replicated by a simulated market. The equilibrium prices are then to be interpreted as planners' prices, or as imputed or shadow prices. To me, this is the strongest reason for studying equilibrium growth theory. In the subsequent chapters, I shall often save space by not emphasizing each time the planning aspect of the equilibrium prices that appear constantly. But I would like to stress now that such an interpretation is far more fruitful than one as an explanation of actual prices in a growing economy. For the latter, equilibrium prices are but a first step, and further examination of various particular influences is important.

In policy analyses, equilibrium growth points out a target path for the economy. We can then view trade cycles not as fluctuations around an average, but as shortfalls of capacity utilization below its ceiling. This can help us in designing better Keynesian policies.

Finally, equilibrium analysis may not help us in planning growth in a precise manner, but it can help us in avoiding the avoidable large errors. Perhaps the analogy of a command economy makes the point more easily. The planners must be well aware that several factors are at work to frustrate their attempts at making and implementing a set of consistent plans. But it seems undeniable that the concept of material balances remains a very useful tool in their thinking and procedures. The outcome may not be within one or two percent of their calculations, but at least they can be fairly sure that they have not made a quite unnecessary provision for millions of ton-miles of transport services. The concept of equilibrium plays a similar role in the analysis of policy in a market economy, and catastrophic errors in economic theory and policy are so common that this seemingly negative virtue is in fact very important. Any rule of discipline in analysis that forces us to think about the complexity of interconnections in the economy must be welcomed.

These remarks suggest the following scheme for analyzing the effects of a historical or planned change in some parameters on a growing economy. First, we examine the permanent pattern of growth (if possible, a steady state) under each parameter configuration, and see how the two compare. Next, we seek a path of equilibrium growth from the old pattern to the new one. The results of the analysis thus far distil the general features of the economic interrelations over time. Then we ask how the particular aspects of the problem affect the picture. Is an initial surprise going to paralyse all agents in the economy for a while? Will delayed responses result in temporary monopolies or market failures? How will the distribution of income change in course of these developments, and how will that affect demands? Answers to these and other questions will supplement and modify the general tendencies inferred from equilibrium analysis. I would claim that such a combination of general equilibrium reasoning and situation-specific examination yields a highly successful method for studying and applying growth economics.

There is of course nothing new about the theoretical part of the above scheme, where an essentially static comparison of equilibria is used in analysing a dynamic transition. The same method, commonly called 'period analysis', has been used with great success by Marshall and Keynes and all their followers, i.e. in virtually all of price theory and employment theory.[6] All readers will have met several instances of such analyses. The added difficulties present, and the added care required, in using the method in a context of growth, are all differences of degree and not of kind.

Nor is there anything new about the proposed combination of general and particular analyses in applications. The position has been excellently expressed by Hicks:[7]

Every historical event has some aspect in which it is unique; but nearly always there are other aspects in which it is a member of a group, often of quite a large group. If it is one of the latter aspects in which we are interested, . . . it will be the average, or norm, of the group which is what we shall be trying to explain. We shall be able to allow that the individual may diverge from the norm without being deterred from the recognition of a statistical uniformity.

As for the method used for discussing such a uniformity,

It will be a 'model', like other models that are used by economists to elucidate the working of economic institutions. We do not suppose, when we use such a model, that it is describing what actually happens, or has happened, in any particular case. It is a 'representative' case, from which particular instances must be expected to diverge, for particular reasons. But when we find a deviation from the model, the model will tell us to ask 'Why?'. If it is a good model, the 'why?' (sometimes at least) will be an interesting question.

If we are to make the best possible use of such an approach, we should be aware of its limitations. Some of these arise from the way in which such analysis is commonly done, while others are inherent defects of the approach. The first kind are usually related to the treatment of saving and investment, and the highly aggregative nature of the simple models. If it is supposed, for example, that Keynesian policies keep the economy at full employment, attention must be paid to possible effects of these policies on saving and investment behaviour. This is almost never done. If it is supposed that the ceiling of an actual disequilibrium path will be well approximated by an equilibrium path, it is implicitly assumed that the fluctuations have no significant effect on the level of the ceiling path (through saving and investment behaviour) or on its rate of growth (through possible effects on technological progress). This may turn out to be valid, but the point of the criticism is that the issue is usually not even discussed. Of course it cannot be considered in full without setting up the more complicated model in just the detail we are trying to avoid, but some simple cases can be studied as tests.

The simple assumptions of constant saving propensities and drastic aggregation pose another problem. The model decomposes in such a way that we can examine growth of output without paying any attention to the determinants of investment. In equilibrium it must equal the supply of saving out of full employment income, and that is all we need to proceed. Further study only serves to determine some asset prices which may or may not be of interest in the context. This is all the more true if there are constant returns to scale, for then the level of production cannot be determined from profit maximization considerations, while on the other hand the appropriate relations between prices are fixed by a zero pure profit condition alone. This is the common complaint that neo-classical models 'do not have an investment function', and are therefore very difficult to relate to the Keynesian models for which they are supposed to provide the target path.

All these problems can be overcome by formulating the most general model of intertemporal equilibrium, but it becomes difficult to find one's way through such general models to concrete conclusions of interest. This poses the unfortunate trade-off between logical rigour and practicality. For the latter, it becomes necessary to use simpler and cruder models to obtain some provisional insights about the economic forces at work. While this calls for care, it does not require undue worry. After all, 'Economic concepts such as wealth, output, income and cost are no easier to define precisely than wind. Nevertheless, these concepts are useful, and economic problems can be discussed.'[8]

This is broadly the aim of my book. Most of the models discussed in the following chapters are designed to illustrate the operations of particular economic forces. I have tried to keep each one as simple as possible, usually by disregarding some other aspects. I hope I have given the readers enough guidance to enable them to appreciate the useful lessons to be learnt from these models as well as to evaluate their shortcomings critically.

The inherent defects of the equilibrium framework are, of course, potentially more serious. The difficulty so far has been that of finding an alternative approach that is free from them, while remaining equally systematic and usable. Current research is slowly opening new and fruitful lines of analysis. I shall mention some such developments briefly in the concluding chapter, and hope that some readers will be tempted to contribute to these developments.

For much of the rest of the book, however, I shall adhere to a setting of equilibrium. Steady states will be used as benchmarks, but an attempt will be made to subject the relevant variables to economic analysis. Characteristics of steady states will be studied, and their stability examined relative to the class of equilibrium growth paths. Simple models will be used in order to illustrate important economic forces, but attempt will be made to point out the special features of these simple models that do not survive in more general models with apparently similar features.

Notes

An outstanding discussion of the methodology of equilibrium growth theory can be found in Bliss (1975a), particularly Chs. 2, 6.

1. Valuable discussions of most of these problems can be found in Parker and Harcourt (eds.) (1969), Lutz and Hague (eds.) (1961). See also any macroeconomics text, e.g. Bailey, (1971, Ch. 12).

2. See Friedman (1966, pp. 23–30).
3. See Samuelson (1973, Chs. 20, 32), Arrow and Hahn (1971, Chs. 11, 12), and Leijonhufvud (1968, Ch. II).
4. See Samuelson (1973, Ch. 30 Appendix), Malinvaud (1972, Ch. 10), and Bliss (1975a, Ch. 3).
5. See Samuelson, (1973, Chs. 3, 19).
6. See Leijohnhufvud (1968, pp. 50–2, 62–6).
7. Hicks, (1969, pp. 3, 42). © Oxford University Press, 1969. Quoted by permission of author and publisher.
8. Robinson (1965, p. ix).

2. Production, Costs, and Prices

Growth theory involves resource allocation over time. Therefore it concerns supply and demand for a set of interrelated commodities, whether from the point of view of a planner or from that of a market. However, there are two new features; one is that some inputs are themselves producible, and the other that some inputs are durable, i.e. they continue to provide factor services for a number of periods. The first does not change the picture much: we only have to relate the marginal cost of production of such a commodity to the derived demand price for it as in input. Input-output models can do this even in a static context. The second is somewhat more important. It requires us to distinguish two prices, one that of the services of such an input in one period, commonly called the *rent*, and the second that of the title to such a stream of rents, viz. the *asset price*. It is clear that the two should be related from a discounted present value calculation, but this brings in some new concepts that are best treated separately.

I shall therefore proceed in stages. For much of this chapter, I shall develop the theory of production at any one point in time, treating capital goods just like any other factor of production, and considering only their services and their rents. In the last section I shall introduce asset prices. Finally, in Chapter 3 I shall introduce the fact that capital goods are themselves produced, thus setting up a complete growth model. The models of Chapter 3 are highly simplified, and are useful only for some preliminary insights into the problems of intertemporal allocation. The subsequent chapters will examine generalizations that allow some more realistic features. This procedure will enable us to classify complications according to the stage where they arise.

Constant returns to scale will rule, except briefly in Chapter 4. For geometric illustration, I shall consider the case where there are only two inputs, a capital good and one type of labour, and only one output, 'national product'. I shall indicate possible generalizations, but their full implications will be developed only in Chapter 6.

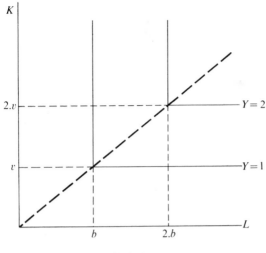

FIG. 2.1

1. Fixed coefficients

The simplest production process is one which requires fixed amounts of each input per unit of output. Suppose one unit of output requires b units of labour and v units of capital. This produces the familiar L-shaped isoquants of Fig. 2.1. Under constant returns to scale, they are scale replicas of each other, the isoquant for output $Y = 2$ being a radial magnification by a factor of 2 of the isoquant $Y = 1$.

Consider equilibrium under such a setting. Let w be the price of labour services (the wage rate), and r that of capital services (the rental rate). Let p be the price of output. The unit cost of production is $(w \cdot b + r \cdot v)$. Given free entry, this cannot be less than p, as positive 'pure' or 'excess' profit cannot persist. Similarly, given free exit, it cannot exceed p if positive output is being produced. There are cases in multi-sector models where we are interested in finding which goods are not produced at all, but otherwise the case $Y = 0$ is not of great interest. Ruling it out, we have the equilibrium condition

$$w \cdot b + r \cdot v = p \qquad (2.1)$$

Of course only relative prices matter, and we can choose output as the numéraire, i.e. take $p = 1$. But even then, (2.1) on its own is not enough to determine w and r. It is only one of a set of equilibrium conditions, and we must consider the factor markets as well. This could lead to different outcomes.

Suppose first that we have here a model of the whole economy, and that at the instant being considered the supplies of capital and labour are fixed at amounts K and L respectively. If $K/v > L/b$, then output $Y = L/b$ can be produced. There is an excess supply of K, therefore we can have an equilibrium only if $r = 0$, and then $w = 1/b$. Similarly, if $K/v < L/b$, we can have an equilibrium with $Y = K/v$, $w = 0$ and $r = 1/v$, with some labour unemployed. Finally, if $K/v = L/b$, we can have an equilibrium with full employment of both factors. However, any w and r satisfying (2.1) will then be compatible with equilibrium in all three markets, i.e. the equilibrium prices will be indeterminate within this range. Of course each of w and r must be non-negative if there is costless disposability of the two factors. This non-uniqueness of equilibrium is not a cause for surprise or concern. In this model, the factor prices affect neither the supplies nor the demands so long as they remain within the permissible range. Similarly, in a planning context, the shadow prices are immaterial for efficient allocation.

However, such indeterminacy arises only when the factor endowments happen to be in just the right proportions to permit an equilibrium with full employment of both factors. Otherwise the equilibrium price of one of the factors must be zero, which is a determinate but unrealistic situation. We shall meet this problem again. It can be avoided or solved in various ways. We can leave the framework of equilibrium. Even within the framework, we can allow factor prices some influence over supply or over demand; the former can result from an income-leisure choice and the latter from factor substitution in production.

As an example of an alternative setting, suppose we are considering not the whole economy, but only the industrial sector of an economy with a large agricultural sector. Then the opportunity cost of labour is the agricultural income, and under some conditions this can be taken to be exogenous as far as industry is concerned. If w is this wage, and $w \cdot b < 1$, then we can have an equilibrium in industry with $r = (1 - w \cdot b)/v$, with enough labour hired at the going wage to man the existing capital.

2. Factor substitution

If factor substitution is possible, the unit input requirements v and b are not fixed. The unit isoquant shows the possible choices of their values, and the actual choice is made to minimize cost. Fig. 2.2 shows some examples of this. Provided the factor supplies are within the range of substitution, it is now possible to find an equilibrium where both factor prices are positive.

From the unit isoquant, we can find v and b as functions of the factor price ratio, $\omega = w/r$. Further, when there are constant returns to scale, changing the output level by a factor of Y at fixed w/r merely changes both input choices by the same factor Y. Thus the inputs per unit of output remain the same, and so does their ratio, $k = K/L = v/b$. Thus we can regard the cost-minimizing k as a function of ω, independent of the level of output. This is an increasing function. A measure of the ease with which the factor combination can be changed in response to a change in factor prices is given by the elasticity of this function. This is called the *elasticity of substitution* in production, and usually denoted by σ. Thus a 1 per cent rise in w/r leads to a σ per cent rise in the desired ratio K/L. If σ is low, substitution is difficult and the isoquants are nearly L-shaped; if σ is high, substitution is easy and the isoquants are nearly straight lines. This is illustrated in the two parts of Fig. 2.2.

Now return to the unit isoquant, and the functions $v(w/r)$ and $b(w/r)$. From these, we can calculate the unit cost of production when the optimum input choices are made; write it as

$$\phi(w, r) = w \cdot b(w/r) + r \cdot v(w/r) \qquad (2.2)$$

It is clear that the function ϕ must be non-decreasing in each argument, since a higher input price cannot lead to a lower unit cost of production even after making all available substitution. Also, ϕ must be homogeneous of degree one: for example, doubling w and r leaves v and b unchanged and, from (2.2), this doubles the unit cost. Finally, ϕ must be a concave function. A simple way to see the intuition behind this is as follows. If factor substitution is not possible, i.e. if v and b are constants, then ϕ will be linear in w and r. If there is any possibility of substituting away from an input as it becomes more expensive, then ϕ

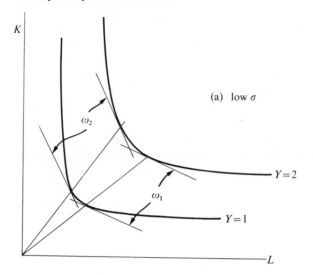

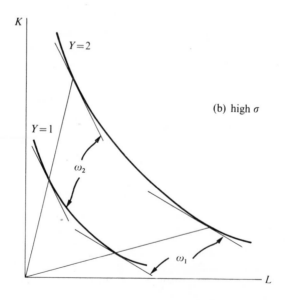

FIG. 2.2

must increase less than linearly, i.e. it will be a concave function. I shall omit the rigorous proof as it is not relevant here.[1]

The reason for interest in the unit cost function is that it embodies all economically relevant information about our technology. In particular, we can find the functions v and b from ϕ. To see this, suppose w and r change by small increments dw and dr. We have

$$d\phi = dw \cdot b + w \cdot db + dr \cdot v + r \cdot dv$$

But v and b were chosen from the unit isoquant by the cost-minimization condition that the slope of the isoquant, $-dv/db$, should equal the factor price ratio, w/r. Thus $w \cdot db + r \cdot dv = 0$, and we can read off the partial derivatives by comparing what remains in the above expression with the first differential

$$d\phi = \phi_w(w, r) \cdot dw + \phi_r(w, r) \cdot dr.$$

Thus the unit input requirements are simply the partial derivatives:

$$b(w/r) = \phi_w(w, r), \qquad v(w/r) = \phi_r(w, r) \tag{2.3}$$

Now let Y be the quantity of output. Under constant returns to scale, the factor demands will be Y times the expressions in (2.3). Thus, given fixed supplies K and L of the factors, the factor market equilibrium conditions are

$$L = Y \cdot \phi_w(w, r), \qquad K = Y \cdot \phi_r(w, r) \tag{2.4}$$

This assumes sufficient substitution to permit full employment of both factors. For the general case, we must allow one of them to be in excess supply and to have zero price. Then the fixed coefficient case can be subsumed in this.

The output market equilibrium condition, generalizing (2.1), is simply

$$\phi(w, r) = 1 \tag{2.5}$$

In (2.4) and (2.5) we have three equations to determine the general equilibrium values of the three unknowns Y, w and r.

We shall soon see another, and in this special case somewhat simpler, way of describing the equilibrium. However, that approach does not generalize to more complex models, and attempted generalizations can be misleading. The method above does generalize more easily, and highlights the interrelations among the variables. This is why I have treated it first and more prominently.

We can now describe some other features of the equilibrium, and also some comparative static properties. First, note that the equilibrium share of wages in national income (or product) is $\pi w = w \cdot L/Y$, and that of rents is $\pi r = r \cdot K/Y$. From (2.4) and (2.5) we can write these as the elasticities

$$\pi w = w \cdot \phi_w(w, r)/\phi(w, r), \qquad \pi r = r \cdot \phi_r(w, r)/\phi(w, r) \qquad (2.6)$$

Since ϕ is homogeneous of degree one, Euler's theorem gives $w \cdot \phi_w + r \cdot \phi_r = \phi$, and therefore

$$\pi w + \pi r = 1; \qquad (2.7)$$

this is the standard result that under constant returns to scale, competitive returns to factors exactly exhaust the product, leaving zero pure profit.

If such a competitive equilibrium is a good approximation to reality, we have here a theory to explain the distribution of income. Within the confines of equilibrium, it is easy to generalize it to allow many types of labour and capital goods. But the framework of equilibrium is a more serious limitation. It is therefore better to think of the above factor shares as those 'imputed' in an efficiency shadow price solution or an idealized market.

It is often useful to know how v and b respond to changes in w and r. The chain rule of differentiation gives $dv = \phi_{rw} \cdot dw + \phi_{rr} \cdot dr$, where I have omitted the arguments (w, r) for sake of brevity. To simplify this, note that $v = \phi_r$ is homogeneous of degree zero. Euler's theorem applied to it gives $w \cdot \phi_{rw} + r \cdot \phi_{rr} = 0$. Substituting, $dv = w \cdot \phi_{rw} \cdot (dw/w - dr/r)$. Using the expressions for the imputed distributive shares (2.6), and defining

$$\sigma = (\phi \cdot \phi_{rw})/(\phi_w \cdot \phi_r) \qquad (2.8)$$

we find

$$dv/v = \pi w \cdot \sigma \cdot (dw/w - dr/r) \Big\rbrace$$

and, similarly, $\qquad (2.9)$

$$db/b = -\pi r \cdot \sigma \cdot (dw/w - dr/r)$$

Now note that $k = v/b$ and $\omega = w/r$, and that a small proportional change in a ratio equals the difference in the corresponding proportional changes in the numerator and denominator. Using (2.7) and (2.9) we have

$$dk/k = \sigma \cdot d\omega/\omega \qquad (2.10)$$

Thus a 1 per cent increase in ω leads to a σ per cent increase in k. Recalling our earlier discussion, we see that σ is the elasticity of substitution, and (2.8) gives a convenient expression for it.

Next, we note that $\pi r/\pi w = (r \cdot K)/(w \cdot L) = k/\omega$, and therefore

$$d(\pi r/\pi w)/(\pi r/\pi w) = dk/k - d\omega/\omega = (\sigma - 1)\, d\omega/\omega.$$

Thus the distribution of income moves in favour of rents as ω (and thus k) increases if $\sigma > 1$. This makes economic sense. If the elasticity of substitution is high, a rise in wages leads to a large reduction in the use of labour, and the calculation above gives us the precise point beyond which the balance tips against the wage bill relative to rents. We shall soon meet another interpretation of this.

It should be stressed that all the relations discussed above are merely consistency conditions between the changes in different variables in the model when an equilibrium shifts, without going into the underlying causes of the shift. That will be done in different contexts later.

One further advantage of the method of this section is that it brings to the fore the important relation (2.5). This is a constraint on factor prices imposed by the zero pure profit condition. For each level of one of the factor prices, it enables us to find the value of the other compatible with the equality of the product price and the unit cost. This is called the factor-price curve or 'frontier'. Since ϕ is increasing, concave and homogeneous of degree one, it is as a mathematical formalism exactly like a production function of intermediate price theory, and thus (2.5) looks exactly like a unit production isoquant, as in Fig. 2.3a. If we regard w as a function of r along this, we can find its slope by the rule for differentiating implicit functions:

$$dw/dr = -\phi_r/\phi_w = -v/b, \qquad (2.11)$$

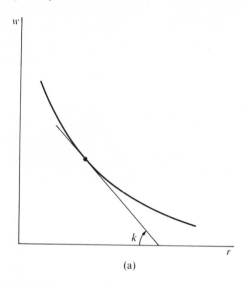

(a)

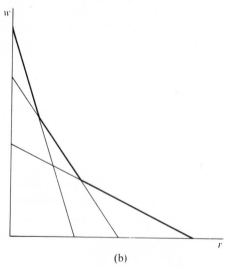

(b)

FIG. 2.3

the cost-minimizing capital/labour ratio. Similarly, the elasticity is the ratio of the imputed distributive shares,

$$-\frac{r}{w} \cdot \frac{\mathrm{d}w}{\mathrm{d}r} = \frac{\pi r}{\pi w} \qquad (2.12)$$

Thus some economically useful information can be read off from the factor-price curve. Similar results are valid with many factors.[2]

It is extremely important to distinguish between this curve and another similar curve that will appear later. Confusion is likely because in one simple case the two curves are formally identical. This latter curve shows the relation between the wage rate and the interest rate in comparing different steady states of a growth model; to avoid confusion I shall call it the wage-interest curve. The point to note is that the factor price of a capital good is the rent, and it is only in special cases that the interest rate serves as a proxy for the rent of one, let alone of several, capital goods.

In the fixed coefficient case, (2.1) shows that the factor price curve is a straight line. If we have several fixed coefficient techniques available, the relevant curve is the outer envelope of the individual straight lines. This is so because at any point inside this envelope, the factor prices are such that a technique on the envelope allows positive pure profit, and this cannot persist in equilibrium. Of course such an envelope has 'corners', where the equalities like (2.11) must be replaced by a pair of inequalities. This is illustrated in Fig. 2.3b. However, I shall leave the development of this to texts on capital theory.

3. Production functions

The more conventional approach to the determination of equilibrium uses a production function, expressing output as a function of inputs. This is treated at length in elementary textbooks on price theory and on growth theory, and therefore I shall merely sketch it here.[3] Writing Y for output and K and L for the respective quantities of capital and labour inputs employed, we have

$$Y = F(K, L), \qquad (2.13)$$

where F is a non-decreasing concave function, homogeneous of degree one. Consider equilibrium at an instant in time, with supplies of the factors fixed by the history up to this instant. If a factor is unemployed in equilibrium, its price must be zero. Then so must its marginal product, for otherwise some pure profit could be made by using a little more of it, and the initial situation would not be an equilibrium. We can therefore use the *supplies* of K and L instead of the actual employment in (2.13) to find the equilibrium output; either the two are equal, or else the difference does not contribute to output.

Now consider the equilibrium conditions in the factor markets. I shall assume differentiability to allow me to present the theory in a simple form. It is possible to do without this, using inequalities, and the only problem that arises is a possible range of indeterminacy of factor prices.

Let output be numéraire. Producers maximize profits given the factor prices. As in intermediate price theory, this leads to the conditions equating the marginal product of each factor to its price:

$$r = F_K(K, L), \qquad w = F_L(K, L) \qquad (2.14)$$

Correspondingly, the distributive shares are:

$$\pi r = K \cdot F_K/F, \qquad \pi w = L \cdot F_L/F \qquad (2.15)$$

Once again, and for the same reason, we can use the supplies of K and L in this.

In (2.13) and (2.14) we now have three equations to determine the equilibrium values of the three unknowns Y, w, and r. Moreover, these equations take a particularly simple form, where each unknown is on the left hand side of one equation, and the right hand sides contain only the known variables, K and L. This is certainly convenient, but also misleading. The problem arises from the common tendency to think of the variables on the right hand side of an equation as causes and the one on the left hand side as the effect. Thus we come to think of a 'marginal productivity theory' where the factor endowments and the technology determine factor prices (and income distribution) independently of demand. This has a tempting simplicity which, however, does not survive beyond the one-good model. With different outputs, their relative prices begin to matter, and it becomes necessary to solve the full general equilibrium problem, including demand aspects, in order to determine factor prices. Of course any general competitive model will include equilibrium conditions which equate the value of the marginal product of each factor in each use to its price. But the three components of this relation — the relevant output and input prices and the marginal physical product — are all unknowns of the whole equilibrium problem. We shall see some examples of such a situation in Chapter 6. With this warning against reading too much from (2.14), I shall use them where convenient in the one-good context.

It should be noted that the composition of output, i.e. what part of it is to be used for consumption and what part for investment, remains to be determined even in the one-good context. For that, demand is indispensable.

Other useful expressions for the equilibrium factor prices can be found using the property of constant returns to scale, and deflating the production function (2.13) by any scale variable. This enables us to derive relations among 'intensive' magnitudes like capital per head, $k = K/L$, output per head, $y = Y/L$, and similarly $l = L/K$ and $1/v = z = Y/K$. We have

$$y = f(k), \qquad z = g(l), \tag{2.16}$$

where each of f and g is a non-decreasing concave function. This is shown in Fig. 2.4.

This form is convenient because under constant returns to scale, marginal products of factors depend only on their relative amounts and not on the absolute scale of production. Mathematically, when F is homogeneous of degree one, each of its partial derivatives is homogeneous of degree zero. Thus we can choose the scale as we wish, and choosing $L = 1$ first and then $K = 1$, we see that

$$r = f'(k), \qquad w = g'(l). \tag{2.17}$$

In each case, the other factor price can be found using the zero pure profit condition $r \cdot K + w \cdot L = Y$, or

$$r \cdot k + w = y, \qquad r + w \cdot l = z.$$

Then

$$w = f(k) - k \cdot f'(k), \qquad r = g(l) - l \cdot g'(l). \tag{2.18}$$

Thus, in each part of Fig. 2.4, one factor price becomes the slope and the other the intercept of the tangent at the given value of k (resp. l).

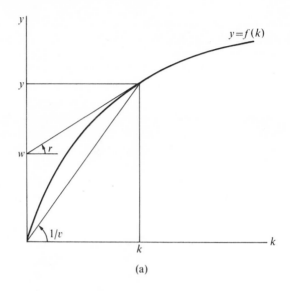

(a)

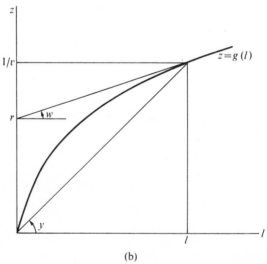

(b)

FIG. 2.4

Finally, we can understand more of the concept of the elasticity of substitution using production functions. Since f is concave, for example, $f''(k)$ is negative, and a higher k corresponds to a smaller r. From Fig. 2.4a, we see that it also corresponds to a higher w. This is what was indicated by the cost function method earlier. We now see that a large change in k will correspond to small changes in w and r if $f''(k)$ is numerically small. In the earlier approach, the same conclusion followed from a large σ. Thus we see that the elasticity of substitution provides information about the rate at which $f'(k)$ changes, i.e. diminishing returns set in. If σ is large, these set in slowly. Thus the effect of a higher k is not fully offset by a fall in the marginal product of capital relative to that of labour, and the imputed distributive shares shift in favour of capital. The opposite is the case if σ is small. We saw earlier that the critical dividing line is $\sigma = 1$, when factor shares are constant, independent of the amounts of the factors. It can be shown that the case $\sigma = 1$ corresponds to the well known Cobb-Douglas production function

$$Y = A \cdot K^\alpha \cdot L^\beta, \tag{2.13a}$$

where A, α, and β are positive constants, and $\alpha + \beta = 1$. It is easy to take partial derivatives and verify that the imputed shares are $\pi w = \beta$ and $\pi r = \alpha$. Also, k is proportional to ω, and therefore the elasticity is 1.

It is worth stating for the record that the production functions for which the elasticity of substitution is constant (CES) are of the type

$$F(K, L) = \{BK \cdot K^{-\rho} + BL \cdot L^{-\rho}\}^{-1/\rho} \tag{2.13b}$$

where BK and BL are positive constants, ρ is a constant with $1 + \rho > 0$, and then it can be verified that $\sigma = 1/(1 + \rho)$.

In general, σ may be different at different points along an isoquant, i.e. σ may be a function of ω (or k). The earlier calculations apply to small changes, i.e. derivatives, using the local value of σ. Of course, if σ stays on the same side of 1 at all points over some range of ω, then corresponding results for finite changes over this range can be obtained by stringing together small ones. i.e. by using integration.

4. Technological change

It is important to establish some terminology. A *technique* is a
particular combination of inputs producing a particular output, i.e. a
production process. The collection of all available techniques, e.g. as
described by an isoquant map or a production function or indirectly by
a cost function, is the *technology*. Thus, when new techniques become
available as a result of research or experience, it is the technology that
changes. Even with an unchanged technology, the chosen technique can
change if factor prices change, say as a result of changes in relative
endowments.

I shall maintain constant returns to scale. Thus, given any technique,
another technique which merely magnifies or shrinks all inputs and
output in the same proportion must also be available. The technology
can then be described by any one isoquant, say the one where $Y = 1$.
Technological change can be described by a shift of it. So long as
previously available techniques are not forgotten, any shift must move
it nearer the origin. There are some particular shifts of this kind which
are analytically convenient, and are frequently used. Fig. 2.5 illustrates
one such type of shift, both for a fixed coefficient technology, i.e. one
where there is only one technique, although there is always the
possibility of wasting some of one input, and one which allows
substitution, i.e. one with several techniques. In each case the shift is by
a constant proportion, in this case $\frac{1}{2}$, parallel to the labour axis. In other
words, comparing each old technique, unit output can be produced
using the same amount of capital as before, but only half as much
labour. This is formally exactly as if more labour is made available, or
the effective labour services provided by each physical unit of labour
such as a man-hour increase by a factor of two. We can then define
'efficiency units' of labour, and work as if the technology is unchanged
when described in these efficiency units. This is what makes such a shift
analytically so simple. Since it acts formally as if more labour were
made available, it is called a 'labour augmenting' shift, or sometimes a
'Harrod-neutral' shift.

Similarly, we can define a 'capital augmenting' shift to be a
proportionate shift parallel to the capital axis. The two can be
combined, one shift parallel to one axis being followed by the second
parallel to the other. If these two are in the same proportion, the overall
result is to shift the isoquant radially towards the origin. Such a shift by

a factor of two, for example, would make the new isoquant $Y = 1$ coincide with the old isoquant $Y = \frac{1}{2}$. We can then call such a shift 'output-augmenting'; it is also called 'Hicks neutral'.[4]

Note that the kinds of shifts discussed above are quite special. For example, if the old technology has fixed coefficients as in Fig. 2.5a, and then substitution is discovered yielding a new isoquant like that in Fig. 2.5b, the change cannot be described by any combination of shifts parallel to the axes. However, the assumption of factor-augmenting shifts is quite common.

Mathematically, for each of K and L we define associated efficiency factors AK and AL, and the factor quantities in efficiency units are then

$$EK = AK \cdot K, \qquad EL = AL \cdot L.$$

The production function in terms of these units is

$$Y = F(EK, EL) = F(AK \cdot K, AL \cdot L) \qquad (2.19)$$

Note that if $AK = AL = A$, this becomes $Y = A \cdot F(K, L)$, the output-augmenting form. The marginal productivity equations (2.14) can be found using the chain rule:

$$r = AK \cdot F_{EK}(EK, EL), \qquad w = AL \cdot F_{EL}(EK, EL). \qquad (2.20)$$

The factor shares become

$$\pi r = EK \cdot F_{EK}/F, \qquad \pi w = EL \cdot F_{EL}/F \qquad (2.21)$$

Notice the formal similarity of these expressions with those for the case of no technological change, (2.15). Thus, in order to find the competitive factor shares, we need to know only the factor supplies in efficiency units, and not the separate information concerning physical units and efficiency factors. We do need that in order to find the prices of the factors. However, we can dually define the prices in efficiency units as well. Since each physical unit of labour has price w, and comprises AL efficiency units, each efficiency unit can be said to have price w/AL. Similarly for capital we have the efficiency rent r/AK. From (2.20), we see that these equal the marginal products of the factors measured in efficiency units.

Measuring prices in efficiency units enables us to define the unit cost function subject to a factor-augmenting technological shift, viz.

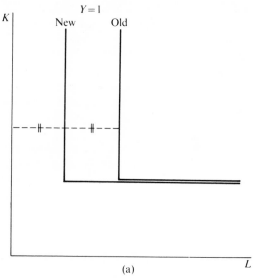

(a)

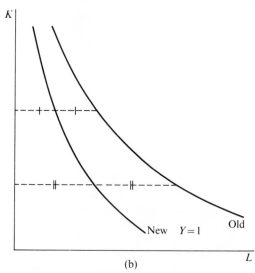

(b)

FIG. 2.5

$\phi(w/AL, r/AK)$. Equilibrium conditions can be expressed in terms of ϕ; this is left as an exercise.

We can also define the elasticity of substitution between efficiency units, and use it in drawing inferences about the imputed factor shares. Thus, if the elasticity of substitution exceeds one, an increase in the capital/labour ratio in efficiency units will be accompanied by a shift of the income distribution in favour of rents.

It is easy to verify that, in the output-augmenting case, the ratio w/r can be expressed in terms of the ratio of the physical quantities K/L, irrespective of the efficiency factor. Similarly, in the labour-augmenting case, r can be expressed in terms of Y/K, irrespective of AL. In fact, these properties provide equivalent characterizations of the two types of technological change. I shall omit the proof of this, as it has no great interest for my present purpose.

In one special case, namely that of a Cobb-Douglas function with a multiplicative shift, it is possible to rearrange terms to express the shift as augmenting either factor, or output. Thus we have alternative ways of writing (2.13a):

$$A \cdot K^\alpha \cdot L^\beta = K^\alpha \cdot (A^{1/\beta} \cdot L)^\beta$$
$$= (A^{1/\alpha} \cdot K)^\alpha \cdot L^\beta$$

This will be useful later. Incidentally, it shows that factor augmentation is a mathematical property of the relevant functions. It does not carry any engineering or welfare implications concerning a change in the quality of that factor.

5. Several factors and goods

It is trivial to generalize the cost function or the production function to the case where several factors produce a homogeneous output. We have equilibrium conditions exactly like (2.4) or (2.14), in each case involving one equation for each factor. We can even define pairwise elasticities of substitution and obtain inferences about imputed factor shares.

Some new problems arise. When there are several capital goods, we have to formulate a mechanism for investment allocation, even though all the investment goods come initially from the same homogeneous output. With several non-produced factors, steady states can be problematic if their supplies are growing at different rates. But these issues are for later treatment; they do not affect the description of equilibrium in production at an instant.

Heterogeneity of goods causes other problems. I shall illustrate these using the case where there is one consumer good and one investment good, since this will be useful in Chapter 6.

Suppose each good has its own production function, F^C for the consumer good C and F^I for the investment good I. Suppose the factors of production are one capital good and one type of labour, with supplies fixed at K and L. We must face one new problem, namely the allocation of the factors to the two uses. Suppose amounts (KC, LC) are used for consumer good production and (KI, LI) for investment good production. These must satisfy the feasibility conditions

$$KC + KI = K, \qquad LC + LI = L \qquad (2.22)$$

The outputs of the two goods are

$$C = F^C(KC, LC), \qquad I = F^I(KI, LI) \qquad (2.23)$$

Since C, I, KC, KI, LC, and LI are all to be determined, this leaves us two equations short of solving the problem. One further condition we can impose is that the allocation should be efficient, i.e. it should yield a point on the transformation frontier between C and I, or a point of tangency between two isoquants in the Edgeworth-Bowley box for production. This yields the condition that the marginal rates of factor substitution in production of the two goods be equal, and this is achieved in a competitive equilibrium since each is equal to the common wage/rental ratio.

However, efficiency alone does not determine the allocation completely. As we can trace out the entire Pareto efficiency frontier in welfare theory by varying the weights attached to the individuals' utilities in a social welfare function, we can determine a particular efficient allocation by maximizing $(q \cdot C + p \cdot I)$ for particular non-negative weights q and p, and then trace out all efficient allocations by varying the ratio p/q between 0 and ∞. The maximization leads to the well-known conditions

$$\left. \begin{array}{l} q \cdot F_{KC}{}^C(KC, LC) = p \cdot F_{KI}{}^I(KI, LI) \\[2mm] q \cdot F_{LC}{}^C(KC, LC) = p \cdot F_{LI}{}^I(KI, LI) \end{array} \right\} \qquad (2.24)$$

If q and p are the respective prices of the consumer good and the investment good, this is achieved in competitive equilibrium through profit-maximization, and the common value of the first line is the rent r and that of the second the wage, w. Of course the prices q and p are specified exogenously in this discussion, and their determination will involve demand. Thus, as was emphasized in Section 2.3, factor prices cannot be determined independently of demand as soon as we have more than one good.[5]

The discussion of efficiency suggests two useful ways of modelling the production side. First, since w and r are common to the two sectors or goods, it is natural to make them independent variables. This is just what the cost function does. Thus we specify cost functions ϕ^C and ϕ^I for the two goods. The demand for labour to produce a unit of the consumer good is then $\phi_w{}^C(w, r)$, and similarly the other demands can be obtained. The factor market equilibrium conditions are

$$\left. \begin{array}{l} C \cdot \phi_w{}^C(w, r) + I \cdot \phi_w{}^I(w, r) = L \\ C \cdot \phi_r{}^C(w, r) + I \cdot \phi_r{}^I(w, r) = K \end{array} \right\} \tag{2.25}$$

We also have the zero pure profit conditions

$$\left. \begin{array}{l} \phi^C(w, r) = q \\ \phi^I(w, r) = p \end{array} \right\} \tag{2.26}$$

Once again, we have four equations and six unknowns. It remains to specify the demands for the two goods, but matters are a bit more complicated. The two demands are related by Walras' Law and therefore provide only one independent equation. In fact Walras' law takes a very simple and transparent form. Since each of ϕ^C and ϕ^I is homogeneous of degree one, Euler's theorem yields

$$w \cdot \phi_w{}^C + r \cdot \phi_r{}^C = \phi^C$$

etc., and then we have from (2.25) and (2.26)

$$w \cdot L + r \cdot K = C \cdot \phi^C(w, r) + I \cdot \phi^I(w, r) \tag{2.27}$$

$$= q \cdot C + p \cdot I,$$

which is the relation of identity between the national product and the national income. Thus the number of independent equations is reduced to five. However, as in all general equilibrium theory, we can only determine relative prices. We can choose a numéraire, whether a single good or a composite one. We often use the consumer good for this role, thus setting $q = 1$ and leaving five unknowns. Of course we know that an equality between the number of equations and the number of unknowns is neither necessary nor sufficient for existence or uniqueness of a solution. Existence is no problem, it is guaranteed by very general theorems which apply in this case. Uniqueness is more problematic, and will be taken up when we consider demand explicitly in Chapter 6.

The second approach stresses the aspect of maximization of the value of output. We define the outcome as a function of the exogenous variables that specify the problem; this is called the *revenue function*.[6]

$R(K, L, q, p) = \max (q \cdot C + p \cdot I)$ subject to (2.22) and (2.23).

Given our assumptions concerning the technology, this function is non-decreasing in all arguments. For each fixed (q, p), it is homogeneous of degree one and concave in (K, L), while for each fixed (K, L), it is homogeneous of degree one and convex in (q, p).

This approach is 'complementary' to the cost function approach. The latter gives the minimum cost of producing a given target output at given input prices, while a revenue function gives the maximum revenue obtainable from given inputs at given output prices. The analogy extends further. As the partial derivatives of a cost function with respect to the input prices yield the input demands, those of a revenue function with respect to the output prices yield the output supplies. Following the earlier proof, we note that

$$dR = q \cdot dC + p \cdot dI + dq \cdot C + dp \cdot I,$$

and for small changes along the transformation curve, $q \cdot dC + p \cdot dI = 0$. Then the partial derivatives can be read off as

$$C = R_q(K, L, q, p), \qquad I = R_p(K, L, q, p) \qquad (2.28)$$

The other partial derivatives of R are also useful. Suppose the maximization problem has been solved, and regard the allocations (KC, LC), (KI, LI) as functions of (K, L, q, p). Then the chain rule of differentiation yields

$$R_K(K, L, q, p) = q \cdot F_{KC}{}^C(KC, LC) \cdot dKC/dK$$
$$+ p \cdot F_{KI}{}^I(KI, LI) \cdot dKI/dK$$
$$= r \cdot (dKC/dK + dKI/dK) \quad \text{from} \quad (2.24)$$
$$= r \quad \text{from} \quad (2.23)$$

Similarly for R_L. This gives two more equilibrium conditions

$$r = R_K(K, L, q, p), \qquad w = R_L(K, L, q, p) \qquad (2.29)$$

The formal similarity between (2.29) and (2.14) is noticeable. However, the former involves output prices, and thus it is no longer possible to determine the imputed factor prices or distribution from the production side alone.

As with the cost function approach, we now have four equilibrium conditions, and it remains to consider demand. This will be done in Chapter 6. The two approaches model the same general equilibrium problem, but differ in their formal structure. Depending on the considerations of mathematical simplicity in the treatment of different variables, some applications are better handled using cost functions and others using revenue functions. There is no difference of economic substance involved in the choice.

6. Asset prices and rents

One other preliminary step is necessary before we can develop complete equilibrium growth models. We must consider the relation between prices and rents of durable assets.[7] Consider one such asset, say a machine. Let $r(t)$ be the rent for its services during the period t, and $p(t)$ the price of the title to it at this date. I shall make a convention, which does not affect anything substantial, that the title at any date is sold *ex* the rent for that period; thus a machine bought in period t begins to earn rents from $(t + 1)$.

The prices are measured relative to some numéraire. Let $i(t + 1)$ be the one-period rate of interest in terms of this numéraire for repayment at $(t + 1)$. Thus a loan of one unit of the numéraire at date t for one period calls for a total repayment of $\{1 + i(t + 1)\}$ at date $(t + 1)$. If the unit of account is a 'safe investment', for example, $i(t + 1)$ will be the rate of normal profit at $(t + 1)$. In our framework of an equilibrium with perfect foresight, even uncertainty will be immaterial.

Now compare the policy of lending one unit of the numéraire for one period with that of buying and holding the machines for the same period. Since $1/p(t)$ such machines can be bought, each of which fetches a rent $r(t + 1)$ in period $(t + 1)$, and can then be sold for $p(t + 1)$, the total proceeds at $(t + 1)$ are $\{r(t + 1) + p(t + 1)\}/p(t)$. In an equilibrium with perfect foresight extending at least up to $(t + 1)$, this must equal $\{1 + i(t + 1)\}$. Otherwise there will remain an opportunity of making a pure profit by suitable arbitrage, i.e. borrowing the numéraire to buy machines or else selling machines and lending the proceeds as numéraire loans, that yields a pure or excess profit. Similarly, in a planning context, the equality will be a condition for efficient allocation of investment, and the relevant prices and rents will be shadow prices and rents.

Another way of seeing the condition is to write it in the form

$$\frac{p(t + 1)}{p(t)}\left\{1 + \frac{r(t + 1)}{p(t + 1)}\right\} = 1 + i(t + 1) \tag{2.30}$$

To interpret this, consider a second system of accounting which uses a machine itself as the numéraire. One machine at date t yields, at date $(t + 1)$, the machine itself as repaid principal, and rental income which is worth $r(t + 1)/p(t + 1)$ machines at that date. Thus we can call $r(t + 1)/p(t + 1)$ the rate of interest in machine units, or the 'own rate of return' on machines. If the rates of interest in our two systems of units differ, this can be consistent with equilibrium if and only if the relative prices of the two units are changing at just the right rate. This is exactly like the equilibrium relation between the rates of interest in two countries and their relative exchange rate changes.

Yet another interpretation is as follows. We have

$$r(t + 1) = i(t + 1) \cdot p(t) + \{p(t) - p(t + 1)\} \tag{2.31}$$

In words, the rent just suffices to meet the interest costs of holding the machine for one period, and the loss in its capital value over the period, to be called the *depreciation*. Of course some assets might increase in capital value, in which case the capital gains must be subtracted from the interest costs, but the algebraic equation (2.31) remains valid.

If time is treated as a continuous variable, we define 'instantaneous' interest rates and rents. Thus, over an infinitesimal time interval $(t, t + dt)$, the interest is $i(t) \cdot dt$ and the rent $r(t) \cdot dt$. Then (2.31) becomes

$$r(t) = i(t) \cdot p(t) - \dot{p}(t), \tag{2.32}$$

where the dot over a function denotes differentiation with respect to time. It is customary to call (2.31) or (2.32) the 'equation of yield' or the 'short-run perfect foresight equation', to indicate the considerations which lead to it.

It should be emphasized at the outset that this is only one of several conditions of intertemporal equilibrium. By itself, it is not enough to determine anything. However, in one very special case the equation takes a particularly simple form. I shall use this case in the next chapter to isolate and illustrate some simple features of growth and capital accumulation. Many textbooks discuss the models as if this case were the general one, and fail to put it in its proper context.

In the special case, there is only one type of machine. There is no technological change, and no physical deterioration of machines. Thus all machines, old and new, have the same price. Further, each new machine can be constructed at the cost of exactly one unit of the consumer good, which is the numéraire. Thus the common price of all machines is always 1, i.e. $p(t) = 1$ for all t. Then (2.31) or (2.32) becomes

$$r(t) = i(t) \tag{2.33}$$

Thus we have a very special, and almost incidental, case where the rental rate also serves as the interest rate or the normal profit rate. If this relation is thought to be generally valid, immense confusion can result. A case in point is the confusion between the factor price curve and the wage-interest curve mentioned before.

The general formula is extremely important and widely applicable. There is nothing to constrain us to think of the durable asset as a machine. It could be fiat money, a bond, land, or a deposit of an exhaustible natural resource. Some of these cases will be considered later. In that context, it will be useful to have the result in a slightly different form, comparing the prices $p_1(t)$, $p_2(t)$ and the rents $r_1(t)$, $r_2(t)$ of any two assets. By considering arbitrage between them directly, or by comparing each in turn to a numéraire, we find

$$\{r_1(t+1)+p_1(t+1)\}/p_1(t) = \{r_2(t+1)+p_2(t+1)\}/p_2(t) \tag{2.34}$$

or in continuous time

$$\{r_1(t)+\dot{p}_1(t)\}/p_1(t) = \{r_2(t)+\dot{p}_2(t)\}/p_2(t). \tag{2.35}$$

The formula is also useful in applied work on investment demand. The price of capital services is the rent, but firms often buy machines outright. Given data on machine prices, (2.32) enables us to calculate the equivalent rents, i.e. the rents that would lead to the same decisions about machine use in an institutional setting where machines are owned by others and rented by the firms using them. Such equivalent rents can then be used, along with the wage and price data, to find the demand for capital services. This is in essence the starting point of the theory of investment behaviour developed by Jorgenson, and widely used in empirical work.[8]

Finally, we can shed light on prices and rents from yet another angle by writing (2.30) as

$$p(t) = \frac{r(t+1)}{1+i(t+1)} + \frac{p(t+1)}{1+i(t+1)}$$

Now suppose the equilibrium with perfect foresight extends up to $(t+2)$. Then there will be a similar relation between $p(t+1)$ and $p(t+2)$. Using it, we have

$$p(t) = \frac{r(t+1)}{1+i(t+1)} + \frac{r(t+2)}{\{1+i(t+1)\}\cdot\{1+i(t+2)\}}$$

$$+ \frac{p(t+2)}{\{1+i(t+1)\}\cdot\{1+i(t+2)\}}$$

This has an obvious interpretation. The right hand side is the sum of present values, discounted to date t, of the rents accruing to a machine bought at date t and sold at date $(t+2)$, together with that of the proceeds of the sale. There being no pure profit in equilibrium, this equals the purchase price. The standard rules for compounding one-period interest rates over successive periods apply, allowing for variation in these rates over time. If the one-period rate is constant over time and equal to i, these will reduce to the familiar sequence $(1 + i)$, $(1 + i)^2$ etc.

The same argument extends to equilibrium over many periods. In general, we define the discount factor between periods t and t' as

$$D(t, t') = [\{1 + i(t + 1)\} \cdot \{1 + i(t + 2)\} \ldots \{1 + i(t')\}]^{-1} \quad (2.36)$$

and then, considering equilibrium from t to T, we have

$$p(t) = \sum_{\tau = t + 1}^{T} r(\tau) \cdot D(t, \tau) + p(T) \cdot D(t, T) \quad (2.37)$$

In continuous time, interest compounds exponentially. This yields

$$D(t, t') = \exp \left[-\int_{t}^{t'} i(\tau) \cdot d\tau \right] \quad (2.38)$$

and

$$p(t) = \int_{t}^{T} r(\tau) \cdot D(t, \tau) \cdot d\tau + p(T) \cdot D(t, T) \quad (2.39)$$

All these are zero pure profit conditions resulting from consideration of arbitrage over several periods.

If the asset, or the whole economy, has a finite and known terminal date, so that $p(T) = 0$ for some fixed T, then we can use such formulae to find asset prices in terms of rents. However, complications arise if an asset can last for ever. Taking limits in (2.37) or (2.39), we see that the asset price at any date equals the discounted present value of subsequent rents into the indefinite future if and only if

$$\lim_{T \to \infty} p(T) \cdot D(t, T) = 0, \quad (2.40)$$

and there is nothing in the nature of equilibrium to guarantee this. Given free disposal, $p(T)$ must be non-negative and therefore the price at t cannot be less than the discounted present value of subsequent rents, but it can exceed the latter.

As an extreme example that helps us understand the phenomenon, consider an 'asset' that yields no rents. It seems sensible that its price should be zero. However, if $p(0)$ is taken to be any positive constant, and $p(t) = p(0)/D(0, t)$ for all t thereafter, we see that (2.37) or (2.39) holds. For example, if the rate of interest is constant and equal to i, we have $D(0, t) = (1 + i)^{-t}$ and $p(t) = p(0) . (1 + i)^t$, and similarly $p(t) = p(0) \cdot \exp{(i \cdot t)}$ for continuous time. In this situation, anyone who buys and holds the asset for ever will never obtain any return and thus make a loss equal to his purchase price. However, if he sells it at any positive date, he will make a capital gain just enough to offset the interest costs, since the price is rising at a rate equal to the rate of interest. Even if successive exchanges merely circulate the asset among the same group of agents, none of them is ever caught out, and the process of self-fulfilling expectations can go on, producing a 'pure speculative boom'.

This considers only one equation in a general equilibrium system, and repercussions elsewhere in the economy may be such as to eliminate the boom. In some cases, the price of some other asset is driven down to zero in finite time, and if the agents in the economy foresee this and react appropriately, the speculative boom in the first asset is avoided. Also, large price changes in one asset can alter the rate of interest, producing another counteracting force. However, this question has not yet been fully resolved.[9]

It is natural to suspect some inefficiency in an equilibrium with a speculative boom, since it involves asset holding without regard to the rents which are the imputed return to its use. There is in fact a relation between such speculation and inefficiency, but the complete story is quite complicated and only a few instances will appear in the chapters that follow.

Notes

As a general background to this chapter, it is important to know the basic microeconomics of producer behaviour, and some elements of welfare economics. Suggested readings for this, in increasing order of sophistication, are Lancaster (1969, chs. 5, 6, 10, and 11), Henderson and Quandt (1971, chs. 3, 5, 7, and 8) and Malinvaud (1972, chs. 3, 4, 5, and 10).

1. See Diewert (1974), Dixit (1976, ch. 7).
2. See Samuelson (1962, note 1).
3. See Solow (1956), (1970, ch. 2), Burmeister and Dobell (1970, § 1–4, 5).
4. See Allen (1967, ch. 13), Uzawa (1961a).
5. See Jones (1965), Burmeister and Dobell (1970, § 4–1, 2, 3).

6. Note that I have defined only one revenue function for the whole economy, but separate cost functions for each sector. This is becuase I am assuming separate production functions for each sector, i.e. that production is non-joint. See Hall (1973), Dixit (1973b).

   Note also that the revenue function enables us to form quantity indices of output change at constant prices. This has implications for interpretations of marginal products; see Bliss (1975, ch. 5), and compare (2.29) below.
7. See Samuelson (1937).
8. See Jorgenson (1963, 1971).
9. See Cass (1972) for a complete analysis of one simple model.

3. One-sector Models

In Chapter 2 we considered a snapshot of the economy at an instant, and obtained some conditions for equilibrium in production. However, in a context of growth, each period is linked to others in various ways, and we must study these links to complete the picture. The concluding section of Chapter 2 looked at one such link, namely the relation between asset prices and rents.

Let us turn to another important link. When production uses durable inputs, outputs of one period are inputs in subsequent periods. This in fact introduces a twofold link. The inputs at date t are outputs dating back to $(t-1), (t-2), \ldots$, and we have to keep track of a long chain of history in order to know the factor supplies at t. Secondly, some outputs at t will become inputs at $(t+1), (t+2), \ldots$. It is therefore natural that the demand for outputs at t should depend on a forward view of the economy at these later dates. In a market economy, an entrepreneur ordering a machine at t will be concerned with the rents he will obtain at later dates, and his demand price will be a discounted present value in the manner examined before. A planner will similarly consider the marginal productivities, i.e. the imputed rents, at later dates. However, these backward and forward links combine, since the conditions at $(t+1), (t+2), \ldots$ will depend on, among other things, the durable goods outputs made available from $(t-1), (t-2), \ldots$, and these latter quantities will depend on, among other things, the rents at $(t+1), (t+2), \ldots$. Thus we are forced to look at all relevant dates simultaneously in order to determine completely what goes on in any of them.

I need hardly say that such a general and complete examination is extremely difficult. We are forced to proceed gradually, beginning with simpler cases and building on the lessons learnt from them.

This will be my plan in Chapters 3–7. I shall begin with a very simple case where most of these links are cut, leaving only the bare minimum essential for any story of accumulation and growth, and then admitting complications one at a time. Let us examine the nature of the various links, in order to find the proper simplifying assumptions. First the backward links. For each type of machine, a detailed list of its numbers installed at all past dates can matter for three reasons. A machine might be specific to the technology of its date, and unable to benefit from subsequent advances. It might also be restricted to a fixed technique chosen at the outset, and unable to adapt by substitution to later factor price changes. Finally, it may deteriorate as it ages. If all these complications are assumed away, then all that will matter will be the total stock of machines of that type in existence at t, and history in detail will not affect the factor services available at t. The simplest set of assumptions for this comprises no technological progress or deterioration by age, and equal substitution possibilities on machines after construction. This will be used in most of Chapter 3, and also in Chapters 5–7 where the emphasis is on forward links. In fact some special kinds of deterioration and technological progress can be allowed with almost no added difficulty, and these cases will be considered in the concluding section of Chapter 3 and the first section of Chapter 4. Later in Chapter 4 the difficult problems posed by the two kinds of specificity will be examined in greater detail.

In order to remove the forward links, we have to ensure that saving, and the volume and the form of investment, are all sufficiently independent of prices at future dates. For saving, this is typically done by postulating 'propensities' which apply to income, or to separate components like wages and rents. In models where there is only one capital good, this is sufficient for our purpose. As we saw in Chapter 2, equilibrium at t can be determined given such a saving function. The desired amount of investment may depend on prices at later dates, but its equilibrium value must equal that of saving. This gives us enough information to find the accumulation of the stock of a single capital good. The general intertemporal equilibrium relation between prices at later dates implied by the condition equating investment demand to saving supply does not affect anything else at t, and may be disregarded. Of course, if there are two or more capital goods, it is not enough to know the total value of investment. We must consider the portfolio allocation conditions, and these will involve prices of assets at $(t + 1)$ in the manner considered in §2.6. Also, if the technique chosen cannot be altered afterwards, the form of investment at t will depend on the factor prices that are expected to prevail at later dates. Once again, all such complications will be assumed away in this chapter, where the models will admit only one good, and stipulate fixed saving propensities. More goods and assets will be considered in Chapters 6 and 7. Forward-looking saving behaviour will be the subject of Chapter 5, and the consequences of specificity of technique will be studied in Chapter 4. In some of these last problems, the technical difficulties are formidable enough to confine our analysis to steady states. This is of course unfortunate, but some useful lessons can still be learnt.

Having outlined the general scheme, I shall state a few common properties of the special models of this chapter before developing each in more detail. All these models will assume, not merely one capital good, but only one good in production. Thus each unit of addition to the capital stock, i.e. investment, is obtained at the cost of one unit of consumption. As we saw in Chapter 2, this has two consequences. First, equilibrium decomposes even further. Factor prices can be found independently of demand, and the split of output into consumption and investment determined later. Secondly, the price of each unit of the capital good relative to the consumer good is always unity, and then the rental rate equals the rate of interest or the normal profit rate. This is convenient, but can be confusing.

1. The Harrod-Domar model

Let us begin with the simplest case, viz. that of a fixed coefficient technology. I mentioned in passing in Chapters 1 and 2 that such a technology in a setting of strict equilibrium produces some very unrealistic outcomes. Now we can examine the problem in greater detail.

Continuing the notation of § 2.1, suppose each unit of output needs the inputs of amounts v and b of capital and labour services respectively. Suppose saving is planned (and in equilibrium, realised) to be a given fraction s of income, and population (and labour supply) grows at a fixed rate n. The resulting model is called the Harrod-Domar model. We saw in Chapter 1 that a steady state requires $s/v = n$, and noted that this would be fortuitous when all three magnitudes are exogenous.

Consider equilibrium growth in this model. It is convenient here to let time progress in a sequence of discrete periods. In later sections it will be better to let it be a continuous variable; nothing of importance hinges on this choice. To provide a simple beginning, suppose full employment of both factors is possible at date 0. As we are confining our attention to equilibria, plans are fulfilled and there is no need to use subscripts on variable names to distinguish actual values from planned ones. Then in equilibrium we have the following relations among the variables.

$$\left.\begin{aligned} K(0) = v \cdot Y(0), \qquad L(0) = b \cdot Y(0) \\ v \cdot r(0) + b \cdot w(0) = 1 \\ I(0) = s \cdot Y(0) \end{aligned}\right\} \qquad (3.1)$$

As discussed before, the factor prices are indeterminate but also immaterial. Within this range of indeterminacy, we have described equilibrium at date 0 without reference to any other date. Thus we see explicitly how the general intertemporal equilibrium has decomposed into a sequence of equilibria for each date. Also, we have

$$K(1) = K(0) + I(0) \qquad (3.2)$$

which is the minimal link necessary to carry out the story of accumulation to the next period. We can then repeat the procedure.

At least, we can attempt to do so. The factor supplies at date 1 are

$$L(1) = (1 + n) \cdot L(0)$$

$$K(1) = K(0) + I(0) = K(0) + s \cdot Y(0) = K(0) + (s/v) \cdot K(0).$$

If full employment of both factors is to persist at date 1, we must have labour and capital services available in just the right proportions dictated by the fixed coefficient technology. We supposed this to be the case at date 0, and that state will continue if and only if the two factors grow at the same rate in the meantime, i.e.

$$s/v = n \qquad (3.2)$$

Thus in the Harrod-Domar model, the only path of equilibrium growth with sustained full employment of both factors is the steady state itself. Of course, such a path is conceivable only in the same fortuitous parametric configuration.

Let us see what happens if (3.2) does not hold. The faster growing factor must be in excess supply at date 1, and this can be so in equilibrium only if it is a free good. In view of (2.1), both factors cannot be free, and the equilibrium value of $Y(1)$ must be such as to require all of the slower growing factor. Consider first the case where this factor is capital, i.e. where $s/v < n$. Now $I(1) = s \cdot Y(1) = (s/v) \cdot K(1)$, so capital again grows at rate s/v between periods 1 and 2. Proceeding in this way, we find that for $t = 1, 2, 3, \ldots$

$$K(t) = (1 + s/v)^t \cdot K(0)$$
$$L(t) = (1 + n)^t \cdot L(0)$$
(3.3)

Given the fixed coefficient technology, only $K(t) \cdot b/v$ men can be employed at date t. The proportion of the labour force employed is $\{(1 + s/v)/(1 + n)\}^t$, which tends to zero asymptotically. Then $w(t) = 0$ and $r(t) = 1/v$ for all positive t.

The case where $s/v > n$ is not quite symmetric. Output can grow only at the smaller rate n, and this leads to a smaller supply of saving and a lower rate of growth of capital at subsequent dates. For example, we have $Y(1) = L(1)/b$, and

$$K(2) - K(1) = I(1) = s \cdot Y(1) = s \cdot L(1)/b = s \cdot (1 + n) \cdot L(0)/b$$
$$= s \cdot (1 + n) \cdot K(0)/v$$

Proceeding in this way, it can be shown that

$$K(t) = K(0) \cdot [1 + (s/v) \cdot \{(1 + n)^t - 1\}/n]$$
$$L(t) = L(0) \cdot (1 + n)^t$$
(3.4)

Now $L(t) \cdot v/b$ units of capital are employed at t. The proportion of capital in use declines over time, but tends to the asymptotic value of $n/(s/v)$, not 0 as for labour in the other case. Of course, any excess capacity is enough to ensure $r(t) = 0$ and $w(t) = 1/b$ for all positive t.

If the situation at time 0 is not one of full employment of both factors, then we must either be already in one of the two regimes described above, or enter one eventually. In any case, equilibrium paths do not converge to any steady state. On the contrary, they veer further and further away from such a state. Also, one of the factor prices is always zero.

It hardly needs saying that such a picture has neither practical nor theoretical appeal. Almost any modification would be an improvement, and several have been suggested. In fact, most expositions and interpretations use some modification from the outset. I have used a very strict equilibrium framework above only to present a stark picture of the difficulties involved.

Modifications which remain within the framework of equilibrium must allow at least one of s, v, and n to be endogenous, capable of responding to economic influences. In many contexts, a purely economic effect on n is thought to be unlikely, and I shall neglect it.[1] Models with flexible v and s will be studied in the next three sections. We shall find that they help us overcome the three problems — existence of a steady state, behaviour of equilibrium paths, and determination of factor prices — in different ways and to different extents.

Other models step outside the equilibrium framework. The simplest change of this kind would be to maintain the full employment of the relatively scarce factor, but to allow a gradual fall in the price of the unemployed factor. However, in the present model this will not alter the asymptotic outcomes. More sophisticated modifications allow Keynesian unemployment. These depend crucially on investment demand, and hence on assumptions concerning expectations. It is then possible to produce stable or unstable disequilibrium paths, irrespective of flexibility in v and s. Some such models will appear in Chapter 8.

All this assumes an unchanging technology. However, technological progress affecting old and new machines alike is easy to incorporate provided it is purely labour-augmenting. Such progress acts exactly like an increase in labour supply as far as production is concerned. If labour supply in physical units is growing at rate n, and the efficiency factor is growing at rate m, then labour in efficiency units grows at the rate $(1 + n) \cdot (1 + m) - 1 = n + m + n \cdot m$, which is approximated by $n + m$ if each of n and m is small. We can then replace n by $n + m$ in the above analysis, measuring the wage in efficiency units. The same applies to the models in the rest of this chapter. We shall see in Chapter 4 that purely labour-augmenting technological change is the only kind that permits steady states with a constant saving ratio.

2. The Solow-Swan model

Let us alter only one aspect of the Harrod-Domar model, and admit a technology with factor substitution. This produces the Solow-Swan model. It is sometimes believed that neoclassical growth theory begins and ends with this model. I hope my remarks at the beginning of this chapter, and the programme to follow, will help the readers to place this model in its proper limited context within the general neoclassical approach.

It is now more convenient to allow time to vary continuously. At any instant t, the factor supplies $K(t)$ and $L(t)$ are fixed. We can then find the equilibrium output $Y(t)$ and the factor prices $w(t)$ and $r(t)$ from (2.4) and (2.5), or from (2.13) and (2.14), or from (2.16)–(2.18). With no technological change, or with purely labour-augmenting change and labour and wage expressed in efficiency units, the functional form of F or ϕ does not change over time. Then, provided we can obtain the time-paths of $K(t)$ and $L(t)$, we can calculate the remaining variables of interest in terms of them. It is sometimes more convenient to work in terms of the intensive or relative magnitudes $k = K/L$ and $l = L/K$. Since we know that $\dot{L}(t) = n \cdot L(t)$, i.e. $L(t) = L(0) \cdot e^{n \cdot t}$, we can then calculate $K(t)$ and proceed.

Investment flow is now the rate of change, i.e. the time derivative, of the capital stock. Using the assumption of the constant saving propensity, we have

$$\dot{K}(t) = I(t) = s \cdot Y(t) \tag{3.5}$$

and

$$C(t) = (1 - s) \cdot Y(t) \tag{3.6}$$

The proportional rate of growth of capital is

$$\dot{K}(t)/K(t) = s \cdot Y(t)/K(t) = s/v(t) = s \cdot z(t) \tag{3.7}$$

In what follows, I shall omit the time arguments when no confusion is likely.

Turning to the ratios k and l, we note that

$$\dot{k}/k = \dot{K}/K - \dot{L}/L = -\dot{l}/l,$$

and therefore, using (3.7), we have

$$\dot{k} = s \cdot y - n \cdot k \tag{3.8}$$

$$\dot{l}/l = n - s \cdot z \tag{3.9}$$

We know the functional relations $y = f(k)$ and $z = g(l)$, where each function is increasing and concave. Then Fig. 3.1 can be drawn as

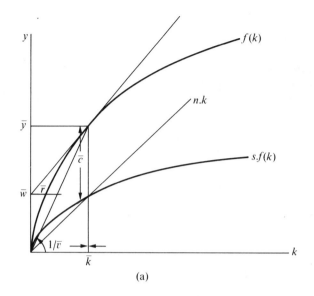

(a)

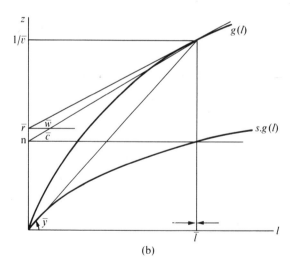

(b)

FIG. 3.1

shown. In each case there can be at most one value of k or l where the right hand side is zero. If the technology allows a sufficient range of variation in v, there will be precisely one such value. This is the steady state, where capital and labour grow at the same rate n, and their ratio is thus constant. If we identify this state by a bar over the variables, we can write the equation defining it as $s \cdot \bar{y} = n \cdot \bar{k}$ or $n = s \cdot \bar{z}$, both of which reduce to the familiar $s/\bar{v} = n$. Unlike the Harrod-Domar case, v can now adjust to take on the particular value $\bar{v}$ to make this true. The figure also shows some other steady state magnitudes of economic interest.

Equilibrium paths are defined by (3.8) or (3.9). From the former, and Figure 3.1(a), we see that to the left of $\bar{k}$, we have $\dot{k}$ positive, i.e. k increasing, while to the right we have $\dot{k}$ negative, i.e. k decreasing. All equilibrium paths corresponding to all possible historical initial values of k therefore converge to the steady state $\bar{k}$. Thus the Solow-Swan model provides one answer to the convergence problem for equilibrium growth that arose in the Harrod-Domar model. However, such convergence will be more problematic when there are more goods.

There are also other problems. The result above is qualitative. Convergence is assured, but it may be extremely slow. In fact, some simulation studies show this to be the case in many situations of interest.[2] Thus we are liable to draw mistaken inferences if we assume that the economy is more or less always in a steady state, or that it jumps to the new steady state soon after a parametric change. Wherever possible, we should try to examine the entire equilibrium path.

Even this may not be enough. A sudden or large parametric change in the real world would lead to a period of disequilibrium. Some time would be needed for expectations and actions to adjust to the new circumstances. In the meantime, another change may disrupt the process once again. While some useful insights can be obtained by analysing equilibrium paths, much supplementary reasoning is necessary in reliable applications.

Let us return to examine further properties of the model. If the range of variation of v is not large enough, a steady state with a positive and finite $\bar{k}$ may not exist. This can arise in two ways, shown in Fig. 3.2. In part (a), all equilibrium paths have k decreasing and tending to zero, while in part (b) they have k increasing and tending to infinity. The asymptotic rate of growth of K can still be constant, but not equal to n.

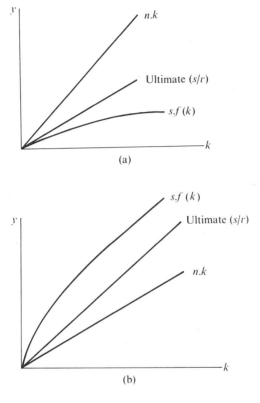

FIG. 3.2

Unlike the Harrod-Domar case, we now have factor substitution, and there need not be any unemployment. We could admit such cases as 'degenerate' steady states, in contrast to the 'proper' steady states discussed before. These possibilities create some technical exceptions to some results; these will be pointed out as they arise.

For a Cobb-Douglas production function, v can range from 0 to ∞, and degeneracy is not possible. In other cases of constant elasticity of substitution, v is bounded above if $\sigma > 1$ and below if $\sigma < 1$, and then values of s and n may be such as to produce a degenerate steady state. This can be verified from (2.13b).

Finally, we can examine in somewhat greater detail the properties of equilibrium paths. For this and for much later work, it will be useful to introduce some new notation. Given any time series $x(t)$, let $G\langle x \rangle$ denote its proportional growth rate, $\dot{x}/x$. Now consider a functional relation $z = z(x, y)$ between any three time series. We can then relate their rates of growth by a simple formula. The Chain Rule of differentiation yields

$$\dot{z} = (\partial z/\partial x) \cdot \dot{x} + (\partial z/\partial y) \cdot \dot{y}$$

Then

$$G\langle z \rangle = \left\{ \frac{x}{z} \cdot \frac{\partial z}{\partial x} \right\} \cdot G\langle x \rangle + \left\{ \frac{y}{z} \cdot \frac{\partial z}{\partial y} \right\} \cdot G\langle y \rangle \qquad (3.10)$$

The expressions in the brackets are the elasticities of z with respect to x and y, and therefore have economic interpretations. For a production function with constant returns to scale, for example, they are the competitive factor shares. Then they add to one, and $G\langle z \rangle$ is a weighted average of $G\langle x \rangle$ and $G\langle y \rangle$. In the Cobb-Douglas case, the weights are constant.

Now consider patterns of equilibrium growth with a constant saving ratio. Applying (3.10) to the production function, we have,

$$G\langle Y \rangle = \pi r \cdot G\langle K \rangle + \pi w \cdot n \qquad (3.11)$$

But $G\langle K \rangle = s \cdot Y/K$, and therefore

$$G\langle G\langle K \rangle \rangle = G\langle Y \rangle - G\langle K \rangle$$

$$= -\pi w \cdot (G\langle K \rangle - n)$$

This shows that $G\langle K \rangle$ is decreasing when it is greater than n and increasing when it is less than n. In other words, not only does the capital/labour ratio move monotonically towards its steady state value, but also its rate of growth moves monotonically towards its steady state value. This applies to proper steady states. In degenerate cases, πw can go to zero and thus arrest the movement of $G\langle K \rangle$ before it reaches n. This throws more light on the problem of degeneracy.

The rate of growth of output need not change monotonically. We see from (3.11) that it is a weighted average of $G\langle K \rangle$ and n, the weights being the imputed factor shares. If $\sigma > 1$, the weight of the faster growing factor increases, and this acts as a force accelerating the output growth. This is called the 'to-him-that-hath-shall-be-given' situation by Meade.[3] This is at least partially offset by the tendency of $G\langle K \rangle$ to move towards n. If there is a proper steady state, this latter force must ultimately prevail. $G\langle K \rangle$ converges to n, and $G\langle Y \rangle$, lying between the two, must do the same. Thus, if $\sigma > 1$ and $G\langle K \rangle > n$, then $G\langle Y \rangle$ may increase for a while, but ultimately it must decelerate and fall back to n.

3. Comparisons between steady states

A steady state is determined by all the exogenous influences on the model, i.e. the saving propensity, the rate of population growth, and the production function. A different set of these data will yield a different steady state. For the Solow-Swan model we know that the equilibrium growth path following a parametric change will converge to the new steady state, and we can examine the whole path without too much difficulty. But we often find it interesting or useful to examine how two steady states corresponding to two different sets of parameters compare with each other, without paying attention to the transition from one to the other. To avoid misunderstanding, it is extremely important to be clear about whether we are comparing steady states or studying transitions. To assist us in maintaining this distinction, we use different terms. It is usual to use comparative words like 'higher', in the former context, and words with dynamic connotations, like 'increasing', in the latter.

A common comparison is that between steady states having the same technology and population levels and growth rates, but different saving propensities. This is illustrated in Fig. 3.3 using the (k, y) diagram; the (l, z) diagram serves equally well and is left as an exercise.[4] Steady states corresponding to the saving propensities s_1 and s_2 are indicated by labelling the relevant variables with subscripts 1 and 2 respectively.

It is easy to see that the steady state with the higher saving ratio has (1) more output per man, (2) a higher capital/labour ratio, (3) a higher capital/output ratio, (in fact, with given n, the steady state v is proportional to s), (4) a higher wage rate, and (5) a lower profit (or rental) rate. The comparison of distributive shares depends on σ. If it exceeds 1 everywhere, for example, we have $\pi r_2 > \pi r_1$.

To illustrate how the results and the terminology differ when we consider transitions, let us examine the corresponding equilibrium path.

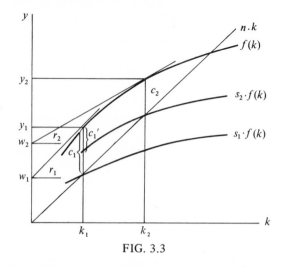

FIG. 3.3

Suppose the economy is initially in the steady state 1, and suppose the saving ratio suddenly jumps to s_2. The labour supply is exogenous and unaffected, and the capital stock cannot change suddenly. Thus, in the first instance, k remains at k_1 and y at y_1. The only immediate effect is that saving per head increases from $s_1 \cdot y_1$ to $s_2 \cdot y_1$, and consumption per head drops from $c_1 = (1 - s_1) \cdot y_1$ to $c_1' = (1 - s_2) \cdot y_1$. The rate of growth of capital jumps from $s_1/v_1 = n$ to s_2/v_1. Along the subsequent equilibrium path, it gradually sinks back to $n = s_2/v_2$. In the meantime, capital grows faster than labour, i.e. there is capital deepening. In this process, y, v, and w are all increasing, and r is falling. The movement of distributive shares depends on σ. Consumption per head steadily increases from its initially fallen level c_1' but we cannot say in general whether the new steady state level c_2 will exceed the old one, c_1.

It is worth pointing out that the various steady state rates of growth are all independent of s, even though the levels of the variables are affected by s. Thus any increase in growth rates resulting from increased saving is only temporary. This is sometimes thought to be an undesirable feature of such models, and I shall re-examine it when discussing technological progress that can be affected by s.

There are two particularly important results concerning comparisons of steady states. The first is that a steady state with a higher wage rate has a lower interest rate. This was shown above when making comparisons for different saving ratios, but it can also be seen more directly. This is because in a one-good model, the interest rate equals the rental rate, and we already have a relation between w and r given by the factor-price curve. Thus we have a wage-interest curve that happens to coincide with the factor-price curve discussed in Chapter 2, and the properties obtained there can be applied to the wage-interest curve. In particular, the slope at any point is the value of k for the corresponding steady state, and the elasticity is the ratio of distributive shares. It is a convex curve, and its curvature can be shown to be proportional to σ.

Next, we can obtain somewhat more precise relations between the various economic magnitudes in a steady state and the saving ratio defining it. We can regard k as a function of s, defined implicitly by the basic equation for the steady state,

$$s \cdot f(k) = n \cdot k \qquad (3.12)$$

All the other variables are known as functions of k and therefore of s. Differentiating (3.12) using the Chain Rule, we find the slope of this function. We have $f(k) + s \cdot f'(k) \cdot dk/ds = n \cdot dk/ds$, and then

$$dk/ds = y/(n - s \cdot r) \qquad (3.13)$$

Fig. 3.1 shows that the curve $s \cdot f(k)$ cuts the line $n \cdot k$ from above, and this verifies that dk/ds is positive. Then we use $y = f(k)$, and therefore $dy/ds = f'(k) \cdot dk/ds$. After some substitution, we find

$$\frac{s}{y} \cdot \frac{dy}{ds} = \frac{r \cdot k}{w} = \frac{\pi r}{\pi w} \qquad (3.14)$$

This is a simple and useful result that is more widely valid, and we shall meet it again. If we believe that the present model is a reasonable approximation to an actual economy, then we can use (3.14) to obtain rough estimates of the long run effects of a change in the saving propensity. If we take the ratio $\pi r/\pi w$ to be roughly $1/3$, we see that a rise in the net saving ratio from 10 to 11 per cent, i.e. a 10 per cent rise, will raise the permanent level of the output path by about 3 per cent.

However, we do not usually desire output for its own sake. Consumption is the more interesting magnitude from the point of view of welfare judgements, and it behaves in a more complex way since there are two opposing forces at work. A steady state with a higher level of output per man also has a higher proportion of that output ploughed back as investment, in order to sustain the higher capital/labour ratio. Diminishing returns to capital ultimately imply a negative net return. If we look at Figure 3.3, we see that for each saving ratio, the steady state consumption level is the vertical difference between the curve $f(k)$ and the line $n \cdot k$. As we consider steady states with different values of s, starting near zero and ending near one, we see that the corresponding value of c is zero at first, then successively higher, and then successively lower again and ultimately zero. The highest value occurs when the two curves are parallel, i.e. when $f'(k) = n$. Mathematically, we have $c = (1 - s) \cdot y = y - n \cdot k$, and $dc/ds = dy/ds - n \cdot dk/ds = (r - n) \cdot dk/ds$, which has the same sign as $(r - n)$. Where c is highest, we have an interesting relation for its value, since in that steady state, $c = y - n \cdot k = y - r \cdot k = w$. The steady state defined by

$$r = n \qquad \text{or} \qquad w = c \qquad (3.15)$$

is called the Golden Rule of Accumulation.

This seems to have a normative connotation. Indeed, if we accept consumption as the ultimate goal of economic activity, it seems obvious to pose the question of whether saving policy should attempt to attain the Golden Rule. However, it is an illustration of the danger of confusing comparisons and transitions. If our choice were to be made from among the collection of steady states, the answer would be yes, provided issues like income distribution were satisfactorily resolved. Actually, the domain of choice is different. Each steady state has its own capital/labour ratio. The economy at the instant when we begin to implement a saving policy has a historically fixed capital/labour ratio, and it cannot be shifted instantaneously to that of the steady state we desire. On the other hand, the same capital/labour ratio is maintained for ever in a steady state, and there is no a priori reason why planned growth should not allow this ratio to change over time. Thus, in comparison with the domain of the collection of all steady states, the domain of choice in practice is different, being narrower in one respect and wider in another. A different approach is therefore necessary to tackle the question of saving policy properly, and I shall take it up in Chapter 5. It will turn out that the Golden Rule has some relation to proper optimum policies, but not a very direct one.

There is one simple normative conclusion that can be drawn now. Suppose the initial saving ratio is such as to yield a steady state above the Golden Rule capital/labour ratio. Suppose we contemplate a slight increase in the saving ratio. We know that the new steady state value of c will be lower than the old one. Considering the transition, consumption per head will drop initially, and in its subsequent climb will not even regain its old steady state level. From almost any welfare standpoint, the policy change will have been a pure waste. Reversing the argument, a slight decrease in s will cause an initial jump in c, and the subsequent decline as the new steady state with a lower k is reached will still leave c above its old steady state value, producing a pure gain. The point is that above the Golden Rule, the economy is weighted down by its own capital stock. A lot of output is being produced solely to equip the growing labour force with the large-quantities of capital, and a policy of some decumulation will yield a Pareto-superior path. The policy for optimum decumulation remains to be found, but some decumulation is desirable, and any policy that maintains the economy permanently above the Golden Rule capital/labour ratio is inefficient. This is a very general result.

In concluding this section, I must emphasize the problems that arise in attempting to generalize from the simple model here. We have obtained several specific and unambiguous results. For example, in comparing steady states, we found that the following were associated together: (1) a higher saving ratio, (2) a higher capital/labour ratio, (3) a higher output per head, (4) a higher wage rate, (5) a lower interest rate, and (6) so long as the Golden Rule is not crossed, a higher consumption per head. At one time, it was hoped by some economists that comparisons of steady states in more general models would yield similar simple and clear results. In particular, it was hoped that capital intensity could be *defined* in many-good models by using the interest rate, with a lower interest rate corresponding to a greater capital intensity. It has since been shown that such hopes are in vain, and most of the above simple results cease to be valid when we admit greater complexity and disaggregation in our models. The Golden Rule is the only truly general result; it is valid so long as the relevant equilibria exist. The wage-interest curve also retains some of its features so long as there is no joint production, but is not in general the same as the wage-rental curve. The association between higher capital or output per man and a higher wage rate depends on the relations of complementarity and substitution among inputs.[5] All other associations soon break down. Similar problems arise for results of monotonic convergence along equilibrium paths. We shall meet some models illustrating these problems in Chapters 6 and 7.

Other comparisons of steady states are left as an exercise. Three useful cases are (1) a change in n, (2) a once-and-for-all, output-augmenting shift in the technology, and (3) a once-and-for-all, purely labour-augmenting shift in the technology.

4. The Cambridge model

We continue with the one-good framework, and revert to treating v as exogenous and constant, but allow s to adjust in response to economic forces. This is done by postulating different saving propensities out of different categories of income. In the version of Kaldor, the saving propensities out of wages and profits are constant but unequal. If the former is sw and the latter sp, it is assumed that

$$0 \leqslant sw < sp \leqslant 1 \tag{3.16}$$

Suppose a proportion πp of income goes to profits and πw to wages, where

$$\pi p \geqslant 0, \quad \pi w \geqslant 0, \quad \pi p + \pi w = 1 \tag{3.17}$$

In a situation of competitive equilibrium, the profit rate will equal the rental rate, and πp will equal the imputed share πr. However, I shall allow some more generality and maintain a distinction between them. Now the aggregate proportion of national income saved is easily seen to be

$$s = sw \cdot \pi w + sp \cdot \pi p \tag{3.18}$$

The condition for sustained equilibrium growth is, as in the Harrod-Domar model,

$$s = v \cdot n \tag{3.19}$$

If $v \cdot n$ lies between sw and sp, then we can find a weighted average of them which equals $v \cdot n$, and the weights serve as the equilibrium values of the shares of wages and profits in income. Solving explicitly, we find

$$\pi w = (sp - v \cdot n)/(sp - sw), \quad \pi p = (v \cdot n - sw)/(sp - sw) \tag{3.20}$$

The existence of a steady state is not now such a fortuitous matter. Owing to the fixed coefficients technology, however, stability of equilibrium growth remains problematic. The only path of sustained full employment growth is the steady state itself, and other equilibrium paths have strange features. As before, start with a steady state and let some disturbance occur to make s exceed $v \cdot n$. In the next period there will be an excess supply of capital, and the equilibrium rent (and thus the profit share) will drop down to zero. Then s will drop to sw, and the growth rate to sw/v, which is assumed to be less than n. In course of time, this will lead to an equilibrium with labour in excess supply, when the equilibrium wage rate (and share) will drop to zero. Then s will jump to sp, and so on. Fluctuations of a singularly unrealistic kind will result.

The usual stories of adjustment in this model therefore involve disequilibrium considerations of some kind. Note that this shows up the limitations of the rigid equilibrium framework, and not necessarily those of the model. I shall postpone further analysis of disequilibrium to Chapter 8, but two simple versions of adjustment mechanisms are worth outlining here.

Let us start both stories at the same point. Suppose the economy has been in a steady state, with a resulting saving ratio $\bar{s} = v \cdot n$. Had this state continued, income in the period being examined would have been $\bar{Y}$, the capital stock $\bar{K} = v \cdot \bar{Y}$, and the labour supply $\bar{L} = b \cdot \bar{Y}$. Suppose some disturbance increases the saving ratio to s'.

If the savers' plans are fulfilled and translated into investment, an excess of capital will emerge. We will have $Y' = \bar{Y}$ and $L' = \bar{L}$, but $K' > \bar{K}$ using obvious notation. We can visualize a state where the scarcer factor is fully employed, but prices move sluggishly towards their equilibrium values. Then the distribution of income will shift gradually away from profits, s will decrease gradually, and stable adjustment will be possible. Recall that such a lagged adjustment of prices did not help in the Harrod-Domar model, since there was no way there in which it could affect the relevant variable, s.

The other story allows Keynesian unemployment. Suppose that investment has become geared to the expectations of the previous steady state. Producers plan to keep capital growing at the rate n, i.e. $I' = \bar{I} = n \cdot \bar{K}$. In the short run, income and output adjust quickly to equate planned saving and investment, i.e. $s' \cdot Y' = I'$, or $Y' = \bar{K} \cdot (n/s') < \bar{K} \cdot (n/\bar{s}) = \bar{K}/v$. There is a shortage of aggregate effective demand,

and both factors are unemployed. If this arises with sticky wages, there will be a squeeze on profits. This will reduce the aggregate saving propensity, and thus exert a stabilizing influence.

It is easy to see that there are unsatisfactory features in both stories. The first does not allow quantity adjustments in the face of disequilibrium, even though it is known that such adjustments can arise from perfectly rational economic responses.[6] The beginning of the second story is undoubtedly very attractive, but it is very difficult to carry it further. Once the growth path veers away from the old steady state, we cannot for very long use the expectations of continuation of that state as the basis for determining investment demand. It is conceivable, for example, that the initial unemployment will make the producers more pessimistic, and reduce investment demand below $\bar{I}$. The multiplier effects of this will be destabilizing, and at least for a while they may be stronger than the stabilizing effects of the fall in s. However, a detailed examination of this will take us into the uncharted territory where Keynesian and general equilibrium models meet.

It is easy to consider equilibrium growth when both s and v are flexible. Since $\pi p = r \cdot K/Y = r \cdot v$, we have from (3.18)

$$s/v = sw/v + (sp - sw) \cdot r \qquad (3.21)$$

Now sw and $(sp - sw)$ are both non-negative, while $(1/v)$ and r are both increasing functions of l (see Figure 2.4(b)). We then have s/v as an increasing function of l, and the proof of stability is exactly the same as that for the Solow-Swan model, following Fig. 3.1(b).

All of this differentiates saving behaviour according to the kind of income. It is also possible to consider behaviour typical of the kind of recipient. If sw is positive, labourers will acquire title to some capital, and their income will come to consist of some wages and some interest on accumulated saving. Kaldor's model attaches different saving propensities to these two categories. Pasinetti, on the other hand, defines two classes of income recipients: labourers, who have some wage income, and capitalists, who have only profit income. Each class saves a fixed proportion of its total income, and the capitalists' saving propensity (sc) exceeds that of the labourers (sl). I shall first look at the results of the Pasinetti model, and then comment on the differences between it and the Kaldor version.

We must now distinguish profit income by recipient, and this is done by distinguishing capital ownership likewise. Let Kl denote the amount of capital owned by labourers and Kc that owned by capitalists, with total capital stock $K = Kl + Kc$. Equations for accumulation of the two are

$$\dot{Kl} = sl \cdot (w \cdot L + r \cdot Kl)$$
$$\dot{Kc} = sc \cdot r \cdot Kc \tag{3.22}$$

In a steady state, we shall require the proportions of capital ownership to be constant, and then each of Kl and Kc must grow at the rate n of growth of labour supply. Thus the steady state is defined by

$$n \cdot Kl = sl \cdot (w \cdot L + r \cdot Kl)$$
$$n \cdot Kc = sc \cdot r \cdot Kc \tag{3.23}$$

From the second of these, we must have either $Kc = 0$ or $n = sc \cdot r$ in a steady state. If we look only at those steady states in which there is a positive amount of capital held by a class that derives its income from profits alone, we must have

$$r = n/sc \tag{3.24}$$

This is a generalization of the result of equation (1.6). This quick determination of the profit rate explains the attraction of this theory for economists who can only see one link in the chain of general equilibrium at a time, i.e. who can only solve one equation at a time. But we must look more closely to see when such steady states are possible.

Consider the other kind of steady state, where $Kc = 0$. Then $K = Kl$ and $Y = w \cdot L + r \cdot Kl$. From (3.23) we have $n \cdot K = sl \cdot Y$, or $n/sl = 1/v$. Finally, $r \cdot v = \pi p$, the proportion of *all* profits in total income. Thus $r \cdot v \leqslant 1$, or $1/v \geqslant r$. In Fig. 3.4 then, we can show all possible steady states on the L-shaped curve ABC (remember we have assumed $sc > sl$). Those along BC are of the Pasinetti type, while those along AB are of the other type, where workers own all capital and there are no pure capitalists.

Thus far in this model we have had no occasion to use any particular properties of the technology, and the argument is valid given only constant returns to scale and diminishing returns to each factor. In

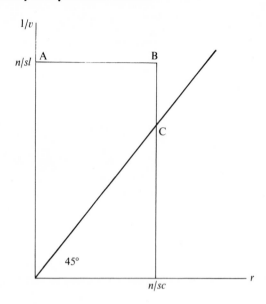

FIG. 3.4

order to fix one steady state out of all the possibilities, we need to specify the technology. This is studied by Meade, who considers three simple cases. For a Cobb-Douglas production function, in the notation of (2.13a), πp is constant and equal to α, the exponent of capital, and thus $1/v = r/\alpha$. This is a ray through the origin in Fig. 3.4. Depending on α, it may intersect either AB or BC, so we may have a steady state of either type. If there are fixed coefficients of production, v is fixed, and the horizontal line at height $(1/v)$ may cut BC, or may by chance coincide with AB, or no steady state may exist. Finally, monetary policy may fix r (although there are difficulties in fixing permanently the real as opposed to the money rate of interest). In this case, the vertical line may cut AB, or may by chance coincide with BC, or no steady state may exist.

Comparisons of steady states corresponding to different values of v, n or one of the saving propensities in the Kaldor or the Pasinetti-Meade model are all very easy to make, and are left as exercises. Stability of equilibrium growth in the Pasinetti-Meade model is not easy to study, but can be examined using geometric techniques of phase diagrams that we shall meet later.[7]

5. Comments on saving behaviour

The treatment of saving by means of fixed 'propensities' is subject to the serious criticism that such behaviour is not in any way forward-looking. This is important since saving is an act undertaken solely for the sake of returns in the future, whether the returns are in the form of consumption, or security, or simply the pleasure from being wealthy. Of course, the simple assumptions may be justified as being in rough agreement with data. But this can be no more than a temporary refuge, like the use of an aggregate Cobb-Douglas production function as a working approximation. It is important to continue more refined analysis of the data, as well as theoretical work on the consequences of various types of forward-looking saving behaviour. Some such theoretical models will appear in Chapter 5.

These remarks apply, obviously enough, to the models of Sections 1–3 which use a single aggregate saving propensity. They apply with almost equal force to the models of Section 4 which allow two saving propensities, for this is at best a small advance as a workable approximation in comparison with the complex reality, and no advance at all as far as admitting a forward view is concerned.

We have in fact seen two separate models involving two saving propensities, and we must now examine the differences between them. They involve different views as to who does the saving in the economy. The reasoning underlying Pasinetti's model seems to be that the consumers do the saving. Then sc exceeds sl because people who derive their income from interest alone are usually richer or, being 'pure' capitalists, are interested in accumulation for its own sake or for the feeling of power it will bring them, and therefore save a greater proportion of their income. This need not always be true. For example, a world in which interest recipients were mostly old age pensioners would look quite different. The implicit institutional assumptions clearly need to be examined more carefully, and the fact that they are concealed behind the simple assumption of constant saving propensities does not make debate or statistical testing easy.

Kaldor's view is different. He sees saving out of profits as done by firms in the form of retained earnings. That is why he differentiates saving by income type rather than by recipient type. Even though workers may have profit incomes, the saving decisions for this part are taken on their behalf by managers of firms who can only be imperfectly controlled by stockholders. While there is truth in this argument, it ignores a host of secondary effects. Workers can notice their imperfect control over managers and respond by altering their saving out of wage income. Also, when firms invest retained earnings, the value of ownership of their shares increases, and the owners of these shares have the additional option of consuming more out of their capital gains if they so wish.[8] Neglecting any such response is rather like assuming that the incidence of a tax stays at the point where it is levied.

It is very likely that in the real world such responses are far from perfect. But it is far from clear whether it is a good halfway house to graft the assumption that households take imperfect or no notice of saving decisions made on their behalf on to an otherwise perfect equilibrium model. On the other hand, it is clear that it is bad to conceal all these complexities behind constant saving propensities. Interactions between corporations' and share-holders' decisions, and their implications for the growth of firms, are becoming very active areas of research. In my opinion, that approach provides a better prospect for understanding the operation and the consequences of saving by firms than is possible with saving propensity assumptions. I shall mention some such models in Chapter 8.

I would like to qualify my criticism of the use of saving propensities by saying that those remarks are made in the exacting spirit of research. In the context of applicability, we should recognize that in skilful hands and used with care, even these crude models have yielded some important practical insights and conclusions.

6. Depreciation

It is very easy to modify the earlier models slightly to take account of one particular type of deterioration of machines as they age. This also provides a simple and useful introduction to the general subject of depreciation.

I mentioned earlier that physical deterioration is one of the factors that can compel us to distinguish machines by the date of installation.

Let θ be the variable denoting this date. Write $I(\theta)$ for the number of machines installed at θ, and $p(\theta, t)$ for the price, relative to the numéraire at date t, of a machine installed at date θ.

Now consider a case where machines lose a constant proportion of their efficacy each year, as if by 'evaporation' or 'radioactive decay'; this is the reverse of a capital-augmenting technological shift. Thus there is a number δ, lying between 0 and 1, such that at any date t, a θ-machine is a perfect substitute in use for $(1 - \delta)$ machines one year younger, i.e. $(\theta + 1)$-machines. Then their prices must obey the relation

$$p(\theta, t) = (1 - \delta) \cdot p(\theta + 1, t)$$

and iterating this,

$$p(\theta, t) = p(t, t) \cdot (1 - \delta)^{t - \theta}$$

Similarly, in continuous time, we have

$$p(\theta, t) = p(t, t) \cdot e^{-\delta \cdot (t - \theta)}$$

In the one-good case, a new machine is a perfect substitute in production for a unit of output, i.e. $p(t, t) = 1$. It is then easy to verify that, in the respective cases,

$$p(\theta, t) - p(\theta, t + 1) = \delta \cdot p(\theta, t) \tag{3.25}$$

and

$$\partial p(\theta, t) / \partial t = -\delta \cdot p(\theta, t) \tag{3.26}$$

Then the short-run perfect foresight equation (2.32) becomes

$$r(\theta, t) / p(\theta, t) = i(t) + \delta \tag{3.27}$$

Thus the loss in value is proportional to the asset price, and the rental rate measured relative to the asset price is the sum of the interest rate and the deterioration rate.

There is another way of looking at this which is often more useful, though the two are of course formally equivalent. Instead of iterating the price relation, we can iterate the information on physical properties of a machine. Thus a machine constructed at date θ will be a perfect substitute in use for $(1 - \delta)^{t - \theta}$ (or $e^{-\delta \cdot (t - \theta)}$ in continuous time) new machines at date t. We can use this to convert all machine quantities into 'new-machine equivalents'. In this unit of measurement, all machines are perfect substitutes in use, and can be aggregated by simple addition. We can then speak of a scalar capital stock. If $I(\theta)$ new machines were constructed at date θ, the number of new-machine equivalents available at date $(t + 1)$ is

$$K(t + 1) = I(t) + I(t - 1) \cdot (1 - \delta) + I(t - 2) \cdot (1 - \delta)^2 + \dots$$

and therefore

$$K(t + 1) - K(t) = I(t) - \delta \cdot K(t) \qquad (3.28)$$

In continuous time, these can be written

$$K(t) = \int_{\theta \leqslant t} e^{-\delta \cdot (t - \theta)} \cdot I(\theta) \cdot \mathrm{d}\theta$$

and

$$\dot{K}(t) = I(t) - \delta \cdot K(t) \qquad (3.29)$$

In the one-good case, of course, the price of each new machine equivalent is 1, and we find that $i(t) = r(t)$, the rent on a new machine equivalent. It is instructive to look at the apparent difference between this and (3.27). By definition, renting out a new-machine equivalent does not involve any loss due to deterioration. At the end of the period, the owner gets back his new-machine equivalent, and that is as if the deterioration is made good by the user. Call the rent corresponding to this arrangement the net rent. In the earlier approach, machines were not converted into new-machine equivalents. The owner therefore received an older machine at the end of the period of renting, and thus bore the deterioration loss himself. Call the rent under this set-up the gross rent. This must exceed the net rent exactly by the deterioration loss, for any discrepancy would create opportunities for arbitrage (buying a net-rental contract to sell a gross one, or vice versa) and thus could not prevail in equilibrium. We then have the result that in the one-good model, the net rental rate equals the interest rate. It is then easy to modify the models of Sections 1–4 to allow for radioactive deterioration of machines. Some care is necessary about sign restrictions. Given free disposability, the gross rental must be non-negative. However, if loss by deterioration is unavoidable, the net rental can be negative, but it cannot be less than $-\delta$.

Most expositions of this subject begin by *defining* depreciation as the rate of physical decay by evaporation, and assert (3.27) and (3.29) directly. With other types of decay, or with technological change, such a simple procedure is no longer valid, and everything has to be defined afresh. This is why I have chosen to begin with the general concept, namely the loss of value through the passage of time. This is what affects the economic calculations of the relevant agents, and it can arise from various causes of which decay by evaporation is only one. It is therefore better to reserve the term 'depreciation' for the general phenomenon, and establish (3.29) as a valid aggregation in the special case.

It is worth mentioning that aggregation over machines of different ages is more generally possible, and we shall meet another case of it in Chapter 4. However, the resulting formulae are not as simple as the one for radioactive decay.

While (3.29) enables us to handle depreciation by radioactive decay very easily in a growth model, one new point arises. A distinction must be made between gross income and net income, and similarly between gross saving and net saving. A saving propensity can then be defined in four ways. There is reason to favour the assumption of constancy of the ratio of net saving to net income. This can be handled very easily in the case of radioactive decay, but in other cases it can be much more difficult.

Another relatively simple instance of physical deterioration is 'sudden death', where a machine provides services at a constant rate for a fixed period T, and then disintegrates with no scrap value. This is the famous 'one-hoss shay'.[9] Consider a steady state where the rate of interest is i, and the rent for the shay over its lifetime is at a constant rate r. We can write the price of a t year old shay as the discounted present value of the rents over the remaining $(T - t)$ years of its life (neglecting pure speculative booms in shays). Also, in the one-good case, the price of a new shay is 1, which means that r and i cannot be independent variables, but must satisfy a constraint implied by this equilibrium condition. After some calculation, it can be seen that the price of a t-year old shay is

$$p(t) = (e^{i \cdot T} - e^{i \cdot t})/(e^{i \cdot T} - 1) \qquad (3.30)$$

and depreciation, i.e. the rate of fall of this, is

$$-\dot{p}(t) = i \cdot e^{i \cdot t}/(e^{i \cdot T} - 1) \tag{3.31}$$

Thus depreciation is initially low, and rises exponentially through the life of the machine. The reason for this is simple. The future rent profile for a $(t + 1)$-year machine is exactly the same as that for a t-year old one except that one year at the end is lost. For a machine that lasts a hundred years, for example, the depreciation as it ages from 5 years to 6 arises from the loss of r in 95 years' time, while the depreciation as it ages from 91 years to 92 is a more immediate loss of r in only 9 years' time. And it is the discounted present value of this loss that accounts for the depreciation.[10]

In general, the rent on a machine will not be constant over its life, nor will it be exogenous. The rent equals the value of output minus the costs of the other factors of production, and both of these magnitudes can change endogenously. An important example is that of 'embodied' technological progress. If the technical specifications of a machine cannot be altered once it is built, but prices of other factors can, then competition for these factors from later and better machines will push up their prices. There may come a time when the variable costs for an old machine exhaust the output. After this time, the owner of such a machine will prefer to keep it idle, for the gross rent from using the machine would be negative. Suppose, for example, that a machine built at θ produces $z(\theta)$ units of output, and requires $l(\theta)$ units of labour, whenever it is used. If output is numéraire, and the wage rate at time t is $w(t)$, then the gross rent is

$$r(\theta, t) = z(\theta) - w(t) \cdot l(\theta)$$

As $w(t)$ rises, the θ-machine is discarded at the date $t = \theta'$ defined by

$$w(\theta') = z(\theta)/l(\theta)$$

A complete model incorporating this possibility will be developed in Chapter 4. Two important implications should be noted at this stage.

First, we have here a cause of depreciation that is quite independent of any physical decay through age. The specifications of the machine in question may remain unchanged, but as relatively more productive machines appear in the rest of the economy and the prices of other factors are pushed up by competition, the rents on this machine decline and so does its price. True economic depreciation then allows for this prospect of 'economic obsolescence'. An attempt is sometimes made to separate out two components of depreciation, the first representing physical decay and thus depending solely on $(t - \theta)$, the age of the machine, and the second representing obsolescence specific to θ, the date of construction or the 'vintage'. Such a separation is not only unnecessary, but also impossible to make in a unique way.[11] We should keep together all the components of value loss under the heading of depreciation.

Second, compared to the one-hoss shay, the model with embodied technological progress involves more rapid depreciation in the earlier years of life of a machine. This is because the rent falls over the life, and the highest rents are being lost in the early years. Given the manifold patterns of depreciation that can arise, simple tax rules like straight line or sum of digits depreciation are unlikely to be correct in any specific case. This has implications for the theory of investment demand. Also, if borrowing possibilities are not perfect, there arises the question of whether the funds accumulated from depreciating according to the rules of thumb provide enough funds for replacement. Of course, in a model of equilibrium, there need be no connection between the repayment of an old loan and the contracting of a new one, and the question is irrelevant there.

We can, however, obtain one very simple rule. Write $D(t)$ for the accumulated depreciation fund at date t. Suppose a new machine is bought at 0, and write $p(t)$ for the price of a t-year old machine. If we arrange matters so that $D(t) + p(t)$ is always equal to $p(0)$, then the moment the machine is useless, i.e. its price falls to zero, we will have just enough in the fund to buy a new one. If the fund is invested at the going rate of interest, we have $\dot{D}(t) = i(t) \cdot D(t) + d(t)$, where $d(t)$ is the flow of new transfers to the fund. Therefore the rule giving the necessary new transfers is

$$d(t) = \dot{D}(t) - i(t) \cdot D(t)$$
$$= -\dot{p}(t) - i(t) \cdot \{p(0) - p(t)\}$$
$$= r(t) - i(t) \cdot p(0), \quad \text{using (2.32)}$$

In other words, the normal return on the initial financial investment

$p(0)$ should be removed as dividends, and the rest of rental income should be transferred to the depreciation fund. This makes perfectly good sense in a framework of equilibrium. Of course several modifications to this rule are necessary to take into account problems like inflation, relative price changes and disequilibrium issues, but these complications are outside our present scope.

Notes

The subject matter of this chapter has a very large background literature. The original and most prominent contributions are as follows.

Section 1.   Harrod (1939), Domar (1946)
Section 2.   Solow (1956), (1970, Ch. 2), Swan (1956)
Section 3.   Phelps (1961), Robinson (1962a)
Section 4.   Kaldor (1955), Pasinetti (1962), Meade (1966a)
Section 6.   Hotelling (1925).

Some further references are cited in footnotes below.

1.   But see Pitchford (1974, Ch. 4).
2.   See Sato (1963), Atkinson (1969).
3.   Meade (1962, p. 28).
4.   See Solow (1970, pp. 24–9) for details of this method.
5.   For details and proofs of these assertions, see Solow (1962), Starrett (1969), Hatta (1975) and Bliss (1975a, Ch. 4).
6.   See Phelps et al. (1970).
7.   See a symposium in the *Review of Economic Studies, 33*(4), October 1966, and Conlisk and Ramanathan (1970), Rau (1975).
8.   See Bliss (1975a, Ch. 6) for a detailed discussion of these points.
9.   See Holmes (1857–8). General equilibrium theorists should carefully read this to the end.
10.   See Meade (1962, Ch. 9 and appendix III) for a detailed discussion of depreciation by sudden death.
11.   See Hall (1968).

4. Technological Progress

Advances in technology are clearly an important part of the experience of growth over the last few centuries, and growth theory has paid a lot of attention to technological progress. It must be confessed that in many ways the result is disappointing. With a few exceptions, the models treat such progress as an exogenous drift of the isoquants. This is at best a description of the phenomenon and not an explanation. However, even such description can be useful, by focussing attention on important relationships among the relevant variables, and providing a better understanding of the forces at work.

In this chapter I shall outline some such models. In the first three sections, I shall consider technological progress that is disembodied, i.e. which affects all existing machines, old and new, alike. It is then enough to work with the stock of machines of each type, and this simplification enables us to probe further some other issues, in particular the study of how technological progress can be influenced by economic forces. In the remaining sections I shall consider the difficult case where technological progress is embodied in new machines, i.e. where a machine cannot benefit from progress that occurs after its construction. The analytical difficulties of the models will force me to confine the discussion to steady states, with a few references to some advanced literature on more general growth paths. Even then, I hope, some useful conclusions will emerge.

1. Factor-augmentation and bias

In Chapter 2 we discussed some ways of describing and classifying shifts of the technology. We can incorporate the same apparatus into a model of growth by making such shifts occur continuously. Assuming that technological progress can be decomposed into labour-augmenting and capital-augmenting forms, for example, we can allow the associated efficiency factors to be functions of time. For sake of simplicity of exposition, I shall assume that these factors grow at constant relative rates, i.e. that the functions are exponential. If mk and ml are the respective rates of growth of the efficiency factors for capital and labour, we can write the production function at time t as

$$Y = F(e^{mk \cdot t} \cdot K, e^{ml \cdot t} \cdot L) \tag{4.1}$$

and similarly for the cost function. The equilibrium conditions can be written at each instant as in equations (2.19) and (2.20) (or alternatively in terms of cost functions) with the values of AK and AL that prevail at that instant.

The next natural step is to assume a constant rate of population growth and a constant saving ratio, and look for steady states. I mentioned before that such states are in fact possible only with purely labour-augmenting technological progress, i.e. when $mk = 0$. We must now see why this is so. The general idea is as follows. Growth at constant rates and with a constant fraction of income saved implies two things. First, a constant ratio of output to capital in physical units, and secondly, a constant imputed distribution of income. However, the latter requires a constant ratio of output to capital in efficiency units. Therefore the two are compatible only when there is no capital-augmentation. Some care is necessary in the logic of the proof, and exceptional cases arise, but the essence of the argument is quite simple.

In the steady state we require $G\langle K \rangle$ and s to be constant, and then $v = s/G\langle K \rangle$ must be constant as well. This is exactly as in Chapter 3. Since K/Y is constant, K and Y must grow at equal proportional rates; let g be the common value. Then we can convert (4.1) into a relation among growth rates, and using (3.10) and (2.21), write it as

$$g = \pi r \cdot (mk + g) + \pi w \cdot (ml + n).$$

Since $\pi r + \pi w = 1$, this becomes

$$g = n + ml + (\pi r / \pi w) \cdot mk \tag{4.2}$$

If we rule out degenerate steady states, i.e. assume that πr and πw are both positive, we find that $\pi r / \pi w$ must be constant, since g, n, ml and mk are all constant. But constant imputed shares are possible in only one of two cases: either EK/EL must be constant, or $\sigma = 1$. Considering the former first, we have

$$mk + g = ml + n.$$

Substituting in (4.2), we find $mk/\pi w = 0$, i.e. $mk = 0$. In the other case of $\sigma = 1$, the production function is Cobb-Douglas, where we can always arrange factors so as to make $mk = 0$. Thus we have proved that proper steady states can exist only when technological progress is, or can be expressed as, purely labour-augmenting. Then

$$g = ml + n. \tag{4.3}$$

This raises two questions. First, is there any reason for expecting technological progress to be purely labour-augmenting? Secondly, what happens if it is not? The answer to the latter is fairly evident, but I shall discuss it in more detail because it provides a good reminder of the relation between imputed shares and substitution, and also because it provides an introduction to a simple and useful geometric technique for studying dynamic systems.[1]

Since we have seen that g and the imputed shares cannot be constant, it is natural to see how they change. To simplify notation, we can suppose that $ml = 0$, or subsume it in n. Now write $x = G\langle K \rangle + mk$, so that $x - mk = s \cdot Y/K$. Taking rates of growth again, we have

$$G\langle x - mk \rangle = G\langle Y \rangle - G\langle K \rangle$$

or

$$\dot{x}/(x - mk) = \pi r \cdot x + \pi w \cdot n - (x - mk)$$

After some simplification, this becomes

$$\dot{x} = (x - mk) \cdot \{mk - \pi w \cdot (x - n)\} \tag{4.4}$$

Next consider πw. In Chapter 2 we found various conditions for consistency of small changes in factor prices and quantities, and later reinterpreted them in efficiency units. If we now take these to be actual changes over time in the process of growth, we can divide equations like (2.10) by the corresponding small interval dt of time to obtain relations among various growth rates. It is then easy to see that

$$G\langle \pi w/(1 - \pi w) \rangle = \{(1 - \sigma)/\sigma\} \cdot G\langle EK/EL \rangle$$

After some simplification in the present case, this becomes

$$\dot{\pi w} = \pi w \cdot (1 - \pi w) \cdot (x - n) \cdot (1 - \sigma)/\sigma \tag{4.5}$$

The two equations (4.4) and (4.5) are a very convenient way of describing how x and πw change through time. If we start with any given pair of values of these variables, we can use the equations to calculate their speeds of change. To the first order, this will tell us their values a short time dt later, and we can repeat the process. In the limit, using integration, we obtain exact solutions.

With only two variables involved, this is easily done geometrically. In the plane, we show x on the horizontal axis and πw on the vertical. At each point $(x, \pi w)$, we can draw a little arrow showing the direction and magnitude of motion compounded of the horizontal and vertical components, as in the parallelogram law for forces. Then we can join successive arrows tail to head, yielding paths of evolution of x and w. Such a diagram is called a *phase diagram*.[2]

In the present instance, only certain regions of the plane are of economic significance. For example, πw must lie in the interval $[0, 1]$. In fact (4.5) shows that $\pi \dot{w}$ approaches zero as πw approaches one of these extremes, and therefore a path starting in the meaningful region will not cross outside it. Also, since I have neglected deterioration, $G \langle K \rangle$ is non-negative, i.e. $x \geqslant mk$. Fig. 4.1 is to be read with this restriction, which does not affect the conclusions derived.

The easiest way to understand the diagram is to think of the plane as being split into regions, classified according to directions of change of the two variables. Since each of the two can increase or decrease, we have four possible combinations, although in the present case one of these falls in a region which is economically irrelevant. To obtain the classification, begin with (4.5) for the case $\sigma < 1$, which is shown in Fig. 4.1a. Here, $\pi \dot{w} > 0$ if and only if $x > n$. Thus we draw a vertical line separating the plane into two regions, with πw increasing to its right and decreasing to its left. Turning to (4.4), and assuming $x > mk$, we have $\dot{x} > 0$ if and only if $mk > \pi w \cdot (x - n)$, i.e. $x < n + mk/\pi w$. This is the region to the left of a hyperbola. In the portion of economic interest, it begins at $x = n + mk$ when $\pi w = 1$, and has x increasing to ∞ as πw goes to 0. Thus we have a rightward component of motion to the left of this hyperbola and a leftward one to its right.

This gives us three regions A, B, and C as shown, with movement to the south-east in A, north-east in B, and north-west in B. These can be joined together to obtain all paths satisfying (4.4) and (4.5). We see that they all converge on the point $x = n + mk$, $\pi w = 1$. A heuristic explanation is as follows. As capital-augmenting technological progress occurs, capital in efficiency units grows relative to labour. However, when $\sigma < 1$, the weight attached to the faster growing factor in

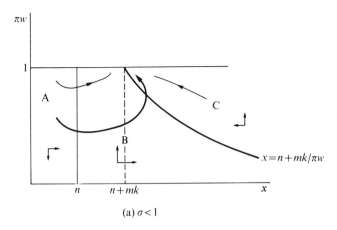

(a) $\sigma < 1$

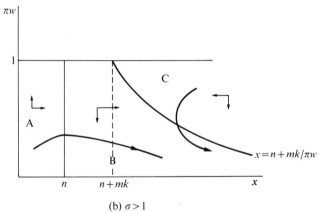

(b) $\sigma > 1$

FIG. 4.1

calculating output growth declines. Thus ultimate output and capital in physical units can only grow at the rate n. Capital in efficiency units grows at the higher rate $n + mk$, but this does not contribute to faster output growth. Of course this does not mean that the technological progress is entirely useless: it does raise the *level* of the output path.

If $\sigma > 1$, the weight attached to the faster growing factor goes to 1, and this accelerates growth faster. This situation is shown in Fig. 4.1b, where all paths have $x \to \infty$ and $\pi w \to 0$. The mathematical derivation of this follows the same lines as given above, and is left as an important exercise to give the reader more familiarity with the new and valuable technique of phase diagrams.

The conclusion we draw from all this is that maintaining a constant saving ratio when there is capital-augmenting technological progress leads to a kind of degenerate steady state. Of course, if the saving ratio were being planned, we would probably lower it through time to obtain some consumption earlier, but I shall not pursue this further. After the discussions of Chapter 5, the matter will become a fairly simple exercise.

Let us turn to the question of why technological progress might be purely labour-augmenting. Clearly there is little reason why exogenous change should obligingly take this form and preserve the convenience of steady states for the theorist. However, if research activity influenced by economic forces is the source of technological progress, then a case can be made for the assertion that in the long run, such change will be labour-augmenting. Suppose individual producers take factor prices as given, and try to alter efficiency multiples so as to reduce unit costs. The cost function is $\phi(w/Al, r/AK)$, and if AL and AK are made to grow at rates ml and mk respectively, the rate of cost reduction at given w and r is seen, using (2.6), to be

$$-\dot{\phi}/\phi = \pi w \cdot ml + \pi r \cdot mk \qquad (4.6)$$

Now suppose the producers can choose the values (ml, mk) on a concave transformation curve, called the 'innovation frontier'. To achieve most rapid cost reduction, they will choose a point of tangency with the straight line contour of (4.6), as shown in Fig. 4.2. If the chosen mk is high relative to ml, then EK will rise relative to EL. If $\sigma < 1$, this will lower πr relative to πw, thus making the cost-reduction contour steeper. Then mk will fall and ml will rise. The opposite will happen if mk is initially too low. Thus, if $\sigma < 1$, which is usually thought to be realistic, we have a stabilizing tendency in the choice of mk and ml. But we have seen that the only stable outcome is $mk = 0$.

This argument is not really satisfactory, for factor prices change in the course of this process, and in time producers will come to expect these changes and include them in their calculations. These complexities can be incorporated into the model, and similar conclusions follow.[3]

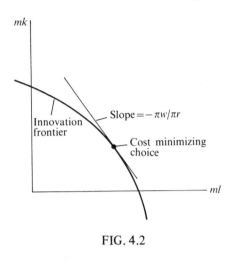

FIG. 4.2

2. Returns to scale

Increasing returns to scale are often thought to be intrinsically linked to technological progress. Thus, even if output at any instant shows constant returns to scale as a function of inputs at the same instant, it is possible that some aspect of this production activity increases the productivities at future dates. Considering the production process extending over time as a whole, where we think of inputs at one date as producing output at the same date and also contributing to output at later dates, this will be subject to increasing returns. The best-known examples of this phenomenon are the case where earlier experience of production raises subsequent productivity (learning by doing),[4] and where investment is a direct cause of productivity increase (a technical progress function).[5]

Increasing returns to scale pose problems for our equilibrium framework. First, if the effects on future productivity are not recognized by individuals, they will act as if constant returns prevail. An equilibrium can then be found as before. However, the scale economies will then become an externality, and the equilibrium will be inefficient. The social marginal benefit from current investment or production (which includes the subsequent effects) will exceed the private benefit (which consists solely of current output). Market economies in such a situation will underinvest. This is a feature of models with learning by doing. On the other hand, if the existence of increasing returns is known to participants, perfect competition is not possible. Marginal product payments to all factors add to more than the total output available. Some elements of monopoly will arise, and the factor market equilibrium will have to be handled differently. This raises important but difficult issues which are not yet fully understood. I shall return to them briefly in Chapter 8, but for now I shall use an *ad hoc* assumption that is common. This supposes that factor shares are scaled down equiproportionately from their marginal product values. In the Cobb-Douglas case, for example, if the exponents α and β add to more than 1, we suppose that the factor shares are $\alpha/(\alpha + \beta)$ and $\beta/(\alpha + \beta)$.

Consider returns to scale on their own for a moment. Steady states are problematic in the same way as we saw above. Save in the Cobb-Douglas case, they require that the returns to scale are channelled through labour alone, i.e. the production function takes the form

$$Y = F(K, L^\nu) \tag{4.7}$$

where F has all the standard properties including constant returns to scale, and it is the fact that $\nu > 1$ which produces increasing returns to K and L. Then in a steady state with $G\langle Y \rangle = G\langle K \rangle = g$, we have

$$g = e_1 \cdot g + e_2 \cdot \nu \cdot n,$$

where e_1 and e_2 are the elasticities of F with respect to K and L^ν. These need no longer have any simple relation to the factor shares, but must add to 1. Then

$$g = \nu \cdot n. \tag{4.8}$$

Comparing this with (4.3), we see that increasing returns can be difficult to distinguish from technological progress, especially in a state of fairly smooth growth. Thus, any given steady state values of g and n can be explained in principle by either (4.3) or (4.8) or some intermediate combination. In practice, the values are such that it would be unreasonable to place the entire burden of the explanation on increasing returns, while placing it all on technological progress gives reasonable numbers. With $g = 3$ per cent and $n = 1$ per cent per year, for example, the former would require $\nu = 3$ (i.e. doubling physical labour would have to increase effective labour eightfold), while the latter would require $ml = 2$ per cent per year.

Now consider how increasing returns to scale can affect technological progress. In the case of learning by doing, the efficiency factor AL for labour is made to depend on some measure of production experience. This may be cumulated past output or investment. In conditions of steady growth almost any proxy will do, and the capital stock is the most convenient. Steady state methods require, and observations suggest, a relation of the form

$$AL = A \cdot K^{\mu}, \qquad 0 < \mu < 1 \qquad (4.9)$$

where A is a constant. The corresponding relation among the growth rates is

$$ml = \mu \cdot g. \qquad (4.10)$$

In conjunction with (4.3), this gives us the steady state growth rate

$$g = n/(1 - \mu) \qquad (4.11)$$

The technical progress function assumes a direct link between the growth rate of capital per head and the rate of labour-augmenting technological progress:

$$ml = \xi(g - n) \qquad (4.12)$$

where ξ is an increasing concave function. The steady state g is then implicitly defined by

$$g - n = \xi(g - n) \qquad (4.13)$$

This is shown in Fig. 4.3.

Having characterized the steady states for the two models, we can do various comparative exercises for each. I shall do this for the technical progress function, and leave learning by doing as a simple exercise. Consider steady states with different saving ratios. We see that they must have the same growth rate. Since $v = s/g$, their capital/output ratios will then be proportional to the saving ratios. If distribution is related to marginal products with minor modifications to allow for returns to scale (e.g. an equiproportionate reduction), then the relative factor shares will differ in a manner depending on the elasticity of substitution that we have met before.

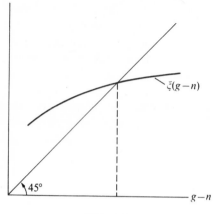

FIG. 4.3

We saw in Chapter 3 that in absence of technological progress, saving policy was powerless in affecting steady state growth rates. In the models above, the same conclusion holds even with technological progress. This has been criticized by Eltis,[6] who argues that the technical progress function should have the saving ratio as its argument instead of the rate of growth of capital. With this change, we will have

$$g = \xi(s) + n \qquad (4.14)$$

and now saving policy can affect the growth rate. Also, we have

$$v = s/[\xi(s) + n] \qquad (4.15)$$

It is easy to see that v is an increasing function of s if ξ is a concave function, and that it increases less than proportionately.

Eltis goes on to discuss a reverse dependence of s on g through the demand for investment, and to analyze the complete model in which both of these are endogenous variables. He also considers the harder case where technological progress is embodied.

I shall leave further refinements and analyses of models of learning by doing and the technical progress function to more advanced treatments.[7]

3. Measurement

A satisfactory treatment of the empirical problems of measurement would need far too much space, and this section must be confined to some very brief remarks on the conceptual issues.[8] The ideal in measurement of growth would be to use data to choose the functional form in (2.19) or some more disaggregated functional relation, and to estimate the parameters involved. Unfortunately, this ideal is unattainable even in principle and with unlimited time-series data on inputs and outputs and their prices. A well known 'non-identification theorem' states that it will remain impossible to sort out in a unique way the rate and bias of technological progress and the returns to scale and elasticity of substitution in production.[9] We must therefore use *a priori* restrictions based on judgement and guesswork, which are themselves impossible to sort out in a unique way. As an illustration of a commonly used device, suppose that technological progress augments capital and labour at the same rate ('Hicks-neutrality') and that constant returns to scale prevail. Note that steady states are not possible except in the Cobb-Douglas case, but this is not a serious problem in the empirical context. With capital and labour inputs each fully aggregated, we can then write

$$Y(t) = A(t) \cdot F(K(t), L(t))$$

or, in terms of growth rates

$$G\langle Y \rangle = G\langle A \rangle + \pi r \cdot G\langle K \rangle + \pi w \cdot G\langle L \rangle \qquad (4.16)$$

Assuming competitive factor markets in equilibrium, price and quantity time-series give us the values of all the remaining variables, and $G\langle A \rangle$ can then be calculated. We can think of the growth of output as resolved into two parts, $G\langle A \rangle$ being attributed to technological progress and the rest to growth of total factor input. As a matter of definition, then, the growth of total input is measured by the competitive-share-weighted sum of proportional changes in the various inputs. Such an expression is called a Divisia index. As πr and πw will change over time (unless $\sigma = 1$), we will have to keep on changing the weights, i.e. use a chain index, over time spans of any appreciable length.

If such estimation is carried out at an aggregate level, we face two problems. First, saving appears to be almost ineffective in promoting growth even in the short run. As an illustrative example, suppose we raise the fraction of income saved by one percentage point. With a capital/output ratio of 3, this will raise $G\langle K \rangle$ by 0.33 per cent, and assuming profits to be a quarter of income, $G\langle Y \rangle$ by 0.08 per cent. In a longer run, diminishing returns will reduce this still further. This calculation is not only very pessimistic but also rather counter-intuitive. In the next section we shall consider models where saving in the short run has an added important role of being a vehicle for technical change.

Next, it turns out that the calculation attributes most (as much as 7/8) of the growth in output to $G\langle A \rangle$. However, attribution is not explanation, and as $G\langle A \rangle$ has been assumed to be exogenous, we are left almost completely in the dark about the forces affecting growth.

Disaggregation improves matters somewhat. Thus if there are different types of capital K_i and of labour L_j, a similar calculation gives

$$G\langle Y \rangle = G\langle A \rangle + \Sigma_i \pi r_i \cdot G\langle K_i \rangle + \Sigma_j \pi w_j \cdot G\langle L_j \rangle \qquad (4.17)$$

Suppose (4.17) is the true relation, but we aggregate $K = \Sigma_i K_i$ and $L = \Sigma_j L_j$ and estimate (4.16) instead. Some elementary algebra shows that

$$\Sigma_j \pi w_j \cdot G\langle L_j \rangle - \pi w \cdot G\langle L \rangle = \Sigma_j (w_j - \bar{w}) \, \mathrm{d}L_j/\mathrm{d}t$$

where $\bar{w}$ is the average wage. This is positive if w_j is positively correlated with $\mathrm{d}L_j/\mathrm{d}t$, i.e. if labour types with higher marginal product are on the whole increasing faster in absolute amounts. Similarly for capital. If this is so, then the true Divisia index of input change will exceed that estimated by aggregation, and less of the growth in output need be attributed to the unexplained technological factors. This does happen in practice, but the extent of it is a matter of debate.

Several attempts have been made to break down the technological factor that has not so far been explained into portions that can be attributed to identifiable influences, such as education, improvements in allocative efficiency and scale economies. This type of work is not usually backed by any satisfactory theory, and often relies on *ad hoc* practices and guesswork. But, given painstaking work by experienced and able economists, a great deal of progress has been achieved in improving our understanding of growth, and some implications for policy have been obtained.[10]

4. Embodied Technological Progress

For the rest of this chapter, technological progress will be exogenous, i.e. not influenced by economic factors, but at least a part of it will be embodied, i.e. specific to machines. Thus a machine can incorporate the latest technology at its date of contruction ('vintage'), but it cannot benefit from any later embodied advances in technology.[11]

While the hypothesis of embodiment is a step towards realism, it greatly increases the complexity of the analysis. It is not generally possible to aggregate machines of different vintages into a scalar capital stock. It can be shown that aggregation requires technological progress to be purely capital-augmenting. Of course steady states need it purely labour-augmenting, and the two are consistent only for a Cobb-Douglas production function. It is on the whole better to retain steady states at the cost of having to keep track of machines of each vintage separately. Even this is not easy. I shall confine the exposition to steady states and their comparisons, and omit some of the messier details of algebra. Some readers, particularly undergraduates, may wish to omit even the remaining details and only look at the general remarks and the conclusions.

Matters are made even more complicated by a second kind of specificity that can arise once we start distinguishing machines by vintage. A machine may embody not merely the technology of its date of construction, but also the technique chosen at that date. Thus the possibility of varying the labour input to suit varying factor prices at later dates may be limited, or even non-existent. As with long-run and short-run cost curves, the isoquant after construction will then be tangent to that before construction at the chosen point on the latter, but more convex. This is illustrated in Fig. 4.4. We can then define an ex ante elasticity of substitution σ_0 and an ex post elasticity of substitution σ_1, with $\sigma_0 \geqslant \sigma_1 \geqslant 0$. Call substitutable capital ($\sigma > 0$) putty, and fixed coefficient capital ($\sigma = 0$) clay; we then have the ex ante-ex post pairs of putty-putty (or putty-'semi-putty'), putty-clay and clay-clay to consider. These terms are due to E. S. Phelps.

It is useful to explain embodiment by analogy with Ricardian rent theory. Machines of different vintages are like plots of land with different productivity. An efficient allocation of labour, whether achieved in a market or by planning, involves using the most modern machines or the most productive plots of land first. In many important

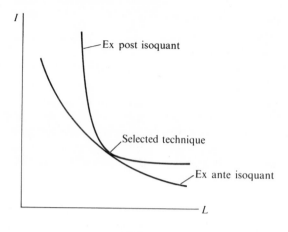

FIG. 4.4

cases, a point is reached where some low-productivity land is left unused. This margin of choice in the allocation of labour, viz. the decision of whether to extend cultivation to slightly less productive plots, is called the *extensive margin*. If more labour became available, it would be used on the plot next in line. Thus the extensive marginal product of labour is the average product on the marginal land. In equilibrium this must equal the wage rate. Then the marginal land would earn no rent, and more productive land would earn a positive rent. If a given plot of land can be cultivated with different degrees of labour intensity, we have another margin of choice, called the *intensive margin*. In this case the intensity of cultivation of each plot of land would be adjusted so as to make the marginal product of labour on each plot of land, i.e. the intensive marginal product of labour, also equal to the wage rate. In fact, if substitution is large enough, the intensive marginal product can be made as high as is necessary by reducing labour intensity sufficiently. Then all plots of land are used, but the less productive ones are used with less labour intensity. This can be thought of as a gradual form of retirement.

There is one important difference between land and machines. Since machines are producible, the observation of high rents on existing machines will induce production of new ones. The competition for labour that ensues will raise the wage rate and reduce the rents. Thus rents on machines are not pure economic rents for all time, and are therefore sometimes called quasi-rents. However, the general points concerning the two margins of choice remain valid. We have to allow for the possibility of economic obsolescence, i.e. of a machine with given physical features gradually becoming uneconomic as the associated variable costs rise. An important new variable thus enters the picture: the economic life of machines. Even if substitution is not possible at the intensive margin, we will find that adjustment of the economic life, i.e. substitution at the extensive margin, can permit steady states and related analyses.

The economic life of machines will be required to be constant in steady states. Outside such states, wage rates may change unevenly, and it is possible that machines which have been idle for a while are brought back into use. In an equilibrium path, such opportunities will have been foreseen and taken into account. Disequilibrium will make matters even more complicated. Few systematic studies of such problems exist, and we do not even have a general answer to the question of whether equilibrium growth paths converge to a steady state. However, stability has been proved in important cases, and generally suspected to be more rapid than is the case in models of disembodied change.[12] I shall keep the exposition relatively simple by confining it to steady states and appealing to stability where appropriate.

The general point to make about models of embodiment is that saving acquires a more important role in them. Added saving yields not only more machines, but also the most modern and productive ones. Interest is then focussed on the effect of saving on growth, and on the extent to which this depends on the degree of embodiment of technological progress.

One of the complications that is important in this study is the fact that the prospect of obsolescence decreases the price of a machine as it ages, i.e. contributes to depreciation. However, unlike the case of radioactive decay, depreciation due to obsolescence cannot be determined without solving for the whole equilibrium. Thus, even though it may be more desirable to assume a given ratio of net saving out of net income, it becomes necessary for the ease of exposition to assume a given gross propensity to save out of gross income. I shall regrettably have to follow this practice.

5. Embodiment: Fixed coefficients

The simplest model with embodiment and obsolescence is the clay-clay model, with no substitution between capital and labour either before or after a machine is built.[13] Output is homogeneous, and units are such that one machine is built using one unit of output. All technological progress is labour-augmenting. Thus a machine in use produces a constant flow of $(1/v)$ units of output, but uses a steadily decreasing amount of labour. Suppose that embodied technological progress at rate me and disembodied technological progress at rate md coexist. Thus a machine built at date θ and being used at date t needs $l \cdot e^{-me \cdot \theta} \cdot e^{-md \cdot t}$ units of labour, where l is a constant. Suppose the labour force at date t is $L_0 \cdot e^{n \cdot t}$, and the gross propensity to save is constant and equal to s.

The simplest way to set up the steady state is to make guesses about the variables and then find conditions for their consistency. It is easy to guess that output will grow at the rate $(n + md + me)$, and the wage rate at $(md + me)$. Thus suppose output at date t is $y_0 \cdot L_0 \cdot e^{(n+md+me) \cdot t}$, and the wage rate is $w_0 \cdot e^{(md+me) \cdot t}$. Let the profit (or interest) rate be i, and the economic life of machines, T.

Consider any date t. At it, machines built at dates θ in the range $(t - T, t)$ are being used. There are $s \cdot y_0 \cdot L_0 \cdot e^{(n+md+me) \cdot \theta}$ machines built at date θ. Each produces $(1/v)$ units of output, employs $l \cdot e^{-me \cdot \theta} \cdot e^{-md \cdot t}$ units of labour, and incurs wage costs $l \cdot e^{-me \cdot \theta} \cdot e^{-md \cdot t} \cdot w_0 \cdot e^{(md+me) \cdot t}$, i.e. $l \cdot w_0 \cdot e^{me \cdot (t-\theta)}$.

Adding together the output from all machines in use, we have

$$y_0 \cdot L_0 \cdot e^{(n+md+me) \cdot t} = \int_{t-T}^{t} \frac{1}{v} \cdot s \cdot y_0 \cdot L_0 \cdot e^{(n+md+me) \cdot \theta} \cdot d\theta$$

Similarly, adding together the employment on all these machines

$$L_0 \cdot e^{n \cdot t} = \int_{t-T}^{t} s \cdot y_0 \cdot L_0 \cdot e^{(n+md+me) \cdot \theta} \cdot l \cdot e^{-(me \cdot \theta + md \cdot t)} \cdot d\theta$$

At this point it will be convenient to define two functions which will simplify notation later. Write

$$\Gamma(x, T) = \int_0^T e^{x \cdot t} \cdot dt, \qquad \Delta(x, T) = \int_0^T e^{-x \cdot t} \cdot dt \qquad (4.18)$$

It is easy to see that both are increasing functions of T, for an increase in T adds positive elements to each integral. Also, as functions of x,

$$\Gamma_x(x, T) = \int_0^T t \cdot e^{x \cdot t} \cdot dt > 0, \qquad \Delta_x(x, T) = -\int_0^T t \cdot e^{-x \cdot t} \cdot dt < 0$$

Using these functions, we can write the two balance equations as

$$v = s \cdot \Delta(n + md + me, T) \tag{4.19}$$

$$1 = s \cdot l \cdot y_0 \cdot \Delta(n + md, T) \tag{4.20}$$

On the machine just about to be scrapped, i.e. with $\theta = t - T$, the wage cost just equals output, i.e.

$$l \cdot w_0 \cdot e^{me \cdot T} = 1/v \tag{4.21}$$

Only the interest rate has not been brought in yet, and to relate it to other prices we must consider the zero pure profit condition for equilibrium. This equates the discounted present value of the quasi-rents (excess of output over wage costs) from a machine over its economic life to the cost of its construction. In a steady state, we can do this for any one machine, say the one built at date 0. This gives

$$1 = \int_0^T [(1/v) - l \cdot w_0 \cdot e^{me \cdot t}] \cdot e^{-i \cdot t} \cdot dt \tag{4.22}$$

or

$$1 = (1/v) \cdot \Delta(i, T) - l \cdot w_0 \cdot \Delta(i - me, T) \tag{4.23}$$

We began with v, l, md, me, n, s and L_0 as parameters, and introduced the variables w_0, y_0, i and T. We then obtained four conditions (4.19)–(4.22) for a steady state equilibrium. Now we ask the usual questions: When do steady states exist? How are they affected by changes in parameters?

First write $g = n + md + me$, and note that $\Delta(g, T)$ increases monotonically from 0 to $(1/g)$ as T increases from 0 to infinity. Then we can find one and only one T satisfying (4.19) so long as $v \leqslant s/g$. Then we can calculate y_0 from (4.20), w_0 from (4.21), and finally i from (4.22). Thus a unique steady state exists when $s \geqslant v \cdot g$. Compare this situation with the Harrod-Domar model and note how the possibility of retiring economically obsolete capital has enlarged the range of parameters compatible with steady states, at any rate in one direction.

It is useful and easy to calculate the steady state distribution of income between the factors. We can write $\pi w = w_0/y_0$, and then some simple algebra yields

$$\pi w = \Gamma(n + md, T)/\Gamma(n + md + me, T) \qquad (4.24)$$

Note that as Γ is an increasing function of its first argument, we can be sure that πw will be in the interval $(0, 1)$. The *aggregate* share of rents in national income will be written as πr in this chapter.

In comparing different steady states, the first point to notice is that n and md enter the equations defining the steady states only in the combination $(n + md)$. In this sense the effects of disembodied technological progress are exactly like those of population growth. It is only the rate of growth of labour in efficiency units that matter for the wage w_0 and output y_0 measured per efficiency unit of labour. However, embodied technological progress does enter separately. We must ask what difference is made by changing the composition of a given rate of technological progress, $m = md + me$, between its embodied and disembodied components. From (4.19), we see that T is unaffected by such a change. From (4.20), (4.21) and (4.24), it is easy to verify that a higher embodied component corresponds to lower values of w_0, y_0 and πw, while a slightly harder calculation using (4.22) shows that it corresponds to a higher value of i.

Consider next the effect of a change in s. It is immediate from (4.19) that a steady state with higher s has lower T, and then from (4.21) that it has a higher w_0. It is slightly harder to calculate from (4.22) that it has a lower i. Finally, a rather messy calculation yields

$$\frac{s}{y_0}\frac{dy_0}{ds} = \frac{\pi r}{\pi w} \qquad (4.25)$$

All these results are fairly easy to interpret. A higher saving ratio increases and modernizes the stock of machines. Both aspects contribute to the rise in the wage rate and output per head. In the new steady state the growth rates are the same as in the old one, but the wage and output paths are at a higher level. The economic life of machines levels off at the new lower value. All these changes decrease the quasi-rents a machine can earn at each date, and the interest rate must fall if this smaller stream is to discount back to the same value as before.

If some input substitution were possible, these changes would induce the choice of a greater capital intensity, and this would have repercussions. For example, such machines would have higher labour productivity, which would be a factor contributing to a longer economic life. Some of the above changes could then be dampened or even reversed. We shall consider some aspects of this problem soon.

Note that the nature of technological progress makes a difference to the elasticity in (4.25). If a greater part of a given total of technological progress is embodied, then (4.24) shows that πw will be lower and therefore the level of the steady state output path will be more responsive to the saving ratio.

6. Embodiment with substitution

The next case is the one where we have equal substitution possibilities on new and old machines, i.e. the putty-putty case. I shall discuss it only to obtain two results of some interest. Suppose $I(\theta)$ machines are built at date θ. Considering production at date t, suppose that $L(\theta, t)$ units of labour working with these $I(\theta)$ machines would produce output

$$Y(\theta, t) = F(I(\theta), L(\theta, t), \theta) \qquad (4.26)$$

where the third argument θ in F indicates the technological knowledge at the date of construction of the machines, and could be put in factor-augmenting forms as appropriate. If $L(t)$ is the total labour supply at t, our allocations must satisfy the balancing equation

$$L(t) = \int_{\theta \leqslant t} L(\theta, t) \cdot d\theta \qquad (4.27)$$

Subject to this, the market or a plan will maximize the total output,

$$Y(t) = \int_{\theta \leqslant t} Y(\theta, t) \cdot d\theta \qquad (4.28)$$

Economic obsolescence can appear here in the form of a corner solution, i.e. $L(\theta, t) = 0$ for θ below the marginal vintage. Carrying through this refinement can be messy, and has no effect on my results; I shall therefore not treat corner solutions separately.

There remains the condition for optimum allocation at the intensive margin. This is to equate the marginal product of labour on all vintages, i.e.

$$F_L(I(\theta), L(\theta, t), \theta) = w(t) \tag{4.29}$$

for all θ. The common value $w(t)$ has to be chosen so that (4.27) is satisfied; it is obviously the imputed wage rate.

Two results follow from this. The first concerns the effect of the saving propensity on the steady state growth path. Suppose $Y(t) = Y_0 \cdot e^{g \cdot t}$, and $I(t) = s \cdot Y(t)$. Differentiating (4.28) totally with respect to s, we have

$$\frac{dY(t)}{ds} = \int \frac{\partial Y(\theta, t)}{\partial I(\theta)} \cdot \frac{dI(\theta)}{ds} \cdot d\theta + \int \frac{\partial Y(\theta, t)}{\partial L(\theta, t)} \cdot \frac{dL(\theta, t)}{ds} \cdot d\theta \tag{4.30}$$

Using (4.29), the second integral becomes

$$w(t) \cdot \int \frac{dL(\theta, t)}{ds} \cdot d\theta = w(t) \cdot dL(t)/ds = 0.$$

This is an instance of the famous Wong-Viner-Samuelson envelope theorem.[14] Since the initial labour allocation is chosen to maximize total output, the first order effect of small changes in this allocation on total output is zero.

To simplify the first integral, we note that by Euler's theorem,

$$Y(\theta, t) = I(\theta) \cdot \partial Y(\theta, t)/\partial I(\theta) + L(\theta, t) \cdot \partial Y(\theta, t)/\partial L(\theta, t)$$

i.e. $\qquad \partial Y(\theta, t)/\partial I(\theta) = \{Y(\theta, t) - w(t) \cdot L(\theta, t)\}/I(\theta)$

Next, $dI(\theta)/ds = Y(\theta) + s \cdot dY(\theta)/ds$. Substituting in (4.30) and simplifying, we find

$$\frac{s}{Y_0} \frac{dY_0}{ds} = \frac{\pi r}{\pi w} \tag{4.31}$$

This generalizes the result (4.25).

The case where each vintage production function is Cobb-Douglas is of particular interest. Here (4.29) yields a constant share of wages in the output of each vintage, equal to the exponent of labour in the production function. If this is the same for all vintages, the aggregate share of wages in output will also equal this exponent, and will thus be constant, independent of the degree of embodiment. The responsiveness of the output path level to the saving ratio will not then depend on the nature of technological progress. It is now easy to guess that the Cobb-Douglas is the dividing line, and that the elasticity of the output level with respect to the saving ratio increases with the degree of embodiment if $\sigma < 1$, and decreases if $\sigma > 1$. The earlier model with $\sigma = 0$ then becomes a special case of this general result.[15]

For the second result to be inferred from (4.29), suppose that the technological progress is purely capital-augmenting, i.e. that (4.26) has the particular form $Y(\theta, t) = F(A(\theta) \cdot I(\theta), L(\theta, t))$. Then F_L depends only on the ratio $A(\theta) \cdot I(\theta)/L(\theta, t)$, and we can solve to write

$$L(\theta, t) = h(w(t)) \cdot A(\theta) \cdot I(\theta) \tag{4.32}$$

where h is some function whose form need not concern us. Using (4.27), we have

$$L(t) = h(w(t)) \cdot \int_{\theta \leq t} A(\theta) \cdot I(\theta) \cdot d\theta \tag{4.33}$$

Write $J(t)$ for the integral on the right hand side. Now

$$Y(\theta, t) = A(\theta) \cdot I(\theta) \cdot F(1, h(w(t))),$$

and from (4.28)

$$Y(t) = J(t) \cdot F(1, L(t)/J(t))$$
$$= F(J(t) \cdot L(t)) \tag{4.34}$$

We have thus reduced the expression for the total output to a simple function of the total labour supply and a fixed weighted sum of the numbers of machines installed at various past dates, the weights being the efficiency factors. In other words, we have aggregated capital of different vintages into a scalar stock, J.

This shows that aggregation of capital across vintages is possible if the technological change is purely capital-augmenting. The converse is also true; thus the conditions required for aggregation are very stringent.[16] It might be of interest to compare the present case with that of exponential physical decay which permitted simple aggregation in (3.29).

6. Embodiment: putty-clay

Finally, I shall turn to consider some important features of the putty-clay case.[17] Here a choice of technique is available in course of construction of a machine, but not thereafter. Once again, only steady states will be discussed.

Now l and v are not technical data. One of them can be chosen by the producer, and the other is then given by a production function like that of Chapter 2, i.e. $1/v = g(l)$. Given the selected values, equations (4.19)–(4.22) remain valid equilibrium conditions. It only remains to add an equation to describe this choice. But that adds many conceptual and technical problems.

Consider an investor contemplating installation of a machine at date 0, and choosing the labour intensity to be associated with it. He knows the equilibrium interest rate i and the wage path $w_0 \cdot e^{(md + me) \cdot t}$. He can then calculate that the machine will have to be scrapped at a date T given by (4.21), or

$$w_0 \cdot e^{me \cdot T} = g(l)/l \tag{4.35}$$

He will take this dependence into account in making his decision. Other things equal, a more capital intensive machine will have a longer economic life: given i, w_0 and me, we have

$$dT/dl = -[g(l) - l \cdot g'(l)] / [me \cdot l \cdot g(l)] < 0 \tag{4.36}$$

The discounted present value of quasi-rents from the machine over its life as a function of the labour intensity is

$$V(l) = \int_0^T [g(l) - l \cdot w_0 \cdot e^{me \cdot t}] \cdot e^{-i \cdot t} \cdot dt \tag{4.37}$$

where T is given by (4.35). Now l is to be chosen to maximize $V(l)$. We have

$$V'(l) = \int_0^T [g'(l) - w_0 \cdot e^{me \cdot t}] \cdot e^{-i \cdot t} \cdot dt$$
$$+ [g(l) - l \cdot w_0 \cdot e^{me \cdot T}] \cdot e^{-i \cdot T} \cdot dT/dl$$

The second term is zero because of (4.35). This is another example of the envelope theorem: after all, the scrapping date is also chosen to maximize net worth. The first order condition for maximization, viz. $V'(l) = 0$, then becomes

$$g'(l) \cdot \Delta(i, T) = w_0 \cdot \Delta(i - me, T) \qquad (4.38)$$

Observe that this implies $w_0 < g'(l) < w_0 \cdot e^{me \cdot T}$. This is very reasonable. The investor, knowing that the capital intensity chosen at time 0 cannot be varied to suit changing factor prices, chooses it initially so as to be suitable on the average in some sense. As the wage is due to rise steadily, the marginal product of labour is kept in excess of the wage at the date of installation, but less than the wage at the date of scrapping. In fact we know that the average product equals the wage at this latter date.

This point can be further clarified by recalling that labour allocation in models with embodied technological progress involves a choice at two margins: extensive and intensive. The marginal product of labour is equal to its average product on the machine at the extensive margin. In the present case, the intensive margin cannot be adjusted.

The linking of these two margins causes a problem for the second order conditions for maximization of V. We find

$$V''(l) = \int_0^T g''(l) \cdot e^{-i \cdot t} \cdot dt + [g'(l) - w_0 \cdot e^{me \cdot T}] \cdot e^{-i \cdot T} \cdot dT/dl$$

$$= g''(l) \cdot \Delta(i, T) + [g(l) - l \cdot g'(l)]^2 \cdot e^{-i \cdot T}/[me \cdot l^2 \cdot g(l)]$$

The first term is negative, but the second is positive, and we cannot in general be sure that the sum will be negative. This can be better understood in terms of the capital/labour ratio, $k = 1/l$. An increase in k has two effects. The first is to increase the rents at each date, and this is subject to diminishing returns for a concave function g. This normal effect of capital 'deepening' is counteracted by the fact that an increase in k prolongs the economic life of the machine and thus lengthens the span of time over which quasi-rents accrue. If the deepening effect is strong, it will prevail over the lengthening effect and the maximand will be a concave function. The deepening effect will be strong if diminishing returns set in rapidly in the function g, i.e. if the elasticity of substitution in it is low. Britto has shown that $\sigma \leqslant 1$ is sufficient to ensure concavity of V. If V is not concave, there will be multiple steady states; this is discussed in detail by Bliss. I shall not go into the matter any further, but having mentioned the possibility and the underlying reason, shall turn to the comparison of steady states.

A glance at the relevant equations (4.19)–(4.22) and (4.38) suffices to show that it is an exceedingly messy problem. While most results of interest have been obtained, some gaps remain. I shall only sketch the results.[18]

The only generally valid association is the wage-interest frontier: steady states with a higher w_0 have a lower i. The rationale behind this is useful to see. Consider V as a function of w_0 and i, as well as the choice variables l and T. The latter are selected to maximise V, so V_l and V_T are both zero. Now the zero pure profit condition $V = 1$ holds in each steady state, and the comparison reduces to $V_w \cdot dw_0 + V_i \cdot di = 0$, i.e.

$$dw_0/di = -V_i/V_w \qquad (4.39)$$

Both partial derivatives on the right are negative, and we have a downward sloping wage-interest frontier. However, the expression in (4.39) does not have a simple interpretation as a ratio of imputed shares in income. The extent of generality of the wage-interest frontier will be discussed in Chapter 6.

As long as the uniqueness condition is satisfied, steady states with a lower i will have a lower l, i.e. a higher k. Further, $-(dk/di)/k$ is an increasing function of σ, the elasticity of substitution in the function $g(l)$. This accords with the general concept of the elasticity of substitution, but the detailed proof is difficult.

The relation between i and T is ambiguous. Bliss explains it as the outcome of two conflicting influences. A lower i is associated with a higher w, which at given k implies lower T, i.e. earlier scrapping. However, a lower i is also associated with a higher k, which at given w implies a higher T on account of the higher labour productivity. This latter influence is non-existent with ex ante fixed coefficients, and increases steadily with σ. Thus there is a critical value of σ, say σ^*, such that a lower i is associated with a lower T if $\sigma < \sigma^*$, and with a higher T if $\sigma > \sigma^*$. The value σ^* depends on the initial equilibrium configuration from which small departures are being examined. It has long been known that σ^* is always less than 1, i.e. with an ex ante

Cobb-Douglas production function a lower i is associated with a higher T. Bardhan has shown that $\sigma^* > 2/3$, while Eltis finds that it will usually lie in the range 0.70–0.83.

The possibility that a low T and a low l may go together in comparing steady states does not contradict (4.36). That relation applies to the choice contemplated by a producer facing given factor prices, while the steady states being compared have different w_0 and i.

Finally, Bardhan has shown that if $\sigma \leqslant 1$, a lower i is associated with a higher s. We can then consider the steady states with different values of i as resulting from an exogenous change in the gross saving propensity in a one-to-one manner.

This is as far as I shall carry the discussion of steady states. We saw that the degree of embodiment matters even in steady states but the difference is not easy to spot. Nor is it easy to detect empirically.[19]

Embodiment of course matters much more outside steady states. Thus if the rate of saving is stepped up and equilibrium growth traced, in the early stages the growth of output benefits from the active process of modernization of the stock of machines, while ultimately only the level at most benefits from the outcome of this process. There is a presumption that the added flexibility due to obsolescence produces a faster approach to the steady state in a model with a greater degree of embodiment, but no general or rigorous results are known.[20]

There is an interesting application of the vintage model that deserves mention. If there are two countries which in isolation would maintain different economic lives of machines, they can both benefit from trade where one country exports its current output and imports used machines. This can be important in relation to issues of growth and planning in developing countries.[21]

Notes

For more general surveys of technological progress, see Hahn and Matthews (1965, Section II), and Kennedy and Thirlwall (1973).

1. For further details see Atkinson (1969).
2. Phase diagrams are explained in detail in Birkhoff and Rota (1969, Ch. 5).
3. See Kennedy (1964), Samuelson (1965), Nordhaus (1969, Ch. 6).
4. See Arrow (1962).

5. See Kaldor and Mirrlees (1962).
6. See Eltis (1973, Chs. 6, 7).
7. E.g. Wan (1971, Ch. 3 §3, Ch. 7).
8. For more details see Nerlove (1967), Jorgenson and Griliches (1967), Denison (1969), Star (1974).
9. See Diamond and McFadden (1965).
10. See Denison (1967), Matthews (1964a).
11. For a general discussion of embodiment, with some simple models, see Meade (1962, Ch. 7), and Solow (1970, Ch. 3).
12. See Phelps (1962), Sato (1966).
13. For a definitive analysis of this model, including proof of convergence of equilibrium growth, see Solow, Tobin, von Weizsacker and Yaari (1967).
14. See Samuelson (1947, p. 34), Dixit (1976, Ch. 3).
15. These results are the outcome of a long debate; see Phelps (1962) and the subsequent discussion, Matthews (1964b), Levhari and Sheshinski (1967), Atkinson (1970b).
16. See Solow (1955).
17. See Bliss (1968), Britto (1969), Bardhan (1969), and the references that follow, for a more thorough treatment. See Cass and Stiglitz (1969) for a proof of convergence of equilibrium paths to a steady state. This convergence can involve damped cycles.
18. These results are compiled from Phelps (1963), Bliss (1968), Bardhan (1969), (1973), Eltis (1973, Ch. 3).
19. See Jorgenson (1966), Hall (1968).
20. See note 12 above.
21. See Sen (1962).

5. Optimum Saving

In almost every preceding chapter I emphasized the undesirability of assuming constant saving propensities, and asserted that a weighing up of intertemporal opportunities and preferences should be a very important aspect of decisions to save and invest. In this chapter, this aspect will be studied in some detail.

I will use the simplest model that is a suitable vehicle for the most basic issues, so as not to complicate an elementary exposition. However, most of the points remain valid in more general contexts, and I shall mention particular ones as they arise. I shall use the one-good model with disembodied labour-augmenting technological progress and no physical deterioration of capital. Even in this model, I shall stick to the central questions and mention details or exceptional cases only in passing.[1]

1. The Keynes-Ramsey formula

It is useful to begin by supposing that the relevant decisions are made by a central planner, and to examine afterwards their relations to market equilibria. To illustrate the idea, look at only two discrete dates in the development of the economy, say dates 0 and 1. The capital stock K_0 (and hence the output Y_0) available at date 0 is fixed by history, and the stock K_2 to be carried forward to date 2 is a given target.

Fig. 5.1 shows Y_0 as the length OA. Suppose consumption $C_0 = $ OB is contemplated at date 0; then AB is left for investment. We can thus measure investment moving from A to the left. The output net of the investment necessary at date 1 in order to meet the capital target gives us the amount C_1 available for consumption at date 1. This is shown by the transformation curve which will be concave given the earlier assumptions concerning production. If the preferences concerning C_0 and C_1 can be represented by a conventional indifference map of convex curves, the optimum choice can be obtained as a tangency solution. This is shown at the point P in the figure. I shall consider solutions at corners later.

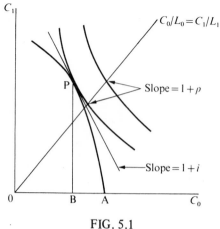

FIG. 5.1

To give more specific content to the analysis, write down the equations of material balance for the two dates, in obvious notation, as

$$K_1 = K_0 + I_0 \quad \text{and} \quad Y_0 = C_0 + I_0$$
$$K_2 = K_1 + I_1 \quad \text{and} \quad Y_1 = C_1 + I_1.$$

Of the variables involved, K_0, Y_0 and K_2 are given, while C_0, I_0, C_1, I_1 and K_1 remain to be chosen subject to the four conditions. This leaves us with one degree of freedom. Suppose K_1 is so chosen, and in terms of it, we write

$$C_1 = Y_1 + K_1 - K_2 \quad \text{and} \quad C_0 = Y_0 + K_0 - K_1.$$

Then the slope of the transformation curve can be written

$$-(\partial C_1/\partial K_1)/(\partial C_0/\partial K_1) = 1 + \partial Y_1/\partial K_1.$$

If the indifference map is represented by a valuation or utility function $U(C_0, C_1)$, the marginal rate of substitution is $(\partial U/\partial C_0)/(\partial U/\partial C_1)$. At the optimum, therefore, we have the equation

$$(\partial U/\partial C_0)/(\partial U/\partial C_1) = 1 + \partial Y_1/\partial K_1 \tag{5.1}$$

or

$$(\partial U/\partial C_0 - \partial U/\partial C_1)/(\partial U/\partial C_1) = \partial Y_1/\partial K_1 \tag{5.2}$$

In words, the rate of decline of marginal utility, measured relative to the the value at the later date, should equal the marginal product of capital. This is the basic formula of the theory. It, or some related version, is called the Keynes-Ramsey formula.

By analogy with similar reasoning which appears frequently in microeconomics, Fig. 5.1 shows how and when such an optimum can be attained as a market equilibrium. Consider consumption at each date as a distinct good, and assign equilibrium prices to the two goods to correspond to the slope of the common tangent to the transformation curve and the indifference curve at the optimum. In particular, take C_0 to be the numéraire and let the price of C_1 be q. If there are no externalities, the producers will maximize $(C_0 + q \cdot C_1)$, the value of their sales to the consumers. This, given the technical possibilities open to them, will lead them to the point P. The same point will also be chosen by the consumers, provided the function U represents their preferences, and their income is at the right level. The last is an automatic consequence of standard accounting identities, when profits are redistributed to consumers.

Readers who have not yet fully grasped the point should remember the discussion in Chapter 1. Equilibrium involving time can be interpreted in terms of futures markets. In this story, all market transactions take place at date 0. The trade in C_1 is then really trade in promises to deliver units of the consumption good at date 1, and the price of each unit promise is q. There are no markets at date 1; only the promised deliveries are made.

The second interpretation has spot markets at each date and borrowing and lending. If we write $1/(1 + i)$ for q, the producers maximize $C_0 + C_1/(1 + i)$, and the consumers' budget constraint is $C_0 + C_1/(1 + i)$ = constant. In common language, i is the rate of interest in terms of which discounted present values are calculated. In a model which recognizes more than one good at each date, there will remain the additional problem of forecasting relative prices at date 1 confidently and correctly before we can complete the story of equilibrium with perfect foresight equivalent to the futures market situation.

Readers will have noticed that some conditions that seem very restrictive had to be imposed before the optimum could be identified with a market equilibrium. I shall return to consider them in some detail later. For the present, let me turn to some other features of the solution.

Our definition makes $(1 + i)$ equal to the slope of the common tangent to the two curves at the optimum. On the production side, this makes $i = \partial Y_1 / \partial K_1$. To relate i to demand conditions, consider a specific form of the function U which is commonly used in this context. If L_j is the size of the population at date j, we write

$$U(C_0, C_1) = L_0 \cdot u(C_0/L_0) + L_1 \cdot u(C_1/L_1)/(1 + \rho) \qquad (5.3)$$

This supposes that at each date consumption is distributed equally over the population, and forms a utilitarian welfare index, discounting future utilities at rate ρ. The function u is supposed to be increasing and concave. I shall defer discussion of problems associated with this choice, and put it to its use as a device for formulating some interesting questions concerning intertemporal choice. For this form, we see that

$$(\partial U/\partial C_0)/(\partial U/\partial C_1) = u'(C_0/L_0) \ / \ [u'(C_1/L_1)/(1 + \rho)]$$

i.e.

$$1 + i = [u'(C_0/L_0)/u'(C_1/L_1)] \cdot (1 + \rho) \qquad (5.4)$$

This looks very much like (2.30), which relates the own rates of return in two price systems and the change in the relative price between the two. Here the consumer good is one unit of account, and a unit of undiscounted utility, called a 'util', is the other. Since one util at date 0 is equivalent to $(1 + \rho)$ utils at date 1, each contributing 1 to the total utility U, we see that ρ is the rate of return in utils. Also, one unit of C provides $u'(C/L)$ additional utils at that date, so this marginal utility is the relative price between the two systems. In fact we can take the analogy further by thinking of consumption as the process of accumulating an asset, namely the total utility U. Saving is the process of accumulating physical capital, and considerations of arbitrage between K and U will lead to (5.4).

From a slightly different angle, we see that there are two different reasons for valuing a unit of C differently when it is available at different dates. First, we may value it less if it occurs later; this is the aspect of 'impatience', and is reflected in ρ. Secondly, if the prevailing levels of consumption per capita at the two dates differ, the marginal valuation of the additional unit will also differ. This is the aspect of intertemporal distribution of consumption. As u has been assumed concave, we have

$$u'(C_0/L_0) \gtreqless u'(C_1/L_1) \quad \text{according as} \quad C_0/L_0 \lesseqgtr C_1/L_1.$$

Given diminishing marginal utility, consumption at date 1 is valued less if there is more of it per head. Of course the feasibility of this depends on the supply side, and emerges from the whole solution of the problem. Thus, in Fig. 5.1, on the line $C_0/L_0 = C_1/L_1$ only the aspect of impatience remains, and each indifference curve has the slope $(1 + \rho)$ where it meets this line. If the marginal productivity of capital is higher here, the optimum will be above this line. The distributive aspect will work in the same direction as that of impatience, and the rate of interest i will exceed the rate of impatience, ρ.

Now remove the restriction of two periods, and consider a longer sequence. From it, pick any three successive dates, $t, (t + 1)$ and $(t + 2)$. Contemplate an alternative plan which has the same history up to t, including K_t, and the same future beyond $(t + 2)$, including K_{t+2}. If varying K_{t+1} subject to these conditions can give a higher value of the objective function, then the whole plan can be thus improved on. Optimality in the two period context, which I shall call 'local optimality', is therefore a *necessary* condition for optimality of a longer plan. We can then use conditions like (5.1) for all two-period segments of it. This takes care of all the intermediate stages of the plan, and needs only to be supplemented by initial and terminal conditions. Rigorous proofs are difficult, and I shall omit them.

2. Optimum growth

Let us use the above rule in a growth model with one good and labour-augmenting disembodied technological progress. It is now easier to have time continuous, but the verbal statement of condition (5.1) can be readily adapted for this purpose. A rigorous proof would require the calculus of variations, and I shall omit it.

I shall use all the previous terminology, except that k and c will be respective amounts of capital and consumption per efficiency unit of labour: $k = K/EL$ and $c = C/EL$. Consumption per physical unit of labour, C/L, will be written $\tilde{c}$. Thus $\tilde{c} = c \cdot AL$. Now $\dot{K} = F(K, EL) - C$, and the usual rules for proportional changes enable us to write

$$\dot{k}/k = \dot{K}/K - E\dot{L}/EL = [F(K, EL) - C]/K - (n + ml)$$
$$= [f(k) - c]/k - (n + ml)$$

or

$$\dot{k} = f(k) - (n + ml) \cdot k - c \qquad (5.5)$$

This corresponds to the condition of material balance. It remains to state the objective function and derive the appropriate local optimality condition. We must now use an integral with exponential discounting over the relevant span of time to replace (5.3):

$$\int L \cdot u(C/L) \cdot e^{-\rho \cdot t} \cdot dt$$

The discounted marginal utility of total consumption at time t is $u'(\tilde{c}) \cdot e^{-\rho \cdot t}$. Its proportional rate of decline is

$$-\frac{d}{dt} [u'(\tilde{c}) \cdot e^{-\rho \cdot t}]/[u'(\tilde{c}) \cdot e^{-\rho \cdot t}]$$

$$= -[u''(\tilde{c}) \cdot e^{-\rho \cdot t} \cdot \dot{\tilde{c}} - u'(\tilde{c}) \cdot \rho \cdot e^{-\rho \cdot t}]/[u'(\tilde{c}) \cdot e^{-\rho \cdot t}]$$

$$= \rho + \epsilon(\tilde{c}) \cdot \dot{\tilde{c}}/\tilde{c}$$

where I have defined

$$\epsilon(\tilde{c}) = -\tilde{c} \cdot u''(\tilde{c})/u'(\tilde{c}), \qquad (5.6)$$

the elasticity of marginal utility, i.e. the relative rate at which undiscounted marginal utility falls as consumption per head increases. If we use an additively separable social welfare function for inter-personal comparisons, then this elasticity is an indicator of the importance attached to equality of incomes among persons.[2] For example, if person A has twice the income that person B has, and $\epsilon = 3$, then the social marginal valuation of an additional unit of income given to A will be $2^{-3} = 1/8$ that of the same additional unit given to B. With an additive valuation function, this will make a redistriubtion of income from A to B desirable, and the strength of this egalitarian concern will increase with ϵ. In the present context, ϵ plays a similar role with regard to the distribution of consumption per head over time. This will be seen shortly. In what follows, it will be extremely convenient for the purpose of simple exposition to assume that ϵ is constant. Even this leaves us with a fairly rich family of utility functions, of which the logarithm is one (corresponding to $\epsilon = 1$).

Finally, we have $\dot{\tilde{c}}/\tilde{c} = \dot{c}/c + ml$, and the marginal product of capital can be written $f'(k)$. Using all these results, the local optimality condition can be written

$$f'(k) = \rho + \epsilon \cdot (\dot{c}/c + ml) \qquad (5.7)$$

the common value being equal to the rate of interest i. Equivalently,

$$\dot{c}/c = [f'(k) - (\rho + \epsilon \cdot ml)]/\epsilon \qquad (5.8)$$

We have in (5.5) and (5.8) two differential equations that govern a path which is feasible and which satisfies the local optimality condition. Suppose we begin planning at time 0, knowing $k(0)$. If we knew $c(0)$ as well, we could solve these differential equations. As a matter of fact $c(0)$ is an important feature of the policy that we are trying to find. In this, it is useful to begin by tracing out the qualitative effects of assuming various values for $c(0)$. Since there are only two variables involved, and since the equations are such that time does not enter directly as an argument in the right hand sides, this can be done very easily in a phase diagram. We met one example of this technique in Chapter 4, and it would be useful to recapitulate the method briefly. Draw a diagram with k on the horizontal axis and c on the vertical axis. At any point (k, c), we can calculate the speeds $\dot{k}$ and $\dot{c}$ of the two variables from (5.5) and (5.8). We can then show the direction of motion at this point by a small arrow attached to it, and having done this for all points, join successive arrows to obtain the possible paths of solutions to the two equations of motion. One new feature that was not present in Chapter 4 now appears: while we know the initial value of k, that of c is unknown. We shall see that the phase diagram helps us find it.

Corresponding to the four possible combinations of each of k and c rising or falling, we have four regions in the (k, c) plane. To find their shapes, observe that

$$\dot{k} \gtreqless 0 \quad \text{according as} \quad f(k) - (n + ml) \cdot k - c \gtreqless 0$$

i.e. as the point (k, c) lies below or above the curve defined by

$$c = f(k) - (n + ml) \cdot k \qquad (5.9)$$

If the point is on this curve, $\dot{k}$ is zero and we have a steady state. To confirm this, note that the implied saving ratio satisfies

$$s = [f(k) - c]/f(k) = (n + ml) \cdot k/f(k) = g \cdot v$$

where g is the steady state rate of growth and v the capital/output ratio. Comparing steady states as in Chapter 3, we see that c is an increasing function of k up to the Golden Rule value k^* where the rate of interest equals the rate of growth:

$$f'(k^*) = n + ml, \qquad (5.10)$$

and decreasing thereafter. Let c^* be the maximum feasible steady state value of c.

Turning to the other differential equation, observe that

$$\dot{c} \gtreqless 0 \quad \text{according as} \quad f'(k) \gtreqless \rho + \epsilon \cdot ml$$

i.e. as the point (k, c) lies to the left or the right of the line $k = \bar{k}$ where

$$f'(\bar{k}) = \rho + \epsilon \cdot ml \qquad (5.11)$$

Fig. 5.2 shows the curve and the line, and the corresponding four regions, for the case where proper steady states exist. The figure also has $\bar{k} < k^*$; the importance of this will become clear shortly. Now define

$$\bar{c} = f(\bar{k}) - (n + ml) \cdot \bar{k} \qquad (5.12)$$

Then both $\dot{k}$ and $\dot{c}$ vanish at $(\bar{k}, \bar{c})$, i.e. the solution to (5.5) and (5.8) starting at this point remains stationary. Using all other possible points of departure, we can trace out solution curves to fill the space. Some other qualitative features can be deduced from the figure. At the boundary between regions 1 and 2 the direction of motion is vertically upward, so solutions can cross from 1 to 2 but not vice versa. Similarly at other boundaries there is one-way traffic. Solution curves must therefore enter regions 2 or 4 from 1 or 3, and exit to a boundary of the whole space. There are isolated but important exceptions. Thus, separating all solution curves which cross from 1 to 2 and all those which cross from 1 to 4, there is just one curve which converges

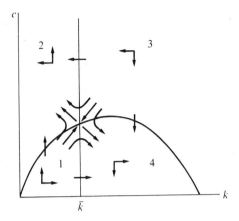

FIG. 5.2

asymptotically to the stationary point $(\bar{k}, \bar{c})$. Similarly, solutions which enter 4 from 1 are separated from those which enter 4 from 3 by a curve which 'emerges' from the stationary point. Combining all this information, we see that the stationary point has two stable solutions converging to it, two unstable ones diverging from it, and all other solution curves are shaped like hyperbolas and ultimately unstable. Such a stationary point is called a *saddle point*. This configuration will have important consequences.

Since the right hand sides of the differential equations (5.5) and (5.8) are both continuous functions, $\dot{k}$ and $\dot{c}$ increase as we move away from the curves where they are zero. Thus the speeds along the solution curves increase as we move away from the stationary point. This needs to be made precise if we are to prove many of the following results rigorously, but the general observation will suffice for my present purpose of showing that the results are plausible.

We can now consider the determination of $c(0)$, given the interval of time $[0, T]$ over which the plan is being drawn, the initial condition $k(0)$, and the target requirement $k(T)$. As Fig. 5.3 shows, there are many solution curves that will permit us to attain $k(T)$ starting from $k(0)$. The paths A, B, C, . . . are successively closer to the stationary point. Movement along them is successively slower, and the time necessary to traverse them longer. We can then select one which takes

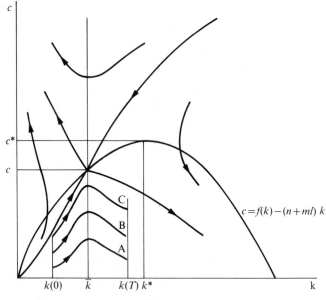

FIG. 5.3

exactly T units of time, and this gives us the optimum policy, including $c(0)$.

If T is very large, the optimum path will approach very close to $(\bar{k}, \bar{c})$ before veering away to its terminal target. What is more, motion in the vicinity of $(\bar{k}, \bar{c})$ being very slow, the path will spend a long time there. This is an important consequence of the saddle point feature. It is in fact possible to show that for any given neighbourhood of the stationary point, if the optimum plan for T years stays T' years in this neighbourhood, then (T'/T) tends to 1 as T tends to infinity. Such 'turnpike theorems' are very common in models of optimum growth far more general than the one I am considering now.

The turnpike property has two important implications. First, $c(0)$ is very insensitive to changes in T or $k(T)$ as long as T is large. This is because the requirement of heading towards a small neighbourhood of $(\bar{k}, \bar{c})$ is sufficient to determine $c(0)$ to a very good approximation. This property is convenient for the policy-maker. The second implication is not. An error in determining $c(0)$, however small, will be greatly magnified in the last stages of a long plan. It is therefore important to be on guard, taking into account any new information as it becomes available or even merely correcting possible errors in calculations. This can be done by means of 'rolling' or 'sliding' plans. For example, a 25-year plan might be made in year 0, and the first five years implemented. In year 5, another 25-year plan is made, taking into account the developments over the last five years and new information. This can continue every five years.

We have so far assumed the time horizon T and the terminal capital target $k(T)$ to be fixed by considerations outside our scope. However, any positive target for capital at the end of the planning horizon must be motivated by some concern for events beyond this horizon. A natural way to handle this is to extend the horizon, and as long as we are unable to state a final date for our concern with certainty, we are compelled to allow an infinite horizon.

If we allow our solution paths to continue indefinitely, almost all of them hit a boundary of the (k, c) plane. Some hit the vertical axis, thus running out of capital, while others hit the horizontal axis to the right of $\bar{k}$, thus accumulating capital for its own sake. It is intuitively clear that neither of these patterns is very desirable as a policy over the indefinite future. This leaves only one avenue of escape: for given $k(0)$, we must choose $c(0)$ so as to place the economy on the stable solution that converges asymptotically to the saddle point. It can be shown that such a policy is indeed optimum, provided $\bar{k} \leqslant k^{*}$, i.e.

$$\rho + \epsilon \cdot ml \geqslant n + ml \tag{5.13}$$

From (5.7) and (5.11), we see that the left hand side is the asymptotic value of the rate of interest in terms of output; call it $\bar{i}$. The right hand side is the steady state rate of growth, g. Thus the condition is

$$\bar{i} \geqslant g \tag{5.14}$$

This reminds us of the discussion of the Golden Rule in Chapter 3, and indeed the violation of this condition is related to inefficient overaccumulation. To see this, examine how the various variables behave in the limit. Consumption per head, $\tilde{c}$, grows at the rate of ml. Undiscounted marginal utility is proportional to $\tilde{c}^{-\epsilon}$, and therefore utility is proportional to $\tilde{c}^{(1-\epsilon)}$. The integrand in the objective function behaves like $\exp(n + (1 - \epsilon) \cdot ml - \rho)$. The integral over the infinite time horizon then converges to a finite value if (5.14) holds as a strict inequality. If it holds as an equality, it is possible to reinterpret the objective function in a suitable limiting sense to prove that the policy in question is optimum.[3] However, if (5.14) is violated, no optimum exists. The intuitive reason for this can be seen by noting that the integrand becomes a growing exponential. Considering small changes in policy, it seems desirable to save a little more in order to consume a little more at a later date: the force of discounting is low or the force of productivity is high. But at the later date, it will again seem desirable to postpone consumption further for the same reason. With an infinite time horizon, this will go on indefinitely and the fruits of the saving policy will never be reaped. Thus we can visualize a succession of policies each better than its predecessor, but the limiting policy at the end of the sequence is the worst rather than the best.[4]

This is just one illustration of the problems that can arise in planning over an infinite time horizon. Optimum policies can fail to exist for other reasons, and there are cases on the borderline of convergence that cannot be salvaged using the modified criterion. On the other hand, 'stop-gap' solutions can be devised to deal with the problem of $\bar{i} < g$ in the above model. These are deep and interesting issues, and readers who enjoy thinking about philosophical questions would do well to follow them up, but this would be a digression that an elementary exposition can do without.[5]

This analysis helps us answer the question of the normative significance of the Golden Rule raised in Chapter 3. Suppose, for example, that we are considering policy starting at time 0 with a given $k(0)$. We could accumulate capital to k^* and sustain consumption at its highest possible steady state level, but this would involve an initial sacrifice of consumption. The two parameters ρ and ϵ govern the benefits of doing this: high values of each of the parameters reduces the benefits, for a higher ρ discounts future utilities faster, while a higher ϵ leads to a smaller value at the margin for the higher levels of consumption per head which occur as benefits of the act of saving. It is only by chance, when (5.14) holds with equality, that the Golden Rule is the asymptotic optimum policy. Otherwise, confining the discussion to cases where an optimum exists, the optimum policy involves less saving and aims for a lower $\bar{k}$. Even if the initial value of k were k^*, it would pay to save slower than at a rate that would maintain the Golden

Rule, or even to dissave if possible, to aim for a lower asymptotic $\bar{k}$. In this case, the initial splurge of consumption is more valuable than a sustained higher level.

We can deduce a few qualitative properties of optimum policies. In the infinite horizon case both k and c move monotonically to their limiting values. For a finite horizon, at most one of them can change direction, and that at most once. This follows since all solution curves are hyperbolic. However, these are rather special consequences of the high degree of aggregation. In a two-sector model where capital is not shiftable between the sectors, for example, the optimum policy can involve repeated oscillations in k and c.

We cannot in general say anything about the saving ratio s along an optimum path. There are a few very special cases where it is constant, but otherwise it may fluctuate. The best we can do in general is to characterize the limiting value $\bar{s}$, and examine its dependence on the parameters. Using the notation of a bar over a variable to denote its limiting value, we have

$$\bar{s} = g \cdot \bar{v} = g \cdot \overline{\pi r}/\bar{i} \qquad (5.15)$$

where $f'(\bar{k}) = \bar{i}$, and therefore $\bar{v}$ and $\overline{\pi r}$ can be expressed as functions of $\bar{i}$. Some rough values will illustrate this. Suppose the annual rates are $n = 1$ per cent, $ml = 2$ per cent and $\rho = 5$ per cent, while $\epsilon = 2$, and the production function is such that $\overline{\pi r} = 0.25$. Then $g = 3$ per cent, $\bar{i} = 9$ per cent and $\bar{s} = 0.08$, which is not unreasonable. But if we change ρ to 0 and ϵ to 1.5, then $\bar{i} = 3$ per cent (barely sufficient for existence of an optimum) and $\bar{s} = 0.25$, which is rather high when compared to experience or casual judgement.

In (5.15) we see two forces acting to determine the ultimate saving ratio. The first is chanelled through the important long run rate of interest $\bar{i}$. A high $\bar{i}$ means that future consumption is discounted heavily, and therefore saving is less desirable. This can occur either because ρ is high, i.e. utils themselves are discounted heavily, or because ml is high, i.e. future generations will enjoy higher living standards through technological progress and this will make it less necessary to save for their sake, or because ϵ is high, i.e. the marginal utility falls rapidly, making the welfare judgement very egalitarian, and values the consumption for the better-off future generations very much less at the margin. The other force is chanelled through g, and a high g

encourages saving, either because it is necessary to save more with a growing population, or because it is more productive to save when there is technological progress.

Thus an increase in n increases $\bar{s}$, while an increase in ρ or ϵ lowers it. Technological progress affects both g and $\bar{i}$ in the same direction, and therefore has an ambiguous effect on $\bar{s}$. For a Cobb-Douglas production function $\overline{\pi r}$ is constant and we can calculate that

$$\partial \bar{s}/\partial ml \gtrless 0 \quad \text{according as} \quad \rho \gtrless \epsilon \cdot n$$

3. Generalizations and comments

To discuss further properties of the optimum policy, it helps to use its connection with an intertemporal equilibrium. If we write $p = u'(\tilde{c})$, we can interpret p as the price of capital in terms of (undiscounted) utils. There are two aspects to this. First in the one-good model, a unit of C and a unit of I (and hence K) are perfect substitutes in production. Both will be produced in positive amounts in equilibrium only if their prices are equal, and the price of C in utils is $u'(\tilde{c})$. Next we have the movement of p over time. The local optimality condition can be written

$$-\mathrm{d}p/\mathrm{d}t = p \cdot f'(k) - p \cdot \rho \tag{5.16}$$

This is just the equation of yield (2.32), since $p \cdot f'(k)$ is the rent in utils, and ρ the interest rate when utils are numéraire.

An important advantage of this interpretation is that it is easy to generalize beyond the one-good model: the relevant condition is that $p/u'(\tilde{c})$ equals the marginal rate of transformation between the consumer good and the capital good in question. Another advantage is that optimum policies which involve 'corner solutions' are very easy to understand and characterize. The simple exposition above neglected some constraints on the choice available that may turn out to be binding. Thus, for example, C must be non-negative, and unless the stock of capital can be consumed (or what amounts to the same thing, borrowed against), C cannot exceed Y. If the latter constraint is binding, no investment goods are being produced, which requires $p \leqslant u'(Y/L)$. Similarly, if the former constraint binds, $p \geqslant u'(0)$. It is common to assume that $u'(0) = \infty$, and this is true of the constant elasticity utility functions used earlier. This rules out the possibility of $C = 0$. A more interesting case is that of the industrial sector of an underdeveloped economy, which can hire labour from the agricultural sector at a going wage w, but must then provide consumer goods on which wage income is spent. Thus the constraint is $C \geqslant w \cdot L$, and if this is binding we must have $p \geqslant u'(w)$. If the economy is productive enough, this constraint ceases to be binding after a while, and then we have $p = u'(\tilde{c})$. In the interim, p must be falling faster than u', or the rate of interest appropriate to production decisions must exceed that appropriate to saving decisions. This has an important bearing on industrial cost-benefit analysis in such economies.[6]

Owing to this ease of interpretation and generalization, advanced treatments of optimum saving usually draw the phase diagrams like Fig. 5.3 with p on the vertical axis instead of c. Of course the two are monotonically inversely related through u', and it is easy to translate one type of diagram into the other. I shall leave this as an exercise.

I shall conclude this section with a few brief remarks on the objective function,[7] considering its use as a value judgement and as a function from which aggregate demand functions might be derived. From either point of view, the use of a special functional form which is a sum or an integral is a major restriction. Preferences can be expressed in this form if and only if the marginal rate of substitution between consumption at two dates is independent of the level of consumption at any third date. This seems rather restrictive. If non-additive functional forms are allowed, the qualitative features of optimum policies can be different. For example, cycles are possible for the optimum path of consumption even in the one-good model. On the other hand, preferences may be such as to penalize fluctuations, particularly downturns, and thus yield smooth optimum paths for consumption even with many goods. Similar arguments will apply to equilibrium growth paths when individuals' preferences cannot be represented by additive functions.

The next point concerns discounting. It is a commonplace to say that individuals discount future utilities, but that the practice is 'ethically indefensible' in a social welfare function. There are two aspects to this. Either individuals might be misinformed, or we may wish to overrule their preferences in any case. The first can arise due to an externality, as when a resource is owned in common and it pays each individual to deplete it fast, or due to secondary or market uncertainty which is faced by individuals but not by society as a whole.

The common argument for overruling individuals' preferences is that each individual might discount utilities which accrue later in his lifetime for reasons of uncertainty or otherwise, but social value judgements should not discount utilities accruing to later generations in the same way. What this argument really points to is a different weakness in the objective function, namely that it pays no attention to the generation structure of the population, and considers all individuals alive at any given date as exactly alike. Even if we admit additivity and all the other restrictions, a better treatment would be the following. Suppose an individual born at date b, when a years of age, consumes $c(b, a)$. Suppose individuals discount utilities at rate α, and the social welfare function discounts utilities across generations at rate β. If $B(b)$ individuals are born at date b, and each lives T years, using u as his undiscounted utility function, the social welfare will be

$$\int_0^\infty e^{-\beta \cdot b} B(b) \cdot \left\{ \int_0^T e^{-\alpha \cdot a} \cdot u(c(b, a)) \cdot \mathrm{d}a \right\} \cdot \mathrm{d}b \qquad (5.17)$$

This is clearly rather difficult to manage. I shall discuss a simple model of this kind in the next section.

A similar treatment of population structure is a desirable addition to the market equilibrium model. There we have the added complication of budget constraints appropriate to each generation. This needs particular care when we consider exhaustible natural resources. Also, when we consider situations between the case of central planning and the pure market, i.e. when government policy is being implemented in part through the market, achievement of the full optimum would typically need lump sum transfers in an intertemporal context, and this can be problematic. As a general point, it should be stressed that considerations of an overlapping sequence of generations put a great strain on the intertemporal equilibrium story. Futures markets are even harder to visualize when not all the agents in the economy exist at any common date. Expectations on part of producers will be of some help; thus owners of a natural resource will expect faster current depletion to lead to greater scarcity in the future and therefore higher prices in the future, and this will put a brake on the current depletion rate. But perfect foresight is hard to accept. Central planning is not a sure answer either, since planners are also imperfectly informed about unborn generations and have to make guesses.

Two issues mentioned above in passing need some amplification. Uncertainty is often thought to be an argument in favour of discounting the future. Economic analysis handles uncertainty by using an expected utility framework.[8] The value of the objective function is found by multiplying the utilities of possible outcomes by their probabilities and adding these products. Thus, if the uncertainty concerns levels of consumption at any date, we should form an expected utility sum at that date. This is not equivalent to discounting at a higher rate, and does not necessarily have the same effect on saving. However, if the uncertainty concerns the length of the time horizon, or survival up to a given date, then we weight utilities at different dates by the probabilities of survival. Since probabilities of survival decrease monotonically for dates further in the future, this has effects very much like faster discounting. Again, we have a possible conflict between individuals' assessment of such probabilities and that of the policy-makers'.

The other issue is that of equity between generations, or more generally over time. I mentioned that ϵ could be regarded as a measure of the aversion to income inequality in the valuation function. If the economy is sufficiently productive, future generations can be given higher levels of consumption per capita. We saw how higher values of ϵ, by increasing $\bar{\imath}$, reduced the value of the saving that achieves this. Suppose we let ϵ go to infinity. Then, whenever we compare two different levels of consumption per capita, the marginal utility of the higher relative to the lower goes to zero. The objective function is then reduced to maximizing the lowest level of utility, which is formally equivalent to Rawls' famous max-min criterion for distributive justice.[9] In an economy capable of growth, this makes it suboptimal to grow, for any saving is a sacrifice for the present and least well-off generation. Verify that $\bar{s} = 0$ in (5.15) when $\epsilon = \infty$ and $ml > 0$. This is not very appealing to the common sense, and Rawls himself does not advocate the strict max-min principle in the intergenerational context.

The situation changes when we consider exhaustible resources. Then the initial generation is not the poorest in an unequivocal way. In fact, since it has at its command the largest amount of such resources of any generation, it is the wealthiest in that respect. It is then possible to work out a sensible combination of capital accumulation and resource depletion to accord with the strict Rawlesian criterion.[20] I shall consider some simple models of this kind in Chapter 7.

4. Life-cycle saving

The problem of optimum saving has so far been considered from the point of view of the whole economy. The same technique can also be applied to an individual who wishes to arrange his consumption stream over his lifetime to maximize a utility integral. We can then recognize that an economy at any instant has several individuals of different ages, and find the total demand for consumption as a function of the prices facing them. This can then be joined to a supply side, and the equilibrium of the whole economy determined. This brings much greater richness to the treatment of saving than is possible with any number of postulated propensities, and yields some interesting results.

In this section I shall outline a very simple model of this kind.[11] My first simplification is to confine the analysis to steady states. Otherwise the wage and interest rates can change over time, and the individuals' saving decisions become extremely complicated. This is best left to more advanced treatments.[12] Another simplification is to use a one-good model without technological change or deterioration of capital on the supply side. Of course exponential decay and labour-augmenting disembodied technological progress are easily incorporated; nor is it difficult to allow an input-output supply side with several capital goods.[13]

Begin with the demand side. In a steady state the wage rate w and the the interest rate i are constant over time. Also, in a competitive framework these are independent of the borrowing and lending decisions of any individual. The formalism of maximization is exactly like that in Section 2, with $n = 0$, $ml = 0$. Replacing physical capital k by the assets owned by the individual, the marginal return $f'(k)$ is to be replaced by i and regarded constant. Then (5.8) becomes

$$\dot{c}/c = (i - \rho)/\epsilon \qquad (5.18)$$

In other words, the consumer will arrange his lifetime consumption stream to be exponentially rising if $i > \rho$, i.e. if the interest rate available exceeds his rate of impatience, and to be exponentially decaying otherwise.

Write λ for the right hand side in (5.18): then the consumption at age t will be $c(t) = c(0) \cdot e^{\lambda \cdot t}$. It remains to determine $c(0)$, and that is most easily done by introducing a lifetime budget constraint in terms of discounted present values. There are various possibilities, and I shall assume a particularly simple one. Suppose the individual receives and leaves no bequests. Suppose he lives for T years, working and receiving a wage for the first T' years, and retiring for the last $(T-T')$. Then the discounted present value of his consumption plan over his life of T years must equal that of his wage stream over his working life of T' years, i.e.

$$\int_0^T c(0) \cdot e^{\lambda \cdot t} \cdot e^{-i \cdot t} \cdot \mathrm{d}t = \int_0^{T'} w \cdot e^{-i \cdot t} \cdot \mathrm{d}t.$$

Using the notation for discounted present values introduced in (4.18), this becomes

$$c(0) \cdot \Delta(i - \lambda, T) = w \cdot \Delta(i \cdot T') \qquad (5.19)$$

This completes the determination of the individual's plan.

All individuals are assumed identical except for their birth dates. Thus at any instant in time, the economy has a collection of individuals of different ages. We must find the consumption demand of each age group and add them. Let n be the rate of growth of population, and choose units so that at date t, there are $e^{n \cdot t}$ births. Now choose and fix any date in the steady state, say the date 0. Then, for each τ in the interval $(0, T)$, there are $e^{-n \cdot \tau}$ τ-year olds who are alive at date 0, having been born at date $-\tau$. Each of these consumes $c(\tau)$. Thus the total consumption is

$$\int_0^T c(0) \cdot e^{\lambda \cdot \tau} \cdot e^{-n \cdot \tau} \cdot \mathrm{d}\tau = c(0) \cdot \Delta(n - \lambda, T).$$

It is more convenient to express this relative to the labour force. At date 0, for each τ in $(0, T')$, there are $e^{-n \cdot \tau}$ workers born at $-\tau$, and thus the total labour force is

$$L = \int_0^{T'} e^{-n\tau} \cdot \mathrm{d}\tau = \Delta(n, T')$$

The consumption demand per unit of the labour force is then

$$c^d = w \cdot \frac{\Delta(i, T')}{\Delta(i - \lambda, T)} \cdot \frac{\Delta(n - \lambda, T)}{\Delta(n, T')} \tag{5.20}$$

Now recall that the values of w and i cannot be independently specified, since they are related by the wage-interest frontier. Remember also that λ depends on i. We can then make the necessary substitutions and express c^d as a function of i alone. It turns out that the graph of this function is U-shaped.

Turning to the supply side, we know from Chapter 3 that in a steady state with k units of capital per unit of the labour force, the ratio of consumption to the labour force is given by $c = f(k) - n \cdot k$. Also $f'(k) = i$, and since f is a concave function, this defines k as a decreasing function of i. We can thus express c as a function of i. We also know that the graph of this function has an inverted U-shape, increasing up to the Golden Rule value $i = n$, and decreasing thereafter.

It is clear that the two curves can in general meet in two points, thus defining two values of i that are compatible with equilibrium for consumption. Moreover, we have the remarkable result that one of these intersections always occurs at $i = n$. We already know the property of the Golden Rule that $c = w$, and from (5.20) we see at once that when $i = n$, $c^d = w$.

In fact the Golden Rule is usually not the general equilibrium. We must also look at other markets, and in particular must have the sum total of assets demanded by individuals equal to the total available, i.e. the capital stock in the one good model since there are no other assets. This condition usually disqualifies the Golden Rule, leaving the other intersection as the equilibrium.

To calculate the demand for assets, we can retrace all the steps of looking at each individual's lifetime asset holding, and then adding over all individuals alive at any instant. However, in a steady state a much simpler method can be used. The assets A must grow at the rate n, and therefore the aggregate expenditure of all individuals at date 0 is $(c^d \cdot L + n \cdot A)$. Their aggregate income is $(w \cdot L + i \cdot A)$. Equating the two, we can solve for the assets per unit of the labour force, $a = A/L$, as

$$a = (c^d - w)/(i - n) \tag{5.21}$$

provided $i \neq n$. For $i = n$, we can interpret this as the limiting value of the right hand side. Similarly, considering the division of the product and the income generated, we have

$$k = (c - w)/(i - n) \qquad (5.22)$$

Now provided $i \neq n$, we see that $c^d = c$ automatically implies $a = k$, and there is no need to consider the asset equilibrium separately. Thus an intersection of our earlier two curves other than the Golden Rule is guaranteed to be a general equilibrium. However, if $i = n$, taking limits on the right hand sides by L'Hôpital's Rule, we see that $a = k$ requires

$$dc^d/di = dc/di \qquad (5.23)$$

i.e. the two consumption curves should be tangent at the Golden Rule. In this case the two intersections are coincident. Of course we know that $dc/di = 0$ at $i = n$, so the mutual tangent is in fact horizontal.

Fig. 5.4 shows the three possibilities. Perhaps the most noteworthy case is (c), where we have an equilibrium with $i < n$. We know that such a steady state is inefficient in the sense that it is possible to make available more aggregate consumption at each instant of time by some decumulation. It should then be possible to distribute this addition in such a way that the lifetime utility integrals for all consumers are raised. Thus the equilibrium is also Pareto inefficient, and suboptimum from the point of view of any welfare judgement like (5.17).

In particular, suppose the welfare judgement applies a zero rate of discount to individuals' utility integrals. Thus the optimum steady state is one in which the common value of this integral is as high as possible. Since, at each instant in time, there exists a balanced age distribution, this is achieved by having a steady state with the maximum aggregate consumption level, irrespective of α. The latter affects only the division of this consumption among people of different ages. Thus the optimum steady state for such a value judgement is the Golden Rule, which occurs as a market equilibrium only in the exceptional case (b).

The possibility of an inefficient steady state also arose in Chapter 3 when the saving propensity was high enough. However, there was little reason to be perturbed about that. The saving behaviour paid no attention to the consumption possibilities anyway, and it was hardly a surprise that it could prove detrimental to them. In the present case,

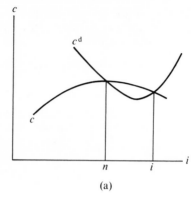

(a)

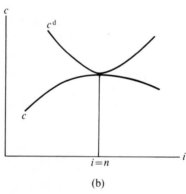

(b)

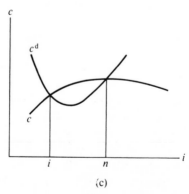

(c)

FIG. 5.4

each individual is taking an optimizing forward-looking view with perfect foresight, but they are all locked into an inefficient equilibrium. This is clearly more serious.

We must therefore examine more closely the question of when an inefficient equilibrium can occur, and what can be done about it. A basic contributing cause is the fact that the economy and its capital stock last for ever, but individuals have finite life-spans and form an overlapping sequence of generations. Thus young savers accumulate capital not merely by acquiring titles to newly built investment goods, but also buying existing capital from older people who are running down their assets. As this can go on for ever, we have the possibility of an equilibrium of self-fulfilling expectations of the kind we met when discussing pure speculative booms in Chapter 2.[14]

To rule out an inefficient equilibrium, it suffices to have $dc^d/di < 0$ when $i = n$. The derivative can be calculated from (5.20), and a rather messy bit of algebra yields the following factors as being conducive to an efficient equilibrium: (i) $\rho \geqslant n$, (ii) T' a sizeable fraction of T, i.e. retirement periods small in comparison with working lives, (iii) T' and T large enough that terms like $e^{-n \cdot T'}$ can be neglected. Different examples in the literature on the subject have different assumptions on these points, and therefore point to different conclusions concerning efficiency.

Conversely, we have inefficiency when $dc^d/di > 0$ at $i = n$. Looking back at (5.21) and (5.22) and taking limits, this means that $a > k$ at this point. In other words, inefficiency arises because at the rate of interest n, the population in the aggregate would wish to hold more assets than can be made possible from the Golden Rule capital stock. However, this suggests a possible policy to restore efficiency. If the consumers do not care about the exact form of the asset, but only for the return, then the government can issue financial assets to satisfy their demand, thus removing the need to accumulate physical capital in excess of the Golden Rule. Such an asset could be interest-bearing money, or national debt. If desired, the Golden Rule itself can be achieved.

The life-cycle model can be enriched by the inclusion of such monetary policies as well as fiscal ones. Bequests can also be incorporated, and empirical work attempted. I shall leave all these refinements,[15] and merely make some general comments on the approach. The hypothesis of life-cycle saving gives a treatment of saving along the same lines as the familiar theory of the consumer's choice, and is therefore much more satisfactory and systematic than the ad hoc approach of saving propensities. We can use (5.20) to derive an expression for the ratio of aggregate saving to aggregate income in the life-cycle model, but this will no longer be a parameter. It will be a complicated function affected by other parameters and the interest rate. In particular, it will depend on n. When we compared steady states in Chapter 3, we treated n and s as independent parameters. This is not possible in the life-cycle approach. An economy with a different rate of population growth will have a different structure of ages at any instant, and therefore different saving behaviour. As to the dependence on the rate of interest, we could simply postulate a saving propensity that was a function of the interest rate, but again there is some advantage in recognizing that interest rate changes affect saving by the young and the old differently. This is because a lower interest rate raises the capitalized value of a young person's future wages, while it lowers the income that accrues from the capital accumulated by an old person. The life-cycle model gives a systematic treatment of this.

Of course there are aspects of saving that are not captured by the life-cycle hypothesis. These have generally to do with uncertainty concerning future incomes, interest rates, tastes etc. All these issues do not arise in an equilibrium framework, and are too difficult to have received a really satisfactory treatment in the context of disequilibrium.

Notes

The subject begins with the classic article by Ramsey (1928), which is still very much worth reading. It has now become common to treat it using a mathematical theorem known as the Maximum Principle; e.g. Cass (1965), Shell (1967). I hope that my approach conveys the economically important insights of that theorem, namely the behaviour of the associated shadow price of capital, without the mathematical machinery. For a simple exposition of a special case, see Black (1962). For an elementary introduction, see Solow (1970, ch. 5), and for more advanced treatments, see Wan (1971, chs. 9–11), Burmeister and Dobell (1970, ch. 11).

1. For a very complete examination of this model, see Mirrless (1967).
2. See Atkinson (1970a).
3. See von Weizsäcker (1965), Mirrlees (1967).
4. For a detailed discussion, see Heal (1973, ch. 13).

5. See Koopmans (1967), McFadden (1973), Hammond and Mirrlees (1973).
6. See Little and Mirrlees (1974, ch. XIV).
7. For a detailed discussion, see Heal (1973, chs. 10, 11).
8. See Baumol (1972, ch. 22), Malinvaud (1973, ch. 11).
9. See Rawls (1971).
10. See Solow (1974b). See also Arrow (1973) for a model of Rawlsian just saving in an economy with overlapping generations, which produces some cyclic behaviour.
11. My immediate source is Hall (1969). See also the important earlier work by Diamond (1965b), Meade (1966b), Tobin (1967).
12. See Cass and Yaari (1967).
13. See von Weizsäcker (1971, Part IV).
14. This problem was discovered by Samuelson (1958). See also the later clarifications by Diamond (1965b), Shell (1971).
15. In addition to the references above, see Atkinson (1971).

6. Two-sector Models

In all the models up to now, output has been fully aggregated. Just as input disaggregation with embodied technological change enables us to study the important concept of the extensive margin, output disaggregation introduces the richer detail of resource allocation among different uses. However, complex models are hard to solve and to comprehend, and we should consider the marginal benefits less costs when introducing complications. There are different ways of distinguishing two or more types of output, and these have different net benefits in different applications.

Broadly speaking, output can be distinguished by demand or by supply considerations, i.e. according to potential use or production relations. The standard two-sector model assumes that the two go together. Thus it has one good used only for consumption and the other only for investment, each produced in its own sector with its own technology. Its main use is to illustrate the new issues, and its direct contribution to realism is debatable. I shall discuss it first in this pedagogical spirit, and then mention some other two-sector models.

In order to highlight the new issues, I shall revert to the other simplifying assumptions of Chapter 3. Thus there will be a scalar capital stock, consisting of accumulated investment. There will be no deterioration of capital and no technological progress. Capital and labour will be shiftable between the two uses, and will be allocated efficiently in an equilibrium. Saving will be specified by fixed propensities. I shall indicate some generalizations in Section 4.

1. Momentary equilibrium

Much of the groundwork for finding an equilibrium at an instant has been covered in Chapter 2, section 5. Either of our approaches – cost function and revenue function – gave us four equilibrium conditions for production, and it only remained to add a saving function. The existence of such an equilibrium follows from standard theorems, but its uniqueness is a problem.

To understand the reason, let us return briefly to the one-good model and examine its equilibrium from a new angle. The producers' desired, i.e. cost-minimizing, capital/labour ratio k_d can be expressed as a function of the wage/rental ratio, ω. This is an increasing function; recall that its elasticity is σ, the elasticity of substitution in production. There can then be at most one value of ω for which $k_d = k$, the ratio of the supplies of the two factors at the instant. Given a sufficiently large range of variation of k_d, there will be exactly one such value. It might be thought that the two ratios could be equal with the same percentage of excess supply or of excess demand for the two factors. But when the output market is in equilibrium, this is not possible. Walras' Law ensures that when one factor is in excess supply, the other must be in excess demand. Thus $k_d = k$ implies equilibrium in both factor markets.

If there is insufficient substitution, we will have an equilibrium at an extreme point, with one factor price equal to zero. In any case, we have a unique equilibrium.

Let us try the same argument in the two-sector case, and see if k_d is an increasing function of ω. When ω increases, the cost-minimizing capital/labour ratio in each sector increases in the familiar manner. However, there are further changes, since output market equilibrium is now compatible with different output compositions, which imply different factor demands. The mathematical details will follow, but the general conclusions can be stated quite simply. The rise in wages relative to rents raises the unit cost of the good which is more labour-intensive in production relative to that of the other. Also, the income of wage-earners rises relative to that of rent-recipients. Both of these affect demand and therefore output composition. If demand shifts towards the relatively capital-intensive good, this will reinforce the substitution effect in each sector, and thus further increase the demand for capital relative to that for labour. The aggregate k_d will increase, which is what we need for uniqueness. However, if demand shifts towards the more labour-intensive good, this will oppose the substitution effects, and the net outcome will be doubtful. Therefore, if we assume that the wage earners have a higher propensity to consume, the demand shift will be favourable for uniqueness if the consumer good is more capital-intensive.

Let us build up this picture in manageable parts, beginning with the effect of factor price changes on output prices. The equilibrium conditions are given in (2.26). Some natural economic interpretations can be obtained by considering proportional changes. For any variable x, I shall write $\hat{x}$ for dx/x. We can then obtain a rule exactly like (3.10). For a relation $z = z(x, y)$ between any three variables x, y, and z, we will have

$$\hat{z} = \left\{\frac{x}{z} \cdot \frac{\partial z}{\partial x}\right\} \cdot \hat{x} + \left\{\frac{y}{z} \cdot \frac{\partial z}{\partial y}\right\} \cdot \hat{y} \qquad (6.1)$$

Then, using (2.6) for each sector,

$$\pi r^C \cdot \hat{r} + \pi w^C \cdot \hat{w} = \hat{q}$$
$$\pi r^I \cdot \hat{r} + \pi w^I \cdot \hat{w} = \hat{p} \qquad (6.2)$$

Of course πr^C denotes the imputed rent share in the consumer good sector, and so on. It is easy to verify that $(1 - \pi w^C)/\pi w^C = k^C/\omega$, k^C being the desired capital/labour ratio in the consumer good sector, and similarly for the other good. Then $\pi w^I > \pi w^C$ if and only if $k^I < k^C$, i.e. the consumer good is more capital-intensive. This will help us in our interpretations.

It is interesting to note that output price changes are weighted averages of the input price changes. Thus an exogenous change of 1 per cent in one of the latter will be dampened, i.e. will cause a change of less than 1 per cent in one of the former. Conversely, output price changes will be magnified in input price changes. This 'magnification effect' is important in similar models in international trade.

Using the fact that the imputed shares in each sector sum to 1, we have

$$\hat{p} - \hat{q} = (\pi w^I - \pi w^C) \cdot (\hat{w} - \hat{r}) \qquad (6.3)$$

Thus an increase in w relative to r raises p relative to q if the investment good is more labour intensive. In particular, if the two goods are equally labour-intensive, relative output prices will be unchanged when input prices change. We can then use these output prices as fixed weights to aggregate the two sectors to one, and reduce the model to the one-good case.[1]

Next we turn to the quantity equations (2.25), interpreting L and K as the quantities desired for efficient production of C and I when the factor prices are w and r. Write $b_C = \phi_w{}^C$, the labour input per unit of consumer good output, and define b_I, v_C and v_I analogously. Now

$$dL = C \cdot db_C + dC \cdot b_C + I \cdot db_I + dI \cdot b_I,$$

which can be transformed into

$$dL/L = (C \cdot b_C/L) \cdot (dC/C + db_C/b_C) + (I \cdot b_I/L) \cdot (dI/I + db_I/b_I).$$

Write $\Pi C^L = C \cdot b_C/L$, the proportion of labour employed in the consumer good sector, and similarly $\Pi I^L = I \cdot b_I/L$. Thus ΠC^L, ΠI^L are non-negative and add to one. Defining ΠC^K and ΠI^K as the proportions of capital employed in the two sectors, we have a similar equation for capital. Using our notation for proportional changes, these become

$$\hat{L} = \Pi C^L \cdot (\hat{C} + \hat{b}_C) + \Pi I^L \cdot (\hat{I} + \hat{b}_I)$$
$$\hat{K} = \Pi C^K \cdot (\hat{C} + \hat{v}_C) + \Pi I^K \cdot (\hat{I} + \hat{v}_I) \tag{6.4}$$

Now $\Pi C^K > \Pi C^L$ if and only if $\Pi C^K/(1 - \Pi C^K) > \Pi C^L/(1 - \Pi C^L)$, i.e. $v_C/v_I > b_C/b_I$, i.e. $k_C = v_C/b_C > v_I/b_I = k_I$, i.e. the consumer good is more capital-intensive. This will also be useful in interpreting some conditions to be derived later.

Subtracting, we can write

$$\hat{K} - \hat{L} = (\Pi C^K - \Pi C^L) \cdot (\hat{C} - \hat{I}) + (\Pi C^K \cdot \hat{v}_C - \Pi C^L \cdot \hat{b}_C)$$
$$+ (\Pi I^K \cdot \hat{v}_I - \Pi I^L \cdot \hat{b}_I) \tag{6.5}$$

Each of $\hat{v}_C$ etc. can be found from equations exactly like (2.9) applied to each sector.

One incidental result will be useful later. Consider the thought-experiment of changing K and L holding w and r constant, and finding the corresponding changes in C and I compatible with equilibrium in production. Then each of the $\hat{v}_C$ etc. will be zero, and only the first term on the right will remain in (6.5). This is a dual 'magnification effect' for quantities. A little algebra yields

$$\hat{I} - \hat{L} = - \frac{\Pi C^L}{\Pi C^K - \Pi C^L} \cdot (\hat{K} - \hat{L}) \tag{6.6}$$

Thus, if the consumer good is more capital intensive, a higher capital/labour ratio at constant prices leads to a lower amount of investment per head. If the consumer good is more labour-intensive, i.e. the investment good more capital-intensive, then $\Pi C^L/(\Pi C^L - \Pi C^K)$ is positive and greater than one, i.e. a 1 per cent rise in the capital-labour ratio at constant prices will raise investment per head by more than one per cent. This is known as Rybczynski's Theorem, and will prove useful soon.

Finally, let us turn to saving and postulate separate propensities out of wages and profits. We have

$$
\begin{aligned}
q \cdot C &= (1 - sw) \cdot w \cdot L + (1 - sr) \cdot r \cdot K \\
p \cdot I &= \quad sw \ \cdot w \cdot L + \quad sr \ \cdot r \cdot K
\end{aligned}
\tag{6.7}
$$

in obvious notation. We assume $sr > sw$. Now consider small changes in this. For the purpose of equilibrium analysis, we calculate demand assuming that sellers of factors can sell all the services they wish at the going prices; these are the 'target' or 'notional' demands. Thus we calculate changes holding L and K fixed at their full employment levels. By differentiating and dividing as above, we find

$$
\begin{aligned}
\hat{q} + \hat{C} &= \gamma^C \cdot \hat{w} + (1 - \gamma^C) \cdot \hat{r} \\
\hat{p} + \hat{I} &= \gamma^I \cdot \hat{w} + (1 - \gamma^I) \cdot \hat{r}
\end{aligned}
\tag{6.8}
$$

where γ^C is the ratio of the consumption out of wages to total consumption, and γ^I is the ratio of the saving out of wages to total saving. Given our assumptions, we have $\gamma^C > \gamma^I$.

Subtracting and using (6.3), we have

$$
\hat{C} - \hat{I} = - \{1 + (\gamma^C - \gamma^I)/(\pi w^I - \pi w^C)\} \cdot (\hat{q} - \hat{p})
\tag{6.9}
$$

This tells us how the relative demands respond to the relative output prices. We can then call the coefficient σ^D, the elasticity of substitution in demand. In fact this is made up of two parts. The first, 1, is the pure substitution effect. The remaining term, $(\gamma^C - \gamma^I)/(\pi w^I - \pi w^C)$, is the income effect arising from the induced changes in factor prices. This is positive given our saving assumption and the assumption that the consumer good is more capital intensive. However, if one of the assumptions is reversed, this part will be negative. There is nothing to stop it falling below -1 and making σ^D negative. This is the point about changes in demand being ambiguous. If $sw = sr$, then $\gamma^C = \gamma^I$, and $\sigma^D = 1$.

Finally, putting all the parts together, we can write

$$\hat{k}_d = (\delta^C \cdot \sigma^C + \delta^I \cdot \sigma^I + \delta^D \cdot \sigma^D)\,\hat{\omega} \qquad (6.10)$$

where σ^C and σ^I are the respective elasticities of substitution in the two sectors, and δ^C, δ^I and δ^D are weights, defined by

$$\left.\begin{aligned}
\delta^C &= \Pi C^K \cdot \pi w^C + \Pi C^L \cdot \pi r^C \\
\delta^I &= \Pi I^K \cdot \pi w^I + \Pi I^L \cdot \pi r^I \\
\delta^D &= (\Pi C^K - \Pi C^L) \cdot (\pi w^I - \pi w^C)
\end{aligned}\right\} \qquad (6.11)$$

It can be verified that the weights are non-negative and add to one. Thus the elasticity of k_d with respect to ω, which can then be called σ, the aggregate elasticity of substitution, is a weighted average of the three separate elasticities. For uniqueness of momentary equilibrium we need $\sigma > 0$. For this, it is sufficient but not necessary to have σ^D positive, and for this in turn it is sufficient but not necessary to have the consumer good more capital intensive when the propensity to save out of wages is lower. It is clearly possible to obtain weaker conditions, i.e. to have a stronger result. Having explained the general principle and working of the model, I shall leave these refinements as exercises. One of the best-known of these conditions for uniqueness is that the sum of σ^C and σ^I should exceed 1.[2]

While the cost function is most suitable for explaining the problem of the uniqueness of momentary equilibrium, growth paths are more easily studied using the revenue function. Let us therefore briefly re-examine the momentary equilibrium in these terms.

As we found in Chapter 3, it is often simpler to work with relative magnitudes. Let us express the various quantities per unit of labour force by the corresponding lower case letters, but let $I/L = j$ in order to avoid confusion with the interest rate. Choose the consumer good to be the numéraire, setting $q = 1$. Then the revenue function becomes $R(k, p)$, the maximum of $(c + p \cdot j)$ subject to the production condition conditions. Using the same arguments as were employed for the one-sector production function in (2.17) and (2.18), we can write the equilibrium conditions (2.28) and (2.29) as

$$j = R_p(k, p), \qquad c = R(k, p) - p \cdot R_p(k, p) \qquad (6.12)$$

$$r = R_k(k, p), \qquad w = R(k, p) - k \cdot R_k(k, p) \qquad (6.13)$$

Now saving per head is $(sw \cdot w + sr \cdot r \cdot k)$, and the final condition for equilibrium becomes

$$p \cdot R_p(k, p) = sw \cdot R(k, p) + (sr - sw) \cdot k \cdot R_k(k, p) \quad (6.14)$$

The question of uniqueness then becomes: given the prevailing k at any instant, does (6.14) provide a unique solution for p?

This will be so if, for each fixed k, the function given by the difference between the two sides, $p \cdot R_p - sw \cdot R \cdot -(sr - sw) \cdot k \cdot R_k$, is a monotonic function of p. Its derivative with respect to p is easily seen to be $p \cdot R_{pp} + (1 - sw) \cdot R_p - (sr - sw) \cdot k \cdot R_{kp}$. Recall that R is a convex function of prices, and therefore R_{pp} is positive. Now examine R_{kp}. This is $\partial j/\partial k$, evaluated at fixed p. By Rybczynski's Theorem, it is positive if the investment good is more capital-intensive, and negative if the consumer good is more capital-intensive. Then our whole expression will be positive if the last term is negative, i.e. if $(sr - sw)$ and R_{kp} are of opposite signs, i.e. if, with $sr > sw$, the consumer good is more capital-intensive. Once again, this is only a sufficient condition. Moreover, we can again express the various terms using elasticities of substitution.

Incidentally, Rybczynski's theorem yields a stronger result that will be very useful. If the investment good is more capital intensive,

$$\hat{j} > \hat{k}, \quad \text{i.e.} \quad \partial j/\partial k > j/k, \quad \text{i.e.} \quad R_{kp} > R_p/k. ^{(3)}$$

It must be admitted that the condition on relative capital intensities is not very plausible, not very intuitive, and not really verified or refuted empirically. Moreover, it is possible to have one sector more capital-intensive for one set of factor endowments and more labour-intensive for another, i.e. there may be reversals of factor intensity. In view of all these complications, we must carefully check uniqueness in particular applications. Matters are of course easier if the propensity to save out of both classes of income is the same.

2. Equilibrium growth
Having examined the problems, I shall now neglect them and assume a unique momentary equilibrium. The next step is to obtain an equation to determine how k evolves along a path of equilibrium growth. Since

$\dot{k}/k = j/k - n$, this equation of motion is

$$\dot{k} = R_p(k, p) - n \cdot k \qquad (6.15)$$

where of course p is defined by (6.14). We could in principle solve for p, obtain the right hand side of (6.15) as a function of k alone, and then examine the solutions as in Chapter 3. However, an indirect approach is more illuminating.

Let us draw in (k, p) space the locus of points defined by (6.14). Momentary equilibrium being assumed unique, this defines p as a (single-valued) function of k. Since we are considering equilibrium growth, the values of k and p at any instant must lie on this curve. Along it, we have

$$\frac{\mathrm{d}p}{\mathrm{d}k} = \frac{sr \cdot R_k + (sr - sw) \cdot k \cdot R_{kk} - p \cdot R_{pk}}{p \cdot R_{pp} + (1 - sw) \cdot R_p - (sr - sw) \cdot k \cdot R_{kp}} \qquad (6.16)$$

We have already assumed the denominator to be positive. The numerator, however, is ambiguous. Recall that R is a concave function of quantities. Thus R_{kk} is negative, and even the capital-intensity condition $R_{pk} < 0$ is not enough to determine the sign of the whole expression. In the special case where $sr = sw = s$, say, the numerator is reduced to $(s \cdot R_k - p \cdot R_{pk})$, which is positive if R_{pk} is negative, and ambiguous otherwise.

Next consider the curve defined by

$$R_p(k, p) - n \cdot k = 0 \qquad (6.17)$$

Since $R_{pp} > 0$, this defines p uniquely as a function of k. For the same reason, the left hand side is positive above the curve and negative below it. Its slope is easily seen to be

$$\mathrm{d}p/\mathrm{d}k = (n - R_{pk})/R_{pp} \qquad (6.18)$$

This is positive when R_{pk} is negative, i.e. when the consumer good is more capital-intensive. If the investment good is more capital-intensive, then Rybczynski's Theorem gives us $R_{pk} > R_p/k = n$ along (6.17), i.e. $\mathrm{d}p/\mathrm{d}k$ is negative along the curve.

Now consider the two curves together, as shown for a complicated case in Fig. 6.1. Where (6.14) lies above (6.17) we must have $\dot{k}$ positive, and the equilibrium will shift to the right along the curve (6.14). Where

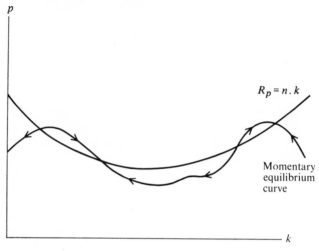

FIG. 6.1

this curve is below the other, $\dot{k}$ is negative and the equilibrium will shift to the left. Where the two intersect, we have an equilibrium with $\dot{k} = 0$, i.e. a steady state.

Thus we see that there can be multiple steady states. Those where (6.14) cuts (6.17) from above will be locally stable, i.e. equilibrium paths beginning with a value of k sufficiently close to the steady state value will converge to that state. The opposite intersections define locally unstable steady states. If there are multiple steady states, they must be alternately stable and unstable. If the extreme ones with positive k are unstable, we can speak of degenerate steady states with zero or infinite k, which will then be locally stable. If there happens to be a unique steady state, all equilibrium paths will approach it, i.e. it will be globally stable.

Although the picture is much more complicated than it is in the one-good case, some simple conclusions can be drawn. All equilibrium paths must converge to some steady state, but not necessarily the same one. Along each equilibrium path, k changes monotonically, but p may oscillate if the slope of (6.14) changes along the way.

We can use the expressions (6.16) and (6.18) to derive the condition for a stable steady state. After some patient simplification, we find the condition

$$sw \cdot w \cdot R_{pp}/k - k \cdot (sr - sw) \cdot \{R_{kp}(n - R_{kp}) + R_{kk} \cdot R_{pp}\}$$
$$+ (1 - sw) \cdot R_p \cdot (n - R_{kp}) > 0 \quad (6.19)$$

The first term is obviously positive. Also, $R_{kk} < 0, R_{pp} > 0$, and by Rybczynski's Theorem, R_{kp} and $(n - R_{kp})$ have opposite signs. Therefore, when $sr \geqslant sw$, the second term is non-negative. The third term is positive if $R_{kp} \leqslant 0$, so this together with $sr \geqslant sw$, suffices for stability. Sufficient conditions in the terms of elasticities of substitution can also be found.[4]

Having characterized the paths of k and p, we can examine other variables defined in terms of these two by (6.12) and (6.13). We can also consider the rate of interest in terms of the consumer good, which is given by $i = (r + \dot{p})/p$, the short-run perfect foresight equation. However, these involve some intricate mathematics, and I shall leave them to more advanced treatments.[5]

We can also simulate equilibrium paths for plausible numerical values of the parameters and the initial conditions. It is found that in a stable case the convergence to the steady state is much more rapid than is typical in the one-good case. This may be thought to be encouraging after all the difficulties we have encountered so far.[6]

3. Comparisons between steady states

Let us turn to some comparisons between steady states. Now that we no longer have a unique steady state for each set of parameters, and some steady states may be unstable, such comparisons are of even more limited interest. It is only in the case of small changes in locally stable steady states that we can use a convergence argument to motivate the comparative analysis. However, within this limited framework, some useful and interesting results can be found.

One particular class of results concerns comparisons of the prices and interest rates. Since production has been assumed to be non-joint, we have the conditions equating the unit cost in each sector to the price of that good. These depend solely on the technology, and hold irrespective of demand or factor endowment conditions. So long as the steady states being compared have the same technology, we can differentiate these equations to obtain the conditions for consistent changes in the variables concerned, irrespective of the exact nature of the parametric shift.

Choose the consumer good to be the numéraire. In a steady state, the relative price p is constant over time, i.e. $\dot{p} = 0$. Then the relevant equations are

$$\left.\begin{array}{c} \phi^C(w, r) = 1, \quad \phi^I(w, r) = p \\[2ex] r = i \cdot p \end{array}\right\} \tag{6.20}$$

and

Let us consider another steady state differing from this by a small extent. Defining proportional changes as in (6.2), we have

$$\pi w^C \cdot \hat{w} + \pi r^C \cdot \hat{r} = 0$$

$$\pi w^I \cdot \hat{w} + \pi r^I \cdot \hat{r} = \hat{p}$$

and

$$\hat{r} = \hat{i} + \hat{p}$$

These can be solved fairly easily in terms of $\hat{i}$. We find

$$\left.\begin{array}{c} \hat{w} = -(\pi r^C/\pi w^I) \cdot \hat{i}, \quad \hat{r} = (\pi w^C/\pi w^I) \cdot \hat{i} \\[2ex] \hat{w} - \hat{r} = -\hat{i}/\pi w^I \\[2ex] \hat{p} = -\{(\pi w^I - \pi w^C)/\pi w^I\} \cdot \hat{i} \end{array}\right\} \tag{6.21}$$

and

We have in effect solved the three equations in (6.20) for w, r, and p as functions of i, and obtained their slopes in (6.21). The property that relative prices can be found given the rate of interest, and independently of the demand conditions, is known as the 'non-substitution property'. It is a consequence of the assumption that there is no joint production. It is not limited to the two-good case; similar results can be obtained for steady state models with arbitrarily many capital goods, giving the wage, and the rent and the asset price for each capital good, in terms of the interest rate.[7]

We see from (6.21) that a higher interest rate goes with a higher rental rate. It is in this sense that the interest rate serves as a proxy for the rental rate, i.e. the proper factor price. We can then convert the factor-price curve into the wage-interest curve. This is implicitly done, and the slope shown, in (6.21). We see that it is a downward-sloping curve, and its elasticity is a ratio of distributive shares, the numerator being capital's share in the consumer good sector, and the denominator being labour's share in the investment good sector. If the two sectors are equally capital-intensive, then we will have $\pi r^C = \pi r^I = \pi r$, capital's share in national income as a whole, and similarly $\pi w^I = \pi w^C = \pi w$. Our result will then reduce to the one-good result as a special case.

It is interesting to write the result somewhat differently as $dw/di = -p^2 \cdot v_C/b_I$. Now, as i increases, w/r falls, and therefore v_C falls and b_I rises. Each of these contributes to d^2w/di^2 being positive, i.e. to a convex wage-interest curve. The effect on p is ambiguous, and depends on the capital-intensities of the two sectors. We see that a higher i gives a lower p, thus reinforcing the other effects, if $\pi w^I > \pi w^C$, i.e. the consumer good is more capital-intensive. Otherwise we have an opposite influence, which could be powerful enough to yield a concave wage-interest curve. In fact, the proportional change in the numerical value of dw/di is $2 \cdot \hat{p} + \hat{v}_C - \hat{b}_I$. Using (6.21) and (2.9), we see that the curvature of the wage-interest curve is proportional to

$$\pi w^C \cdot \sigma^C + \pi r^I \cdot \sigma^I + 2 \cdot (\pi w^I - \pi w^C)/\pi w^I$$

In the case of fixed coefficients in both sectors, the curvature depends solely upon the relative capital intensities. This is a well-known result.[8]

It should be emphasized that since steady states with different i have different p, the relation between r and i is non-linear and fairly complicated. It is therefore important to maintain the distinction between the rent and the interest rate.

Let us turn to comparisons of various quantities in the steady states. It is now important to specify the cause of the underlying change. The usual comparison is to consider a steady state in relation to another having a slightly higher value of one of the saving propensities. It is easy to see that in Fig. 6.1, the effect of a rise in sw or sr is to raise the curve defined by (6.14) upward. This shifts a stable steady state to the right, i.e. raises the steady state k. The shift is a movement along the curve defined by (6.17), and thus yields a lower value of p if the investment good is more capital-intensive, and a higher value if the consumer good is more capital-intensive. Once we know the effect on p, we can use the earlier results to find the effects on i, r, and w. We see that a steady state with a higher value of one of the saving propensities has higher values of k and w, and lower values of r and i. Thus, so far as local comparisons of stable steady states are concerned, the two-sector model does not differ from the one-sector case.

It is also easy to generalize the result concerning consumption. The steady state consumption per head can be found from (6.12) by substitution of appropriate values of p and k. If we have a different steady state with the same technology and the same n, these values move along the curve (6.17). Then we have

$$\mathrm{d}c/\mathrm{d}k = (-p \cdot R_{pp}) \cdot \mathrm{d}p/\mathrm{d}k + (R_k - p \cdot R_{pk})$$

Using (6.18) and (6.20), this simplifies to

$$\mathrm{d}c/\mathrm{d}k = (i - n) \cdot p \qquad (6.22)$$

This confirms the Golden Rule, and its associated results, for the two-sector model. A steady state with a higher level of capital per head has more consumption per head so long as the Golden Rule is not crossed, and lower consumption per head thereafter.

Finally, some comments on the relationship between p and i, which is known as the (price) Wicksell Effect. The result we have obtained is that a steady state with a lower rate of interest, i.e. with more capital per head, has a lower relative price of capital if the consumer good is more labour-intensive, i.e. the investment good is more capital-intensive. This has a simple explanation. Comparing steady states with the same growth rate, the amount of investment required to maintain the steady state is proportional to the initial amount of capital. Now suppose the investment good is more capital-intensive. If output prices were held constant, by Rybczynski's Theorem the output of the investment good would increase by a greater proportion than the amount of capital input. To maintain the balance between demand and supply, the relative price of the investment good has to fall.

The Wicksell Effect stops us from aggregating output into a scalar: the weights required for aggregation would be different in different steady states. It also adds to the model the question of determination of the value of p, and outside of steady states, this variable price raises problems of uniqueness and stability. However, the existence of equilibria is not threatened. Nor is the validity of various marginal conditions, including $r = R_k(k, p)$, although all the relevant magnitudes are endogenous and must be found from a full solution of the general equilibrium problems. It is thus important to realize the precise importance of the Wicksell Effect, to avoid the impression that it makes no difference at all, or that it undermines the very basis of equilibrium growth models.[9]

4. Some generalizations

Several simple modifications can be imposed on the above development of the basic two-sector model. It is almost trivial to allow 'radioactive' deterioration of capital, although a bit of care is necessary in setting up the equilibrium correctly if capital being used in different sectors can deteriorate at different rates. We can also develop the model in the manner of Pasinetti, distinguishing saving propensities by recipient type rather than by income type.[10] Disembodied technological change in either sector can also be considered. This brings in one new aspect, since the conditions for such technological progress to be compatible with steady states are rather more complicated than the simple requirement of labour-augmentation for the one-good case.[11] I shall leave it to the interested reader to follow these lines further.

Another interesting point is the appropriate sectoral classification. Most of our earlier results hinge on the relative capital intensity of the two sectors, and we have very little intuition or facts about that. However, there are particular instances where a clearer classification into two sectors is made possible by a clear distinction according to production relations or institutions. An example of this occurs in the theory of economic development, where dual economy models offer a distinction between industry and agriculture. Now industrial products can be used for consumption or for investment, while agricultural output is largely specialized to consumption. Such models offer some interesting and realistic features, but their study would take us too far into a relatively specialized area.[12]

One modification that I shall pursue in somewhat more detail concerns the treatment of saving, arising from the definition of income. It is an implicit assumption of the models which use fixed saving propensities that the saving is done by individuals. Even if we accept that they do not take a forward view, i.e. that they neglect rents or interest rates at later dates, we are forced to allow one complication.

When the price of capital relative to that of the consumer good can change through time, individuals will come to recognize the fact that they are making capital gains or losses. From their point of view, there is nothing to distinguish this from the income arising from current productive activities. Similarly, they have no reason to distinguish additions to their wealth due to capital gains from those due to new acquisitions of investment goods. Therefore it seems worthwhile to study the case where the rate of change of wealth depends on the current income including capital gains. To keep the algebra simple, I shall do this assuming a common propensity to save out of all categories of income. Writing s for this propensity, the saving function is

$$p \cdot I + \dot{p} \cdot K = s \cdot (C + p \cdot I + \dot{p} \cdot K)$$

Deflating by labour, and using (6.12), this can be written as

$$(1 - s) \cdot \dot{p} = \{s \cdot R(k, p) - p \cdot R_p(k, p)\}/k \qquad (6.23)$$

If this replaces (6.14), the determination of momentary equilibrium changes in a fundamental way. It is no longer possible to determine p given k, even within some discrete set of multiple solutions. Literally any value of p is compatible with equilibrium at an instant, provided $\dot{p}$ adjusts to make (6.23) true. It is then conceivable that, given the initial k, the economy will start off with any value of p, with the rates of change of the two variables given by (6.15) and (6.23), and go on following the path in (k, p) space defined by the solutions of this pair of simultaneous differential equations. There may be some other considerations, not reflected in any short-run equilibrium conditions, which rule out some or most of these paths, but that remains to be seen. In the meantime, we must see where such behaviour would lead to, and the method of phase diagrams, familiar from Chapter 5, can be applied in order to do this.

Let us first look at (6.15). We know that the curve defined by $\dot{k} = 0$ in the (k, p) space is upward-sloping if the consumer good is more capital-intensive. Further, since R_{pp} is positive, we know that $\dot{k}$ is positive above this curve and negative below it.

Let us turn to (6.23), and the curve defined by $\dot{p} = 0$, i.e.

$$s \cdot R(k, p) - p \cdot R_p(k, p) = 0. \qquad (6.24)$$

The partial derivative of the left hand side with respect to p is easily seen to be $-(1 - s) \cdot R_p - p \cdot R_{pp}$, which is negative. Therefore (6.24) defines p as a single-valued function of k, and p is negative above this curve and positive below it. Along the curve, we have

$$\mathrm{d}p/\mathrm{d}k = \{s \cdot R_k - p \cdot R_{pk}\}/\{(1 - s) \cdot R_p + p \cdot R_{pp}\} \quad (6.25)$$

The denominator is positive. If the consumer good is more capital-intensive, the numerator is positive and the curve is upward-sloping. In the opposite case the sign of the numerator is not determinate in general. However, at a point of intersection with the other curve, we have $R_{pk} > R_p/k = n$ by Rybczynski's Theorem, and then

$$s \cdot R_k - p \cdot R_{pk} < s \cdot r - n \cdot p = s \cdot r - p \cdot j/k = -s \cdot w/k < 0.$$

The slope elsewhere does not affect the nature of the solution materially.

Next we note, after some simplification, that the $\dot{k} = 0$ curve has a greater algebraic slope than the $\dot{p} = 0$ curve if

$$(1 - s) \cdot (n - R_{kp}) \cdot R_p + R_{pp} \cdot (n \cdot p - s \cdot R_k) > 0 \quad (6.26)$$

As above, we have $(n \cdot p - s \cdot R_k) > 0$. Thus, if $R_{kp} < 0$, (6.26) will hold. If $R_{kp} > 0$, then Rybczynski's Theorem again gives $R_{kp} > n$, and (6.26) may or may not hold. Thus two possibilities arise when the investment good is more capital-intensive.

The resulting phase diagrams are shown in Fig. 6.2. Part (a) shows the case where the consumer good is more capital-intensive, and we see that the system is stable. Part (b) shows one subcase of the case where the investment good is more capital-intensive. Here we have cycles, and we cannot say in general whether they will be stable or unstable. There may even be closed loops. Part (c) shows the other subcase. Here we have a saddle-point. For each value of k, only one value of p will yield a path approaching a steady state. All other paths will diverge to extreme values.

All three cases raise problems, albeit of different kinds. The problem of instability associated with the saddle-point is perhaps the most obvious, and will appear again in different forms. The point is that there is nothing in the nature of equilibrium with limited foresight to stop the economy from embarking on one of the unstable paths. In the model above, for example, expectations of immediate capital gains

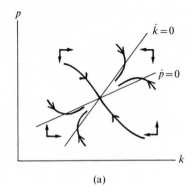

(a)

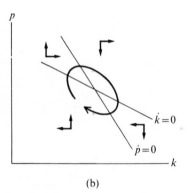

(b)

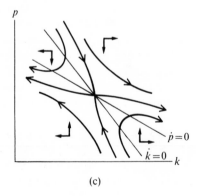

(c)

FIG. 6.2

affect saving, which changes the price of capital just enough to fulfil the expectations along an equilibrium path. If there is a finite time when one of the variables is driven to zero or to infinity, the boundary conditions will stop it from changing any further. If the perfect foresight of individuals extends sufficiently long, they will respond to this, and thus alter the whole path. However, the turnpike property of a saddle-point implies that the time can be quite long. Also, we cannot in general place an upper bound on the time required for this to happen from all initial conditions, and so must allow perfect foresight over the infinite horizon to rule out all errant paths. Even worse, there are cases where the extreme values are approached only asymptotically, and even infinite horizon perfect foresight may not then be enough. Clearly the demands made on a market economy if it is to avoid an unstable outcome are too severe to be credible in practice.

What is not so clear is that the stable case is almost as undesirable. Remember that we are now speaking of stability in the (k, p) space, and not in k alone as in our earlier models. If such joint stability prevails, there is nothing whatever in a market economy — not even infinite horizon perfect foresight — that will enable it to select a particular path. Given k, any initial p, and any subsequent path, can become an equilibrium. It is true that no path yields an extreme outcome. But individuals are not indifferent to the choice, and markets provide no mechanism to enable them to detect that a different choice could have been made. We have come to accept some degree of non-uniqueness of equilibria, but such a total lack of determination is worrying. Given its serious demands, a saddle-point situation at least enables us to select an isolated path, which converges to a steady state. In this sense, the case of a stable phase diagram is worse than that of a saddle-point.

The saddle-point instability will recur later, and I shall have more comments then. I shall now turn to another type of saving mechanism, namely the forward-looking optimum saving policy in the Keynes-Ramsey sense. The way in which the one-sector theory of this was developed in Chapter 5 enables us to set up the two-sector case without effort. The conditions of allocative efficiency in production obviously remain valid. Thus we have (6.12) and (6.13), interpreting w, r, and p as the appropriate shadow prices. Next, let i be the shadow rate of interest in terms of the consumer good. From the arbitrage condition (2.32) we have $i = (r + \dot{p})/p$. Next, considering the marginal rate of substitution in consumption over time, we have $i = \rho + \epsilon \cdot \dot{c}/c$ as in Chapter 5. Now $c = R - p \cdot R_p$, and therefore $\dot{c} = -p \cdot R_{pp} \cdot \dot{p} + (R_k - k \cdot R_{kp}) \cdot \dot{k}$. Also, we know that $\dot{k} = R_p - n \cdot k$. We can put all these together to obtain two differential equations in k and p, and examine them in a phase diagram. Unfortunately, this is easier said than done, and does not introduce any really new conceptual issues. I shall therefore leave it as a tedious exercise.[13]

5. Models with two assets

Let us turn to another situation involving a division of the economy into sectors, where the outputs of both sectors are capital goods of different types. This means that the problem of determining the composition of output involves a portfolio allocation among two assets. If in addition the outputs can serve as consumer goods, we must consider the saving decision as well. The two are usually discussed together in the literature on the subject. However, the issues posed by portfolio allocation are quite independent of the saving behaviour. To highlight these new problems, I shall consider a stripped-down model of an 'economy' which consists of nothing but capital goods producing more capital goods.

Suppose, then, that goods K_1 and K_2 used as inputs produce outputs I_1 and I_2 of investment of the two types. Let p_1 and p_2 be the prices of the assets, expressed in some system of accounting, and define the revenue function $R(K_1, K_2, p_1, p_2)$, which is the maximum of $(p_1 \cdot I_1 + p_2 \cdot I_2)$ subject to the technological constraints. As before, the function R is increasing in all arguments, concave in (K_1, K_2), convex in (p_1, p_2), and homogeneous of degree one in each pair separately. The imputed rents are $r_i = \partial R/\partial K_i$, and the supplies of outputs $I_i = \partial R/\partial p_i$, for $i = 1$ and 2. Then the differential equations for the capital stocks are

$$\dot{K}_1 = \partial R/\partial p_1, \quad \dot{K}_2 = \partial R/\partial p_2 \qquad (6.27)$$

and the arbitrage condition (2.35) for efficient portfolio allocation is

$$(\dot{p}_1 + \partial R/\partial K_1)/p_1 = (\dot{p}_2 + \partial R/\partial K_2)/p_2 \qquad (6.28)$$

the common value being the rate of interest in terms of the chosen numéraire.

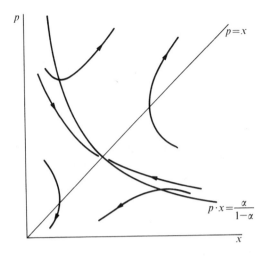

FIG. 6.3

This has some important consequences, and I shall illustrate them using a particular case that yields a solution.[14] Write

$$R(K_1, K_2, p_1, p_2) = K_1{}^\alpha \cdot K_2{}^{1-\alpha}\sqrt{(p_1{}^2 + p_2{}^2)} \qquad (6.29)$$

This is a kind of Cobb-Douglas production function for a joint product which is then split into the two goods. We can then calculate (6.27) and (6.28). Choose the second good as the numéraire, setting $p_2 = 1$, and define $x = K_1/K_2$. Then it is simple to see that

$$\dot{x} = x^\alpha \cdot (p - x)/\sqrt{(p^2 + 1)},$$
$$\dot{p} = x^{\alpha-1} \cdot \sqrt{(p^2 + 1)} \cdot \{(1 - \alpha) \cdot p \cdot x - \alpha\} \qquad (6.30)$$

We can now draw a phase diagram in x and p, which is shown in Fig. 6.3. It is a saddle-point.

We see that on the unstable paths, the relative prices and quantities of the goods move together. This suggests a simple rationale for the effect. The expectations of relative capital gains on one asset raise the relative demand for it, in the meantime fulfilling and continuing the expectations. This can be like the pure speculative boom problem of Chapter 2, but the precise relation is not always clear. However, the reasoning suggests that saddle-point instability of equilibrium growth should be a perfectly general feature of models with two or more assets, and this is indeed so. This can be seen by reinterpreting (6.28) slightly. So far, at each t, we have been choosing one of the goods at t, typically the consumer good, as the numéraire. Suppose instead we look at the whole intertemporal equilibrium at once, and choose and fix some good at some fixed date, say the consumer good at date 0, to serve as the numéraire for all goods at all dates. Then all prices are automatically expressed in present value terms, and the rate of interest, i.e. the own rate of return to the numéraire, is zero. Then (6.28) becomes

$$\dot{p}_1 = -\partial R/\partial K_1, \qquad \dot{p}_1 = -\partial R/\partial K_2 \qquad (6.31)$$

Now it is a very general property of systems of $(2 \cdot n)$ differential equations in $(2 \cdot n)$ variables, which are derived from a function satisfying the properties of our R, by differentiation in the manner of (6.27) and (6.31), that the solutions display a saddle-point instability. Given any set of values of the K_i, we can generally choose only one set of values of the p_i to obtain stable paths leading to the stationary point; all other paths diverge. Many general competitive dynamical systems can be fitted into this framework.[15]

The problem is called the Hahn instability following its first discovery, and similar problems have since been noticed.[16] The problem, of course, is that the demands of foresight placed on a market economy if it is to avoid one of the unstable paths seem far too severe to be fulfilled in practice. The earlier warnings against reading too much into this continue to hold, and again a stable phase diagram would be at least as undesirable. Also, numerical simulations indicate that the amount of time necessary before it becomes reasonably clear that something is wrong is not excessive, and may well be within the extent of foresight of a well-functioning decentralized economy.[17]

The Hahn problem can arise whenever there are two or more assets. These need not even be machines. Models where the second asset is money, or land, or an exhaustible resource, all pose the same problem of divergence of relative prices and quantities. I shall consider land and exhaustible resources in more detail in the next chapter. Growth models with money have received a great deal of attention.[18] However, with the exception of the peculiarities associated with an infinite horizon in Chapter 5, money is essentially related to disequilibrium and uncertainty, and there is little room for it in a model of strict equilibrium growth. I shall therefore mention models with money only in relation to some aspects of disequilibrium in Chapter 8.

There is one simple model involving two capital goods that deserves a mention. This is just like our standard two-sector model, except that investment is specific to each sector, i.e. a machine installed in the consumer good sector cannot later be shifted for use in the investment good sector. Clearly, in a steady state where the relative quantities of outputs of the two sectors stay constant, we never need to contemplate such a shift. Therefore the introduction of non-shiftability makes no difference in steady states. However, it does matter, and adds to realism, outside steady states. This is particularly important in the case of an industry-agriculture sectoral division as in dual economy models.

It is easy to state what happens on account of nonshiftability, although the mathematics is sometimes difficult. If labour is shiftable, the wage rate will be equal in the two sectors. When capital is non-shiftable, the rental rates can differ. If the quantities of capital in the two sectors are KC and KI, the equilibrium conditions in obvious notation are

$$\left.\begin{array}{c} \phi^C(w, r^C) = 1, \quad \phi^I(w, r^I) = p \\ C \cdot \phi_w{}^C(w, r^C) + I \cdot \phi_w{}^I(w, r^I) = L \\ C \cdot \phi_r{}^C(w, r^C) = KC, \quad I \cdot \phi_r{}^I(w, r^I) = KI \end{array}\right\} \quad (6.32)$$

Once again, we can specify demand in order to determine the momentary equilibrium so far as the total output I is concerned. However, it remains to specify the allocation of this to the two sectors, where it will then be bolted down. With the possibility of one-for-one substitution ex ante, we suspect that the allocation mechanism will be rather delicately balanced, and this is indeed the case. We calculate the demand price for capital in the two sectors, in terms of the discounted present values of future rents. In a strict equilibrium framework, the sector with the higher demand price will secure all the output of investment goods at that instant, and this higher demand price will then equal the supply price p as calculated above from the zero pure profit condition. In a less rigid framework, we can allow delayed adjustment. In either case, it is possible to have some overshooting, and consequent cycles. Saddle-point problems of a kind also arise, and the initial prices have to be chosen just right to ensure stability of the quantities. The new feature is that the quantities need not move monotonically to their steady state values.[19]

6. Multi-sector models

From now on, we can generalize the models in many ways. Some cases of importance will be considered in Chapter 7, retaining only one capital good but introducing natural resources. We can also build greater abstraction in the form of several goods in an activity analysis framework. This leads to capital theory. All these open up vast areas that could not be adequately tackled in one or two chapters. I hope I have given some hints in connection with one- or two-sector models that will enable the readers to acquire some intuition for these further developments, and then pursue them in advanced treatments.[20] To recapitulate briefly, comparing steady states, the Golden Rule is a truly general result. The downward-sloping wage-interest frontier is common to all models without joint production, but its curvature comes to depend on ever more complicated capital intensity and substitution conditions. All other monotonic associations fall by the wayside. Outside of steady states, saddle-points become common features of equilibrium paths.

Notes

My treatment of the basic two-sector model is compiled from Hahn (1965), Jones (1965), Dixit (1973b) and Mirrlees (1975). I hope readers will contrast it with the conventional treatment of Uzawa (1961b, 1963), Meade (1962, ch. 8 and Appendix II) or Burmeister and Dobell (1970, ch. 4), and observe how much conceptual simplicity results from using cost and revenue functions instead of production functions.

1. See Hicks (1946, pp. 312–3). This is why the attempt by Samuelson (1962) to extend one-sector theory to a more general case using the wage-interest frontier is such a failure: it works only when the general case can be exactly aggregated to a one-good model. However, that is a story for capital theory.
2. See Drandakis (1963), Burmeister and Dobell (1970, ch. 4).
3. This may seem a surprising property of the revenue function, and it certainly does not follow from concavity alone. In fact it is due to the assumption of non-jointness of production in the two sectors. Without this assumption, the signs and interpretations of ΠC^K and ΠC^L would be doubtful; see Dixit (1973b).

4. See Burmeister and Dobell (1970, ch. 4), Hahn (1965), Hahn and Matthews (1965).
5. Particularly Mirrlees (1975).
6. See Ramanathan (1973).
7. See Stiglitz (1970).
8. See Harcourt (1969).
9. See Swan (1956, Appendix), Bliss (1975a, Ch. 5) and Harcourt (1969) for more on the Wicksell Effect.
10. See Stiglitz (1967).
11. See Diamond (1965a), Burmeister and Dobell (1970, ch. 5).
12. See Dixit (1973a).
13. See Uzawa (1964), Shell (1967).
14. This example is modelled after Caton and Shell (1971).
15. See Cass and Shell (1975), Brock and Scheinkman (1975).
16. See Hahn (1966, 1973), Shell and Stiglitz (1967).
17. See Atkinson (1969).
18. See Solow (1970, ch. 4), Foley and Sidrauski (1970).
19. See Bose (1968, 1970), Dasgupta (1969), Ryder (1969).
20. In addition to the references cited earlier (Chapter 3, note 5), see Burmeister and Dobell (1970, chs. 7–10), Wan (1971, ch. 11), and Dorfman, Samuelson and Solow (1958), Gale (1960), Bliss (1975a), Malinvaud (1953, 1960), Starrett (1970a, 1970b), von Weizsäcker (1971) as a small selection from the available literature.

7. Natural Resources

The theory so far has admitted only two types of inputs in production, namely labour and capital goods. In this chapter I shall examine the effect of natural resources on growth. The importance of such non-producible inputs available in limited amounts is being increasingly emphasized in both theory and practice. We will find some support for the general view that growth is more difficult to sustain when such resources are important than it would be in a world where only capital and labour matter. However, we will discover some complex inter-relations among all variables and policies. These will imply some results that run counter to crude intuition, and show that the ways in which a market economy can fail to be efficient are more subtle than we might at first think.

For conceptual tidiness, we classify natural resources into two types. The first kind produce a constant *flow* of services over time; land would be the example commonly used. The second kind, like fossil fuels, come as a fixed amount of *stock*, and the distribution of this over time into a stream of service flow can be varied. As usual, actual resources are rarely of either pure type. The quality of land can deteriorate over time, and the stock of many exhaustible resources can be augmented by recycling. However, useful principles can be learnt by studying each pure type, and in applications we can combine and modify these principles to suit the facts of the case. Finally, prospects of new discoveries and of technological change bring in uncertainty. This is a difficult and relatively unexplored area, and is not amenable to an equilibrium approach. I shall have to limit its discussion to a few simple remarks.

For simplicity of exposition, I shall assume away other difficulties and use a one-good model without physical deterioration of capital and with only disembodied technological progress. Also, I shall introduce new features one at a time when discussing exhaustible resources. Thus, in section 2, I shall consider the question of resource depletion neglecting both capital and labour. In section 3 I shall introduce capital, and sections 4–6 will include labour as well.

1. Land

The important point about land is that if there are constant returns to scale when all factors of production are included, there will be diminishing returns to capital and labour alone. This reduces the growth possibilities, unless there is sufficient land-augmenting technological progress, or sufficient substitution of other inputs for land is possible.

A model illustrating this runs into serious technical problems[1] if the extent of substitution that is possible between land and capital differs from that between land and labour. Since my aim is to illustrate the basic issues introduced by land, it will be helpful to avoid these complexities. This can be done by assuming a production function of the form

$$Y = \bar{F}(F(K, L), R) \tag{7.1}$$

where R is land, and where F and $\bar{F}$ both show constant returns to scale in the arguments. This is as if capital and labour produce an intermediate product

$$J = F(K, L), \tag{7.2}$$

which is then combined with land to produce final output $Y = \bar{F}(J, R)$. Now only two elasticities of substitution matter, viz. that between capital and labour in the production of J, say σ, and that between J and R in producing output, say $\bar{\sigma}$. In each case, the imputed factor shares will move in the same direction as the relative amounts of the two factors if the relevant elasticity of substitution exceeds one, and in the opposite direction if it is less than one.

Write πj for the imputed share of the composite J in national income, and πr and πw for the imputed shares of capital and labour respectively within J. Thus the separate imputed shares of capital, labour and land are $\pi j \cdot \pi r$, $\pi j \cdot \pi w$, and $(1 - \pi j)$ respectively. Now suppose the labour force grows at rate n. Suppose technological progress is disembodied and factor-augmenting, the respective rates of capital, labour and land augmentation being 0, ml and mr. As usual, we reinterpret (7.1) using efficiency units, and use (3.10) twice to obtain the corresponding relation among the growth rates:

$$G\langle Y \rangle = \pi j \cdot G\langle J \rangle + (1 - \pi j) \cdot mr$$
$$G\langle J \rangle = \pi r \cdot G\langle K \rangle + \pi w \cdot (n + ml) \tag{7.3}$$

Now assume a constant propensity to save, s, and no physical deterioration of capital, so that $G\langle K\rangle = s \cdot Y/K$. Writing $z = Y/K$ as usual, we have $G\langle z\rangle = G\langle Y\rangle - G\langle K\rangle$, i.e.

$$G\langle z\rangle = \pi j \cdot \pi w \cdot (n + ml) + (1 - \pi j) \cdot mr - (1 - \pi j \cdot \pi r) \cdot s \cdot z \quad (7.4)$$

Since $\pi j \cdot \pi r$ must be less than 1, this has a stabilizing influence. Too high a value of z makes $G\langle z\rangle$ negative and thus lowers z. This encourages us to think of a steady state to which any equilibrium path will converge. However, the existence of a steady state poses a problem similar to that we faced in Chapter 4. I have already assumed one lesson from that and ruled out capital-augmenting technological progress. In addition, we need the other two resources growing at equal rates in efficiency units, i.e. $n + ml = mr$, and then capital will ultimately grow at this common rate. Otherwise there will be only degenerate steady states, with a zero imputed share for one of the factors.

As an example, consider the case where there is no land-augmenting technological progress, i.e. $mr = 0$. Now (7.3) yields

$$G\langle Y\rangle = \pi j \cdot \pi r \cdot G\langle K\rangle + \pi j \cdot \pi w \cdot (n + ml)$$

Consider first the case where $\bar{\sigma}$ exceeds one. So long as $G\langle J\rangle$ is positive, πj will rise over time. This will accelerate growth, raising πj further. Ultimately πj will tend to 1, and land will become an unimportant factor in growth. If σ also exceeds one, there will be a further accelerating tendency similar to that we saw in Chapter 4. If $\bar{\sigma}$ is less than 1, on the other hand, πj will tend to zero, and then ultimately so will $G\langle K\rangle$. Thus the limitation imposed by land will become increasingly important and ultimately stop growth altogether.

Empirical work suggests values of $\bar{\sigma}$ around 2, and of σ near 1.[2] If this much substitution is possible in the long run, we have reason to be optimistic about the possibility of growth with land; in fact we might expect some acceleration as capital accumulates and substitutes for land.

Economies of scale also offer a force offsetting the limits that might arise on account of land; the simple theory of this is easy to develop along the same lines as in Chapter 4, where steady states with scale economies are discussed.

The general theory of equilibrium growth with land involves some mathematical difficulties, and does not yield sufficiently important results in return. I shall therefore merely state the general conclusions, which should be evident from the discussions of Chapter 6. First, land is an asset competing with capital, and the equation of arbitrage between the two leads to the familiar saddle-point instability. Secondly, as the price of land in terms of output changes, individuals include the resulting capital gains or losses in their income, and this can affect their saving behaviour. This can produce complicated patterns of growth as in the model of Chapter 6 involving saving out of capital gains.

I shall turn to a special case that yields some simple but useful results. As usual, the one exception to the steady state requirement of equal growth of all factors in efficiency units arises if the production function is of the Cobb-Douglas form, when technological progress can be expressed in such a way as to fulfil such requirements automatically. Thus suppose the production function is

$$Y = e^{m \cdot t} \cdot K^{\alpha} \cdot L^{\beta} \cdot R^{\gamma}, \qquad (7.5)$$

where α, β, and γ are non-negative. Now the familiar growth rate calculation shows the rate of growth in the steady state to be

$$g = (m + \beta \cdot n)/(1 - \alpha) \qquad (7.6)$$

This needs $\alpha < 1$, but non-constant returns to scale are permissible. A question of particular interest is whether rising output per capita is possible, i.e. whether g exceeds n. If $\alpha + \beta + \gamma = 1, g > n$ if and only if $m/\gamma > n$. Now m/γ would be the rate of technological progress if it were written to be purely land-augmenting:

$$Y = K^{\alpha} \cdot L^{\beta} \cdot \{R \cdot e^{(m/\gamma) \cdot t}\}^{\gamma}$$

Thus the condition for sustained growth in output per capita is that the rate of technological progress in purely land-augmenting form should exceed the rate of population growth. This appears sensible.

Next consider consumption along a steady state. We have $C = (1 - s) \cdot Y$, and

$$g \cdot K = \dot{K} = s \cdot Y = s \cdot e^{m \cdot t} \cdot K^{\alpha} \cdot L^{\beta} \cdot R^{\gamma}.$$

Solving for K and substituting back in the expression for Y, we find

$$C = (1 - s) \cdot (s/g)^{\alpha/(1-\alpha)} \cdot \{L_0^{\beta} \cdot R^{\gamma}\}^{1/(1-\alpha)} \cdot e^{g \cdot t}, \qquad (7.7)$$

where L_0 is the value of L at $t = 0$. Now suppose we are offered the choice of any steady state we like, with given L_0, R, and g. The only element of choice is the saving ratio s, and the only factors in (7.7) affected by it are the first two. Thus we choose s to maximize

$$(1 - s) \cdot (s/g)^{\alpha/(1 - \alpha)}$$

A simple differentiation gives the solution $s = \alpha$. Since α is the imputed share of capital in national income, this is just the familiar Golden Rule of Accumulation in one of its guises. Its significance was discussed at length in Chapters 3 and 5, and those remarks continue to apply.

2. Depletion plans

Let us turn to resources of which a fixed stock is available, and this stock is depleted through use. Suppose the amount available at time 0 is S_0. A pattern of depletion $R(t)$ into the indefinite future will be feasible if

$$\int_0^\infty R(t) \cdot dt \leqslant S_0 \tag{7.8}$$

Equivalently, we can write $S(t)$ for the stock remaining at time t, so that $R(t)$ is its absolute rate of decrease:

$$\dot{S}(t) = -R(t) \tag{7.9}$$

and we need $S(0) = S_0$, and $R(t)$ and $S(t)$ non-negative for all t.

To set the question of the choice of a depletion plan in its simplest context, suppose that for each conceivable depletion plan, the rest of the economic allocation questions are solved and the outcome expressed as a function of the depletion plan. Let the objective function also be so expressed, and suppose it takes the form

$$\int_0^\infty u(R(t)) \cdot e^{-\rho \cdot t} \cdot dt \tag{7.10}$$

The problem is to maximize (7.10) subject to (7.9).

The mathematical formalism is exactly the same as that in the analysis of optimum saving in Chapter 5. We need only set $L = 1$, $n = ml = 0$, and replace K by S and C by R. Finally, $F(K, L)$ is identically zero, and therefore so is $f'(k)$. The fundamental condition of local optimality then says that the rate of decline of discounted marginal utility should be zero, i.e. that

$$u'(R(t)) \cdot e^{-\rho \cdot t} = \text{constant} \tag{7.11}$$

This is very easy to explain in terms of the efficiency of inter-temporal allocation. The opportunity cost of using a unit of the resource at one time is simply its use at some other time. Therefore in an optimum allocation the marginal gains from using it at any two dates should be equal when discounted back to time 0.

As usual, the common value of the marginal benefit and the marginal cost can be thought of as a shadow price. We will obtain results that are easier to interpret by reference to earlier work if we use the undiscounted price of the resource relative to utility, i.e. define

$$p(t) = u'(R(t)) \tag{7.12}$$

Then (7.11) yields

$$p(t) = p(0) \cdot e^{\rho \cdot t} \tag{7.13}$$

These two equations show two important aspects of the shadow price of an exhaustible resource. Such a resource is durable only so long as it is not used, i.e. it is used up when it is used. Correspondingly, the yield on such an asset comes either from its services, i.e. the rent, or from capital gains, but not both. In an equilibrium where some of the resource is being used up at time t and some is being held over for the future, these two must be equally attractive. Thus on the one hand, capital gains alone must suffice to meet the interest costs of holding the asset. Since the interest rate in utility terms is ρ, this means that the price must be rising over time at the rate ρ, as is expressed in (7.13). On the other hand, the rent must equal the whole asset price. Of course the rent equals the marginal gain that accrues from use, and thus we have (7.12).

This principle has very general validity. Suppose, as we soon shall, that the resource, along with capital and labour, is an input for the production of a homogeneous output. Take the output to be the numéraire. Then the rent for the use of the resource, and therefore its price, must equal its marginal product. Also, the capital gains on the unused resource must meet the interest costs, and therefore the price must rise at the rate of interest, now expressed in terms of the new numéraire and hence equal to the marginal product of capital.

The discussion so far has neglected extraction costs, but they do not affect the principle greatly. The price of the resource exceeds the marginal extraction cost to allow for its shadow scarcity price, i.e. the pure or economic rent. It is this component, or the difference between the price and the marginal extraction cost, that must now grow at the rate of interest. The formal proof is easy to see if we interpret u in (7.10) as being net of extraction costs. Then $u'(R)$ becomes the difference between the marginal benefit and the marginal extraction cost. Since this simple modification can be made mentally, I shall make the mathematics simpler by neglecting such costs in what follows.

As an example permitting an explicit solution, consider the familiar constant elasticity utility function, for which

$$u'(R) = R^{-\epsilon}, \qquad \epsilon > 0$$

Now (7.11) yields

$$R(t) = R(0) \cdot e^{-(\rho/\epsilon) \cdot t} \tag{7.14}$$

where $R(0)$ is constant, and using (7.12), we have

$$p(0) = R(0)^{-\epsilon} \tag{7.15}$$

It remains to determine the constant $R(0)$, and this must be done using the constraint (7.8). We have

$$S_0 \geqslant \int_0^\infty R(0) \cdot e^{-(\rho/\epsilon) \cdot t} \cdot \mathrm{d}t = R(0) \cdot \epsilon/\rho,$$

since the integral is formally the same as the capitalized value of a consol with a coupon of $R(0)$ and an interest rate (ρ/ϵ). Now it is clear that the constraint must hold as an equality, for else some of the stock will never be used. We can then solve for $R(0)$ and write

$$R(t) = (\rho \cdot S_0/\epsilon) \cdot e^{-(\rho/\epsilon) \cdot t} \tag{7.16}$$

This example, highly simplified though it is, illustrates some important phenomena. This makes it easier to recognize and understand similar results when they appear in more complex models. First we have the obvious remark that in the absence of any offsetting forces, exhaustible resources will lead to declining levels of resource use and consumption in the long run. Offsetting forces do exist in the form of capital accumulation and technological progress. However, given these other things, the recognition that exhaustible resources are important will lead us to expect lower rates of growth. In Chapter 5 we saw that saving policy in the long run depends crucially on the asymptotic rate of interest $\bar{\imath}$. If consumption per capita grows at the rate m, we have $\bar{\imath} = \rho + \epsilon \cdot m$. Now a lower value of m will mean a lower $\bar{\imath}$, which will increase the importance of saving and capital accumulation. Thus resource limitations provide an argument for faster, not slower, growth of capital. This is the first important result that runs counter to the popular view.

Next consider the question of whether an optimum depletion policy can be attained in a market economy. As usual, in a highly idealized setting the answer would be yes. In (7.12) and (7.13) we have the equations that will provide producers just the right incentives if $p(t)$ is made the market price of the resource at t. There is the minor problem that the producers are only in a 'neutral' equilibrium. They have no positive reason for departing from the optimum plan, but they have no positive reason for choosing it in preference to another plan. This is like the problem of determining the size of a competitive firm under constant returns. There are also more serious difficulties. Perfect foresight is as always hard to accept, and there can be important uncertainties from the point of view of individuals. Also, we have the problem that (7.12) and (7.13) provide no mechanism for determining the initial price $p(0)$. Any value of it can be chosen, and the profile over time kept growing at the rate of interest. The implied depletion plan can be found from (7.12). In the iso-elastic case, (7.15) gives us the link between the choice of $p(0)$ and the choice of $R(0)$ and thence of $R(t)$. If $p(0)$ is chosen too low, $R(0)$ will be chosen too high, and the stock S_0 will be exhausted at some finite date. Perfect foresight extending that far will then enable the market to avoid the choice of such a $p(0)$. However, if $p(0)$ is chosen too high, $R(0)$ will be too low, and some of the initial stock will never be used. This cannot be detected by perfect foresight extending over a finite horizon, no matter how long. It is doubtful whether perfect foresight extending over the infinite horizon is any better. It is possible to think of an equilibrium with a speculative boom in which each individual realizes his capital gains at a finite date, and no one is ever caught out holding the unused stock. In all, the idea of an optimum market equilibrium is very shaky indeed.

Finally, consider the complicating case where $\rho = 0$. Now a mechanical application of (7.16) gives $R(t) = 0$ at all times, which is clearly not optimum. The problem is that (7.11) becomes $u'(R(t)) = $ constant, requiring $R(t)$ to be constant, but the only constant flow that can be provided from a finite stock over an infinite horizon is zero. In fact this points to a discontinuity. With no discounting and a concave utility function, the thinner we spread the stock over time, the higher the value of the utility integral. But the limiting policy of zero use is far from being the best. To see this explicitly, note that $u'(R) = R^{-\epsilon}$; on integrating we have

$$u(R) = R^{1-\epsilon}/(1 - \epsilon) + \text{constant}.$$

The additive constant can be neglected. Now suppose $\epsilon < 1$, and consider the policy of maintaining $R(t) = S_0/T$ over the interval $[0, T]$ and zero thereafter. The utility integral becomes

$$T \cdot (S_0/T)^{1-\epsilon}/(1 - \epsilon) = T^\epsilon \cdot S_0^{1-\epsilon}/(1 - \epsilon),$$

which increases steadily with T and can be made indefinitely large by choosing T large enough. In the limit, we have $R(t) = 0$ at all times, and the integral suddenly collapses to zero. If $\epsilon > 1$, letting $R(t) = 0$ makes the integrand infinite, and this raises further and deeper problems. However, in either case the conclusion must be that no optimum policy exists. There is little that can be done about this problem, but we should be aware of it.

3. Capital accumulation

For the rest of this chapter I shall consider the policies of resource depletion and capital accumulation jointly. The interesting question is whether capital accumulation on its own can overcome the limits to growth posed by the resource constraints. The answer of course depends on the extent of substitution that is possible. To highlight this aspect, in this section I shall examine a model where there are constant returns to scale in capital and the resource. Labour will not be a scarce factor of production, and the welfare judgement will be simplified by assuming that the population level is constant and set equal to 1 by choice of unit. In this setting, the growth possibilities will be seen to depend on how the average and marginal products of capital behave in the limit as capital is accumulated relative to the resource use. This in turn relates to the elasticity of substitution between the two.[3]

Writing K for the capital stock and R for the resource flow, suppose output is given by a production function $F(K, R)$ satisfying all the properties required for the analogous function of capital and labour in Chapter 2. Now capital accumulation is given by

$$\dot{K} = F(K, R) - C \tag{7.17}$$

where C is consumption. Resource depletion must satisfy (7.8) or (7.9), and the plan is to be chosen to maximize

$$\int_0^\infty u(C) \cdot e^{-\rho \cdot t} \cdot \mathrm{d}t$$

I shall assume u to be iso-elastic for expository convenience.

The conditions for optimality should be obvious from earlier discussions. The saving plan should satisfy the Keynes-Ramsey formula (5.7), which in the notation of this section becomes

$$\rho + \epsilon \cdot \dot{C}/C = F_K, \tag{7.18}$$

where I have omitted the arguments in the marginal product $F_K(K, R)$ for brevity. Next, if we write p for the shadow price of the resource relative to output, we have seen that equilibrium in use requires $p = F_R$, the marginal product of the resource flow, and that equilibrium in asset-holding requires $\dot{p}/p = F_K$. We can combine these to write

$$F_K = (\mathrm{d}F_R/\mathrm{d}t)/F_R \tag{7.19}$$

These are the basic equations of the model, but the solution can be found more easily in terms of other variables. First, for the purpose of this section alone, write $k = K/R$. Now we can exploit the formal analogy with the production function of Chapter 2 and define $f(k) = F(K, 1)$, and the rent for capital services is $r = f'(k)$. The zero pure profit condition is $f(k) = r \cdot k + p$. This can be seen from (2.17) and (2.18).

Also, since p serves the same role as the wage rate did in Chapter 2, we have the relationship between proportional changes:

$$G\langle K/R \rangle = \sigma \cdot G \langle p/r \rangle,$$

where σ is the elasticity of substitution between K and R. For expositional convenience, I shall assume σ to be constant. Using (7.19), we can write this relation as

$$G\langle k\rangle = \sigma \cdot \{r - G\langle r\rangle\} \tag{7.20}$$

Next we differentiate the zero pure profit condition to write $f'(k) \cdot \dot{k} = r \cdot \dot{k} + \dot{r} \cdot k + \dot{p}$, i.e. $\dot{r} = -\dot{p}/k = -r \cdot p/k$. Then $G\langle r\rangle = -p/k$. Substituting in (7.20) and using the zero pure profit condition, we have

$$G\langle k\rangle = \sigma \cdot f(k)/k \tag{7.21}$$

This shows that k increases steadily through time. Then so does its *absolute* rate of increase $\dot{k} = \sigma \cdot f(k)$, and therefore k tends to ∞ with t. However, its *relative* rate of increase can go to zero if $f(k)/k$ does.

Next, I shall introduce two variables that are easily examined and convey useful information. Define $h = C/K$; taking growth rates and using (7.17) and (7.18) we find

$$G\langle h\rangle = \left\{ \frac{f'(k) - \rho}{\epsilon} \right\} - \left\{ \frac{f(k)}{k} - h \right\}. \tag{7.22}$$

Also define the depletion rate $d = -G\langle S\rangle = R/S$; its reciprocal is the amount of time the existing stock would last at the current rate of use, which is a variable commonly discussed in the popular literature on resources. Now

$$G\langle d\rangle = G\langle R\rangle - G\langle S\rangle = G\langle R\rangle + d, \tag{7.23}$$

and

$$G\langle R\rangle = G\langle K\rangle - G\langle k\rangle.$$

Then, using (7.17) and (7.21), we can write

$$G\langle d\rangle = d + \left\{ \frac{f(k)}{k} - h \right\} - \sigma \cdot \frac{f(k)}{k} \tag{7.24}$$

The solution is now clear in principle. We know the initial values K_0 and S_0. If we assume values of R_0 and C_0, we can use the above differential equations to calculate the time-paths of the relevant variables. Then it remains to choose R_0 to satisfy the stock constraint, and C_0 to rule out paths that run out of capital or accumulate it to an inefficient extent as in Chapter 5. To carry out this programme rigorously is quite difficult, and entails some careful considerations of limits. I shall omit these details and describe what happens in the final stages as k becomes large.

It is clear from (7.22) and (7.24) that the solutions will depend crucially on the limiting values of $f(k)/k$ and $f'(k)$. In fact, by L'Hôpital's Rule, the two limits are equal. Write η as their common value. This is the important average (and marginal) product of capital in the limit as production is attempted using a relatively negligible amount of the resource. Using the explicit form (2.13b) of the production function with a constant elasticity of substitution, it is easy to verify that if $\sigma < 1$, then $\eta = 0$, while if $\sigma > 1$, η will be positive. The case $\sigma = 1$ permits rather more detailed analysis, and will be examined in a slightly different context in the following sections.

In the long run, the right hand side of (7.22) is approximately equal to $h - \{\rho - \eta \cdot (1 - \epsilon)\}/\epsilon$. This implies that h must ultimately equal $\{\rho - \eta \cdot (1 - \epsilon)\}/\epsilon$, for if it strayed above this value, $G\langle h \rangle$ would be positive, pushing h still higher, and ultimately the capital stock would be exhausted. Similarly, if h strayed below this value, it would be pushed further down to zero, involving permanently too little consumption and too much accumulation. For an economically meaningful solution, this ultimate value of h must be positive, which requires

$$\rho - \eta \cdot (1 - \epsilon) > 0$$

This, in fact, turns out to be the condition for convergence of the utility integral and hence for the existence of an optimum policy.

Assuming this asymptotic value, say $\bar{h}$, for h, we see from (7.24) that d must ultimately equal $\bar{d} = \bar{h} + (\sigma - 1) \cdot \eta$. Otherwise a similar cumulative instability will cause the resource stock to be exhausted in finite time, or some of it will never be used. Note that when $\bar{h}$ has been ensured to be positive, so will $\bar{d}$, since the added term $(\sigma - 1) \cdot \eta$ is positive if $\sigma > 1$ and zero if $\sigma \leqslant 1$.

It is now easy to establish the long run trends of the major variables. We have from (7.17) that $G\langle K \rangle = \eta - \bar{h}$, and from (7.21) that $G\langle k \rangle = \sigma \cdot \eta$, in the long run. Using these, we find that ultimately $G\langle C \rangle = G\langle K \rangle = (\eta - \rho)/\epsilon$, and $G\langle R \rangle = -\bar{d}$.

Thus we see that ultimately the resource flow must decline, while capital accumulates relative to the resource flow. Whether this will enable sustained growth of consumption depends on whether the ultimate average and marginal product of capital exceeds the rate of impatience. If $\sigma \leqslant 1$, η is zero and we have to accept declining consumption if ρ is positive. If $\sigma > 1$, it is possible to have η large enough to enable sustained growth.

All this applies to the long run growth rates. The detailed study of the time-paths of the levels is quite difficult, and is probably best left to numerical solutions in particular cases. However, one important general result can be obtained. We have $G\langle C \rangle = \{f'(k) - \rho\}/\epsilon$. As k increases, this falls. Starting from a position with relatively little capital, this will be positive at first, even if ultimately $f'(k)$ falls below ρ. Correspondingly, the consumption level will rise at first and then decline. This contrasts with the model of Chapter 5 which neglected resources, and found that the consumption path was monotonic. It also shows that popular anti-growth arguments can be misconceived. Even if resource limitations are going to force us to accept declining consumption in the long run, this is compatible with rising consumption for a while. The time when $G\langle C \rangle$ should change from positive to negative values along the optimum path needs to be found from a detailed solution of the equation for k, and cannot be asserted from simple intuition.

It is worth pointing out one consequence of relaxing the assumption of a constant elasticity of substitution. Under this assumption, we saw that k goes to infinity asymptotically. If σ is variable, and an increasing function of k, then k will grow still faster, and can in fact reach ∞ in finite time. This means that production from then on will be carried out using capital alone, and the depletion plan will use up all of the available stock of the resource at this point. I shall omit detailed consideration of this.[4]

4. Steady states

The next step is to introduce labour as a factor of production, assuming constant returns to scale to capital, labour and resource inputs considered together.[5] This complicates the analysis, and I shall simplify it somewhat by confining it to the case of a Cobb-Douglas production function. I have examined the effects of a non-unitary elasticity of substitution in a slightly different context in the previous section, and shall point out some further extensions in the concluding section. However, within its limitations, the Cobb-Douglas case yields some explicit, interesting and instructive results. I shall build these up in stages. In this section and the next one, I shall assume a constant saving ratio and examine steady states and equilibrium growth paths. In Section 6, the saving ratio will be variable, to be chosen to maximize a utility integral as in Chapter 5.

Suppose output is given by

$$Y = A \cdot e^{m \cdot t} \cdot K^{\alpha} \cdot L^{\beta} \cdot R^{\gamma}, \qquad (7.25)$$

where A is constant, m is the rate of output-augmenting technological progress, and α, β, γ are all non-negative and add to 1. Suppose the population grows at a constant rate n, the labour force at time t being $L = L_0 \cdot e^{n \cdot t}$. The resource flow R is subject to the stock constraint (7.8). There is no deterioration of capital.

Let us attempt to find conventional steady states, with a constant saving propensity s, a constant rate of growth of capital and output, g, and now also a constant rate of resource depletion, δ. Thus, as in (7.16),

$$R = \delta \cdot S_0 \cdot e^{-\delta \cdot t}. \qquad (7.26)$$

Taking growth rates from (7.25) and solving for g, we find

$$g = (m + \beta \cdot n - \gamma \cdot \delta)/(1 - \alpha). \qquad (7.27)$$

The most important point to note is that g is not exogenous, but can be varied by varying the depletion rate. This has implications for the consumption path. If we use the steady state relation $g \cdot K = s \cdot Y$, substitute for Y from (7.25) and solve for K, we can substitute back in (7.25) and then find

$$C = (1 - s) \cdot (s/g)^{\alpha/(1-\alpha)} \cdot \{A \cdot L_0{}^{\beta} \cdot (\delta \cdot S)^{\gamma}\}^{1/(1-\alpha)} \cdot e^{g \cdot t} \quad (7.28)$$

This is similar to (7.7), and it might be tempting to deduce the Golden Rule for the choice of s. This would follow if δ were fixed, but when we compare consumption paths with different growth rates, these can cross one another and an explicit welfare judgement must be introduced.

The matter is made even more complex by the fact that it is not efficient to have steady states in which s and δ are fixed at arbitrary values. Efficient asset use requires that the marginal product of the resource should grow at a rate equal to the marginal product of capital, for the reasons discussed in detail in Sections 2 and 3. In the Cobb-Douglas case, the marginal product of the resource is $\gamma \cdot Y/R$ and that of capital is $\alpha \cdot Y/K$; this is easy to verify by simple differentiation from (7.25). Then the condition is

$$\alpha \cdot Y/K = G\langle Y \rangle - G\langle R \rangle,$$

i.e.

$$\alpha \cdot g/s = g + \delta.$$

We can solve this for one of s and δ in terms of the other:

$$s = \alpha \cdot (m + \beta \cdot n - \gamma \cdot \delta)/(m + \beta \cdot n + \beta \cdot \delta) \qquad (7.29)$$

or

$$\delta = (\alpha - s) \cdot (m + \beta \cdot n)/(\beta \cdot s + \alpha \cdot \gamma) \qquad (7.30)$$

In particular, we see that a higher δ corresponds to a lower s. Also, since we must have $\delta > 0$ and $s \geq 0$, there are implied limits of $s < \alpha$ and $\delta \leq (m + \beta \cdot n)/\gamma$ on the possible choices. Perhaps surprisingly, this rules out inefficient capital accumulation with $s > \alpha$.

Sustained growth of output per capita is possible if $g > n$, i.e. if $(m - \gamma \cdot n - \gamma \cdot \delta) > 0$. If $m > \gamma \cdot n$, we can choose a positive δ so as to satisfy this. The condition can be written as $m/\gamma > n$, which is the expected condition requiring the rate of technological progress written in purely resource-augmenting form to exceed the rate of population growth.

There is one particularly important case that presents some problems. It might be argued that when we recognize the finiteness of resource stocks, it is odd to allow exponential population growth for ever. It is also of interest to examine a case without technological progress, to see whether capital accumulation alone can overcome the limitations posed by resources. However, if we take $m = 0 = n$, we find that $s \geq 0$ requires $\delta \leq 0$, and it seems that an efficient steady state is not possible. We shall see later that it is still possible to sustain a positive level of consumption, but this is done with a steadily increasing capital/output ratio and a steadily decreasing depletion rate, which is not a steady state as we know it.

5. Equilibrium growth

The next issue is that of equilibrium growth with a fixed saving propensity. This is governed by the same principles as those for steady states, except the constancy of the various growth rates. Thus, taking growth rates from (7.25), we have

$$G\langle Y \rangle = m + \alpha \cdot G\langle K \rangle + \beta \cdot n + \gamma \cdot G\langle R \rangle.$$

The accumulation equation $\dot{K} = s \cdot Y$ can be written as $G\langle K \rangle = s \cdot Y/K$. Finally, the condition for efficient asset allocation is

$$\alpha \cdot Y/K = G\langle Y \rangle - G\langle R \rangle.$$

It is easier to analyze this using some transformed variables. The reason is that it is preferable to use variables which are capable of going to positive and finite values in the long run, rather than to 0 or infinity. In this case the output/capital ratio $z = Y/K$ and the depletion rate $d = R/S$ serve this purpose. Taking growth rates and substituting from the three basic equations above, and finally recalling $\dot{z}/z = G\langle z \rangle$ etc., we find the differential equations

$$\dot{z}/z = \{(\beta \cdot n + m) - z \cdot (\beta \cdot s + \alpha \cdot \gamma)\}/(1 - \gamma) \qquad (7.31)$$

$$\dot{d}/d = d + \{(\beta \cdot n + m) - \alpha \cdot (1 - s) \cdot z\}/(1 - \gamma) \qquad (7.32)$$

It is possible to solve (7.31) explicitly by separation of variables, substitute the solution into (7.32) and then solve that. However, it is much simpler to examine the solutions in a phase diagram. This is very easy to draw, since each of the curves $\dot{z} = 0$ and $\dot{d} = 0$ is a straight line. I shall therefore leave this as a very useful exercise to the reader for developing familiarity with phase diagrams, and show the outcome in Fig. 7.1. The two lines intersect at the point $(\bar{z}, \bar{d})$ given by

$$\bar{z} = (\beta \cdot n + m)/(\beta \cdot s + \alpha \cdot \gamma) \qquad (7.33)$$

$$\bar{d} = (\alpha - s) \cdot (\beta \cdot n + m)/(\beta \cdot s + \alpha \cdot \gamma) \qquad (7.34)$$

Comparing (7.30), we see that this is just the efficient steady state of Section 4. As there, an economically meaningful solution requires $\alpha > s$.

We see that the steady state is a saddle-point. While z goes to $\bar{z}$ on all paths, d goes to 0 or to ∞ on all but the two stable paths. The reason should by now be very familiar. As usual, it is better explained in terms

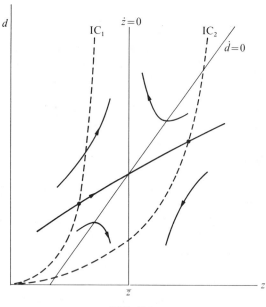

FIG. 7.1

of the price of the resource relative to output, p. Efficiency in use requires the price to equal the marginal product of the resource, i.e.

$$p = \gamma \cdot Y/R = \gamma \cdot e^{m \cdot t} \cdot K^\alpha \cdot L^\beta / R^{1-\gamma}.$$

Thus, at any instant, the price is inversely related to the depletion rate. The choice of too high a depletion rate is equivalent to the choice of too low a price. As Fig. 7.1 shows, the depletion rate then always remains too high, and the price always too low, leading to the entire stock being exhausted in finite time. To see this rigorously, we note from (7.32) that as z goes to $\bar{z}$ and d goes to infinity, $\dot{d}/d^2$ goes to 1. Integrating this, we see that only a finite amount of time is necessary for d to go to ∞. In the opposite case, an initial choice of too low a depletion rate and too high a price produces a path where some of the stock is never used; a rigorous proof follows similar lines. The principle of all this is exactly the same as that governing (7.13) and (7.15) in Section 2, but the details are more complex since the rate of change of the price,

$$\dot{p}/p = \alpha \cdot Y/K = \alpha \cdot z,$$

is now variable and endogenous. I have omitted the rigorous proofs as they do not add anything of economic significance. The important conclusion is that the stable paths are the only desirable ones, but the ability of a market economy to select them is very doubtful. As we saw in Section 2, the error that is more difficult to avoid, even with very long foresight, is that of setting the price too high and discouraging resource utilization too much. This is again a somewhat counterintuitive conclusion.

One important detail remains to be supplied to complete the description of the path. We must state the initial conditions in terms of the transformed variables. Taking K_0, L_0 and S_0 as given, we find from (7.25) the relation

$$z_0 = \{A \cdot L_0{}^\beta \cdot S_0{}^\gamma / K_0{}^{1-\alpha}\} \cdot d_0{}^\gamma \qquad (7.35)$$

since $\gamma < 1$, this defines a parabolic curve in the (d, z) space, of which Fig. 7.1 shows two instances. The first, IC_1, arises when the coefficient in (7.35) is small, i.e. when K_0 is large relative to L_0 and S_0, while the other, IC_2, arises in the opposite case. In each case, the initial point should be chosen where the curve defining the initial conditions meets one of the stable paths into the saddle-point.

Thus we see that if the initial capital stock is large relative to the labour force or the resource stock, the initial values of z and d should be chosen to be low relative to the steady state values, and they should increase steadily through time. The opposite should happen if the initial capital stock is relatively low. The calculation to choose the appropriate policy is quite a complex one, involving estimation of the relevant parameters and computation of the initial condition curve and the stable paths. Thus simple statements about current use do not give much guidance about the desirability or shortcomings of the current policies. We should not feel undue alarm at the observation that there is only 50 years' current use of oil left, nor undue complacency at the observation that at the current rate of use, coal will last 1000 years. The only general qualitative conclusion that can be drawn is the result that a wrong initial choice will lead to ever-increasing error if followed relentlessly. This emphasizes the need for a constant monitoring of depletion plans. A similar result in Chapter 5 pointed out the need for constant monitoring of optimum saving plans. The next step, of course, is to put the two together.

6. Optimum saving and resource use

Let us now abandon the assumption of a constant saving propensity, and decide the optimum saving policy jointly with the depletion policy. Given the way I have built up the model, this is quite easy to do. Equations (7.31) and (7.32), derived from the production function and the condition of efficient resource allocation, are still valid. We need only note that s is no longer an exogenous constant. The rule that helps determine it is familiar from Chapter 5 and from Section 3 of this chapter: the marginal utility of consumption should be kept declining at a rate equal to the marginal product of capital. Using the familiar notation, this becomes

$$\rho + \epsilon \cdot G\langle C/L \rangle = \alpha \cdot Y/K. \tag{7.36}$$

As in Section 3, it is easier to work in terms of $h = C/K$. After some simple substitutions, we find

$$\dot{h}/h = h - z \cdot (1 - \alpha/\epsilon) - (\rho/\epsilon - n) \tag{7.37}$$

We can note that $h = z \cdot (1 - s)$ and write (7.31) and (7.32) as

$$\dot{z}/z = \{(\beta \cdot n + m) - z \cdot (\beta + \alpha \cdot \gamma) + \beta \cdot h\}/(1 - \gamma) \tag{7.38}$$

$$\dot{d}/d = d + \{(\beta \cdot n + m) - \alpha \cdot h\}/(1 - \gamma) \tag{7.39}$$

Rigorous and detailed solution of these three differential equations will be very complicated. I shall omit such details, and only develop the argument sufficiently far to make the important results plausible.

First observe that the equations for h and z do not involve d. We can therefore analyze them independently in a phase diagram. Once again, the curves $\dot{h} = 0$ and $\dot{z} = 0$ are straight lines, and their derivation can be left as an exercise. Fig. 7.2 shows the result. Two cases arise depending on the sign of $(\epsilon - \alpha)$. In each case we find a saddle-point, and for familiar reasons only the stable paths are desirable. Along these, we find that each of h and z moves monotonically to its steady state value. The two increase or decrease together in case (a), but in case (b) one rises while the other falls.

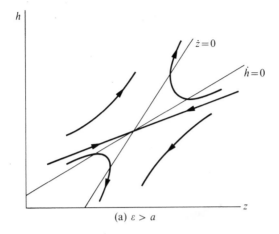

(a) $\varepsilon > a$

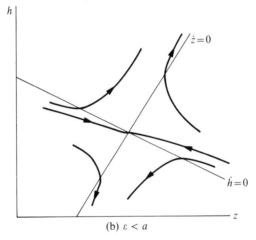

(b) $\varepsilon < a$

FIG. 7.2

Two other general conclusions can be drawn at this stage. We have from (7.36) that $G\langle C/L \rangle = (\alpha \cdot z - \rho)/\epsilon$. As z is monotonic, this can change sign once. For example, if z is initially high and then declines to a value $\bar{z}$ below ρ/α, then C/L will rise for a while and then fall. This is similar to the non-monotonic behaviour we found and discussed in Section 3. The other result is new. We see from (7.23) the resource flow changes according to the equation $G\langle R \rangle = G\langle d \rangle - d$, and from (7.39) this equals $\{(\beta \cdot n + m) - \alpha \cdot h\}/(1 - \gamma)$. As h is monotonic, this can change sign once. Thus, along the optimum path, it is possible to have the resource use increase for a while and then decrease, or vice versa. This poses further problems for simple intuition, and further increases the importance of more careful work concerning resource use policy.

Now consider the time path of d. Suppose a stable path for the other two variables leading to their respective steady state values $\bar{z}$ and $\bar{h}$ has been found, and consider (7.39). It can be seen that its solution must be such as to keep the right hand side near zero in the long run. Otherwise d will go either to 0 or to ∞, leaving some of the resource totally unused in the former case and exhausting it all in finite time in the latter. This is exactly like the argument accompanying (7.24).

There is still one degree of freedom in the solution. We could choose any initial point (z_0, h_0) on a stable path in the phase diagram for z and h, although, given this choice, we would then have to choose d_0 to ensure a solution that had the desirable long run property. However, we know from the production function that z_0 and d_0 must be related as in (7.35). Thus we must choose that initial point (z_0, h_0) which will produce a d_0 for which (7.35) will hold. This completes the solution. I shall omit the mathematical details of existence and uniqueness considerations.

The next step is to obtain and examine various steady state values. Setting the right hand sides in (7.37)–(7.39) to zero and solving, we can write

$$\bar{z} = \frac{\beta \cdot \rho + \epsilon \cdot m}{\alpha \cdot (\beta + \gamma \cdot \epsilon)} \tag{7.40}$$

$$\bar{d} = \frac{\rho \cdot (1 - \alpha) + m \cdot (\epsilon - 1)}{\beta + \gamma \cdot \epsilon} - n \tag{7.41}$$

$$\bar{h} = \frac{\rho \cdot (\beta + \alpha \cdot \gamma) + m \cdot (\epsilon - \alpha)}{\alpha \cdot (\beta + \gamma \cdot \epsilon)} - n \tag{7.42}$$

We can also calculate the asymptotic saving ratio $\bar{s} = 1 - \bar{h}/\bar{z}$,

$$\bar{s} = \alpha \cdot \frac{n \cdot (\beta + \gamma \cdot \epsilon) + m - \gamma \cdot \rho}{\beta \cdot \rho + \epsilon \cdot m} \tag{7.43}$$

For these to be within economically meaningful ranges, the

parameters must satisfy certain restrictions. These also give conditions for convergence of the utility integral, and hence for the existence of an optimum path. The conditions are easily written down, but rather uninformative, and I shall omit them.

We can also calculate the asymptotic rate of interest $\bar{\imath} = \alpha \cdot \bar{z}$, and the asymptotic rate of growth of capital (and also output and total consumption), $\bar{g} = \bar{s} \cdot \bar{z}$. Then it can be verified that $\bar{s} = \alpha \cdot \bar{g}/\bar{\imath}$, which is a simple generalization of the result of (5.15), where resources did not matter and the ultimate growth rate was exogenous.

From (7.36), we can also calculate the ultimate rate of growth of consumption per capita; it equals $(m - \gamma \cdot \rho)/(\beta + \gamma \cdot \epsilon)$. This is positive if $m/\gamma > \rho$, i.e. if the rate of technological progress in purely resource-augmenting form exceeds the rate of impatience. We saw before that sustained growth of consumption per capita was technically possible if this rate of technological progress exceeded the rate of population growth; we now see when such growth will be chosen on an optimum path.

Finally, we can see how the long run properties of optimum paths depend on the parameters. First, if $m/\gamma > \rho$, it is easily verified that a higher ϵ implies a lower $\bar{s}$ and a higher $\bar{d}$. This is easy to interpret, for we have a path with a rising standard of living, and are making the welfare judgement more egalitarian. This produces a redistribution in favour of the worse off, i.e. the earlier generations, by saving less and depleting the resource faster. Next, if we increase γ and lower α at the same time, this lowers $\bar{\imath}$. Thus the greater the importance of the resource relative to capital in production, the greater the role of saving. I shall leave further results of this kind as exercises.

The analysis needs to be sharpened in the case of a stationary economy, i.e. one with constant population and technology and no discounting of the future for reasons of pure impatience. This case can be argued to be of some importance in an economy limited by resources, and therefore we should study it further. The problem is that when $m = n = \rho = 0$, we find $\bar{z} = \bar{d} = \bar{h} = 0$, and $\bar{s}$ takes the form $0/0$. To avoid this problem, we work directly in terms of s. Using the relation $(1 - s) = h/z$, considering proportional changes in it and substituting from (7.37) and (7.38), we find

$$\dot{s} = \alpha \cdot z \cdot (1 - s) \cdot (s - \bar{s})/(1 - \gamma) \tag{7.44}$$

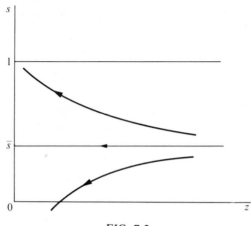

FIG. 7.3

where

$$\bar{s} = (1 - \gamma + \gamma \cdot \epsilon)/\epsilon \qquad (7.45)$$

The other two equations become

$$\dot{z}/z = - z \cdot (\beta \cdot s + \alpha \cdot \gamma)/(1 - \gamma) \qquad (7.46)$$

$$\dot{d}/d = d - \alpha \cdot z \cdot (1 - s)/(1 - \gamma) \qquad (7.47)$$

The phase diagram for z and s is shown in Fig. 7.3. We see that unless s is maintained constant at the value $\bar{s}$, the path will either go to $s = 1$, or cross $s = 0$ and then become infeasible or run out of capital. Eliminating these with the usual reasoning, we must conclude that the optimum policy is to maintain the saving ratio constant at the value $\bar{s}$. This is positive; we also need it to be less than α in order to have $\bar{d}$ positive. The condition for this is easily seen to be

$$\epsilon \cdot (\alpha - \gamma) > 1 - \gamma.$$

This needs $\alpha > \gamma$, and then $\epsilon > (1 - \gamma)/(\alpha - \gamma)$

Now we can use the value $\bar{s}$ in (7.46) and (7.47) to examine the behaviour of z and d. This produces a phase diagram exactly like Fig. 7.1, with $\bar{z} = \bar{d} = 0$ and thus only the top right portion of the diagram is of relevance. We see that both z and d should fall monotonically to zero along the stable path. In fact we can say rather more about the capital/output ratio $v = 1/z$, for

$$\dot{v} = -\dot{z}/z^2 = (\beta \cdot \bar{s} + \alpha \cdot \gamma)/(1 - \gamma)$$

is constant, and therefore v increases linearly.

We have $G\langle C/L \rangle = \alpha \cdot z/\epsilon$, which is positive at all times, but goes to zero asymptotically. Thus the level of consumption per capita is rising at all times, and goes to a finite limit. We see that capital accumulation alone makes this possible, but the ultimate outcome is not a conventional steady state, since the capital/output ratio is steadily rising and the depletion rate is falling. This point was mentioned in Section 4.

It is easy to see that a higher ϵ implies a lower $\bar{s}$. This is again due to the increase in egalitarian concern, since we have some growth in the level of consumption per capita, even though the rate of growth ultimately falls to zero. In the Rawlsian limit as ϵ goes to infinity, we have $\bar{s} = 1 - \gamma$, $G\langle C/L \rangle$ is always zero, and then consumption and output are constant along the optimum path. Thus we have a combined policy of capital accumulation and resource depletion to provide the highest common standard of living for all generations.

7. Further extensions

It is possible to remove the restriction of the Cobb-Douglas production function when considering the three-factor model of the last three sections. This increases the possibilities of non-monotonic paths; for example the resource use per capita can fall, then rise, and finally fall again along an optimum path. The elasticity of substitution again governs the possibility of sustaining growth in the long run, and the effect is similar to that in the model of Section 3 which neglected labour.[6]

In applications, it is obviously very important to allow much more disaggregation, with different resources and different capital goods substitutable to different extents. However, such disaggregation does not yield many general qualitative results.

A more important consideration is that of uncertainty. This is also quite difficult to handle. Only a simple kind of uncertainty, namely about the date at which a new technology will enable us to do without the resource altogether, has been studied in detail.[7] It is found that such uncertainty has the effect of raising the discount rate, as in the simple optimum saving theory with an uncertain lifetime. However, much important and useful work remains to be done.

Notes

The classic analysis of the economics of exhaustible resources is by Hotelling (1931). For simple expositions, see Solow (1974) and Heal (1975). The popular prophesies of the dire consequences of resource depletion are too numerous to list; one of the best known, presented as a model, is that of Meadows et al (1972). For critiques of this, see Nordhaus (1973a) and Kay and Mirrlees (1975). For further empirical work based on principles discussed in this chapter, see Nordhaus (1973b) and Manne (1974).

1. For analysis that faces these difficulties squarely, see Meade (1962, Appendix I).

2. See Nordhaus and Tobin (1972).

3. For a rigorous analysis of this model, including all the details of proofs that I have omitted, see Dasgupta and Heal (1974).

4. On cases where the resource stock *should* be used up in finite time, see Hotelling (1931) and Dasgupta and Heal (1974).

5. The analysis of sections 4—6 is based on Solow (1974b) and Stiglitz (1974). Readers interested in rigorous proofs and details that I have omitted should consult these.

6. See Ingham and Simmons (1975).

7. See Dasgupta and Heal (1974).

8.   Disequilibrium Models

I have conducted the whole discussion of growth so far in a fairly rigid
framework of intertemporal equilibrium. I defended this approach in
Chapter 1, claiming that it yielded some valuable insights and
preliminary conclusions concerning problems of resource allocation in
a growing economy. I hope that the subsequent models, especially those
in Chapters 4, 5, and 7, have gone some way towards substantiating this
claim. Further, I claimed that the great complexity of complete
disequilibrium, and the fact that it often raises considerations specific
to individual cases, make it useful to think in two stages in applied
work, formulating an equilibrium model and then altering it to allow
particular features of disequilibrium. I cited some such work, mainly by
Denison, in support. But it would be desirable to unify the two stages.

Of course the preceding chapters are far from being a complete
account of equilibrium growth theory. I have left several topics to
more advanced or specialized treatments. Two significant omissions
were the examination of non-steady-state growth with embodied
technological change, and the general theory of multi-sector models.
I have also omitted all details of how various growth policies might be
implemented in a mixed economy, and how the restrictions on
available policies affect the optimum choices.[1] I have not considered
growth with international trade,[2] or growth with uncertainty in an
expected utility framework.[3] Finally, even with the most advanced
techniques, not all questions concerning equilibrium growth have been
answered, and much work remains to be done. However, the marginal
cost of further progress here is rising rapidly. Naturally, systematic
treatment of disequilibrium is now a growing priority. In this chapter,
I shall outline very briefly some existing work on this. I hope to
provide some pointers to possible developments, and enable the reader
to put particular models in their proper context.

This is a vast and uncharted area, and any attempt to select, group
and evaluate different approaches is bound to be subjective. I have been
relatively eclectic, but cannot hope to do the problem full justice.

The difficulties arise in the following way. Once we leave the setting of equilibrium with perfect foresight, some markets fail to clear, some plans are not fulfilled, and some expectations turn out to have been wrong. With interrelated markets, wrong expectations concerning one price or quantity can lead to the failure of another market to clear. To set up a model of disequilibrium, we have to specify which markets fail to clear, how the actual transactions in these markets occur when this happens, and how the various plans, expectations and then the realizations of various prices and quantities alter in response to it. There is a bewildering range of possibilities to choose from, and often a seemingly slight difference in assumptions can lead to a major difference in results.

Differences among disequilibrium models can arise not only in the details of assumptions, but also in the overall view about their relation with equilibrium models. Thus suppose that some parametric change disturbs an equilibrium. This will lead to a disappointment of the prevailing expectations, and a consequent path of disequilibrium. However, given the new values of the parameters, it is possible to conceive of a new equilibrium where expectations are once again fulfilled. The question is whether, assuming the new parametric configuration lasts indefinitely, the disequilibrium path will converge to the new equilibrium. Thus we can ask whether Keynesian unemployment can persist for ever, or whether firms that are not maximizing profits can survive in the long run. On this question of compatibility with an underlying equilibrium model, there are two approaches evident in disequilibrium models. Some simply ignore the question, claiming that in practice another disturbance will change the parameters once again before the equilibrium could be attained. I think this is a mistaken argument of practicality, for assumptions concerning compatibility with a hypothetical equilibrium have important repercussions on the *disequilibrium* behaviour of the model. Other models attempt to study the outcome under hypothetical stationary circumstances, some finding compatibility and others, not. In each case, it is usually possible to find interesting reasons for the results, and these suggest further lines of investigation.

With such variety of approaches and lack of consensus, it is not possible to set down simple representative models. Also, some approaches have not been tried for building growth models, although they hold some promise for such applications. I shall therefore concentrate on discussing the general settings, and not on developing particular models in any detail.

1. Income-expenditure models

Keynesian unemployment is obviously a very important kind of disequilibrium. Attempts to incorporate it into a setting of growth usually begin with the simplest Keynesian model, namely the income-expenditure model. This is then altered to allow accumulation, and the consequent changes in investment and output. It is assumed that output is determined by effective demand, there being sufficient supplies of all factors to leave some unused capacity and unemployment.

Investment thus becomes the driving force, determining output through the multiplier. If we make investment demand depend on the expected change in output through an accelerator, we have the most famous Keynesian growth model, namely Harrod's 'knife-edge problem'. This has been discussed at length in the literature at all levels, and it is unnecessary to repeat the details.[4]

The general outline is as follows. The expected change in output determines investment demand through the accelerator, and this in turn determines the actual output and hence the realized change in output through the multiplier. If the actual change happens to coincide with the expected change, this will be a situation of equilibrium as far as the output market is concerned. This is not a general equilibrium of the economy as we have considered it so far, since there is involuntary unemployment in the factor markets. It can be shown that such a path of equilibrium growth in a limited sense exists, i.e. there is one particular value of the growth rate which, if expected by producers, will also be realized through the process outlined above. This is called the warranted growth rate, and the corresponding growth path the warranted path. In the simple one-sector model, it is easy to show that the warranted growth rate g equals s/v, where s is the saving propensity and v is the accelerator coefficient. If there are constant returns to scale and fixed coefficients, v can be taken to be the capital/output ratio.

Given some assumptions, we find unstable growth on either side of the warranted path. If the expected growth rate exceeds the warranted, then the actual growth rate exceeds the expected. If expectations are adaptive, i.e. if they are shifted towards the latest observation, then in the next period the expected growth rate will be raised, the actual growth rate will be still higher, and so on. There will be a similar cumulative downward movement if the expected growth rate is less than the warranted one. Thus the warranted path will be a knife-edge: accidental disturbances on either side of it will lead to unstable movements of the actual path away from it.

The precise assumptions that lead to this result depend on whether the expectations are formed in terms of levels or growth rates. However, in general terms we can say that the instability is caused by an inherent instability of the multiplier-accelerator mechanism, together with the volatility of adaptive expectations. For example, if it is believed that growth will revert to the warranted path and that any disturbance is a temporary phenomenon, i.e. if expectations are regressive, then we will have stable growth. Further, given the existence of some excess capacity, it is questionable whether investment demand will be given by a fixed-coefficient accelerator. A flexible accelerator using a stock-adjustment principle seems more appropriate. This is conducive to stability, but it is no match for very volatile expectations.[5] Finally, the capital/output ratio (or at least that for new investment, which is what is at issue) might itself be variable. This point will be taken up again, but it should be abundantly clear that there is a very wide range of possible assumptions, which can be combined to yield any desired conclusion.

I shall turn to another issue. The knife-edge problem as defined above concerns the relation between the actual growth rate and the warranted growth rate. The equilibrium paths of Chapter 3 can in this terminology be thought of as studying the relation between the warranted rate s/v and the natural rate n, i.e. the rate of growth of labour in efficiency units. There was a time when the two issues were confused, but in recent years it has been thought that there is little or no connection between them. In fact there is an important connection of this kind, and it is clearly stated by Harrod.[6] Suppose the warranted rate exceeds the natural rate. With fixed coefficients, actual growth at a rate above the natural rate cannot be sustained for ever. In course of time the unemployed labour will be used up, and then the actual growth rate will have to drop to, or below, the natural rate, which has been assumed to be below the warranted rate. Given adaptive expectations, in course of time the expected rate will also fall below the warranted rate, thus setting off a cumulative downward movement.[7]

Thus we see that the question of the discrepancy between the warranted rate and the natural rate does have a bearing on the knife-edge problem, and also that factor substitution, by removing the rigid labour constraint and allowing the warranted rate to change, does contribute to reducing this inevitability of the knife-edge instability.

However, in disequilibrium there are other effects, and factor substitution does not guarantee stability. One example of this arises from the need to distinguish between nominal and real interest rates in a monetary economy. If there is effective arbitrage between monetary assets and real assets, then the real rental rate will equal the real rate of interest, i.e. the nominal rate *minus* the rate of increase of the price level. Now suppose the capital/output ratio depends on the real rate, and that the nominal rate is sticky in the short run because of the speculative component of liquidity preference. Suppose s increases to make $s/v > n$. In principle, an increase in v can restore the equality. However, in the short run an increase in s is deflationary. This raises the real rate, thus lowering v and raising s/v still further. Thus the disequilibrium adjustment of v could be destabilizing, at least in the short run. Contrast this with the adjustment of v along an equilibrium path in the one-sector models of Chapter 3, where monotonic stability was guaranteed.

Let us now ask whether the warranted rate can remain persistently below the natural rate. A model developing this possibility has been put forward by Kahn and Robinson.[8] Here it is supposed that all wage income is consumed, and a constant proportion sp of profits is saved. Further, the rate of profit does not equal the rate of interest. The idea is that the latter applies to risk-free loans. Now a steady state viewed in the aggregate has no uncertainty, but this is compatible with some uncertainty at the level of individual firms that is in a relative sense washed out in aggregation. The greater the uncertainty, the more must be the risk premium by which the profit rate exceeds the interest rate in order to bring forth a given amount of investment. Also, a higher average growth rate can be argued to involve greater uncertainty. Thus we can make the warranted growth rate an increasing function of the profit rate, say $g = g(r)$. Assuming a diminishing marginal effect of the risk premium on accumulation, this yields a curve like that shown in Fig. 8.1. Also, as in the Cambridge models of Chapter 3, we must have $g = sp \cdot r$. As Fig. 8.1 shows, this allows two positions of equilibrium.

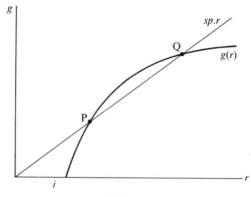

FIG. 8.1

If the rate of profit falls when there is too much saving relative to the accumulation that producers are willing to undertake, and rises when the opposite is true, then the lower equilibrium P will be unstable and the upper one, Q, will be stable. Thus we have the possibility of a low profit, low growth 'trap' in this model. Also, the model does not require the warranted growth rate to equal the natural rate. While it could not remain above the latter for long, it can persist below the natural rate, with the consequent permanent unemployment.

Of course this requires the interest rate to remain fixed for ever. It is clearly not to be supposed that inelastic expectations and the consequent speculative liquidity preference are long run phenomena. Further, even though the nominal rate may be sticky, or held fixed by monetary authorities, the real rate can adjust through price level changes. Finally, if the money wage falls in response to the persistent unemployment, this can have a real balance effect which lowers the interest rate. In conclusion, the model obtains its result of a kind of equilibrium with permanent unemployment only by neglecting many relevant economic forces.

This is a common weakness of income-expenditure models – they are unable to handle relative price changes at all satisfactorily. A model that considers prices, and makes precise the difference between neoclassical and Keynesian assumptions, is presented by Sen.[9] He argues that the crucial neoclassical assumption is to let investment adjust passively to saving. We have seen in Chapter 3 how this is accomplished by changes in future prices that have no effect on the instant in question. Sen shows how, by making investment demand exogenous, we can allow other variables to adjust. One way is to keep full employment of labour but allow the price level to adjust. This affects the interest rate and hence the factor shares. If investment were affected in turn, this would produce a rather Wicksellian story. The other approach is to allow employment to adjust. In either case, the real wage can be kept equal to the marginal product of labour by proportionate changes in the money wage and the price level.

In a similar model, Solow and Stiglitz[10] allow some further disequilibrium and consequent adjustments. The output market can fail to clear, and rationing rules and price changes are specified when this happens. The wage rate responds to unemployment, while employment adjusts with a lag to output. Thus at any instant the real wage need not equal the marginal product of labour and the output price need not equal marginal cost. Investment demand is again exogenous. This model is capable of generating various short-run paths, including cycles.

However, exogenous investment demand is a very restrictive assumption even for short-run dynamics. It may be motivated by the idea of a sticky interest rate. However, all the models discussed so far have used such essentially monetary ideas without considering money at all. Introducing money explicitly, and allowing it to effect the interest rate and absolute prices, yields some further interesting results. This will be the subject of the next section.

2. Monetary models

The special importance of money is essentially connected with disequilibrium. We could introduce money as just another asset in a model of full intertemporal equilibrium, but this would not be very interesting. Consider the textbook case of non-interest-bearing money distributed without charge. Taking money as numéraire, let p be the price of goods in a one-sector model, and let r be the real rate of interest. The yield on capital is then $r + \dot{p}/p$. The yield on money being zero, the equilibrium condition (2.35) would become $r + \dot{p}/p = 0$. This would produce the saddle-point instability familiar from Chapter 6, but little else of interest. It is more usual to allow $r + \dot{p}/p$ to be non-zero, and to make the demand for money a decreasing function of it. However, this is motivated by arguments about the convenience of money as a liquid asset, and these arguments have no real place in a setting of equilibrium with perfect foresight. Such a model has an indirect use, for it shows how some disequilibrium models where money has a real place can be constructed by altering some specifications. It is with this view that I shall briefly outline an equilibrium model with money.

Let M be the stock of money, growing at a rate μ. Both the level and the rate of growth of the money supply are exogenously fixed. Let p be the price of goods relative to money, and write $\pi = \dot{p}/p$, the rate of inflation. Let the rest of the notation be as in the Solow-Swan model of Chapter 3. Now individuals regard real cash balances as wealth, and additions to them as income. Thus wealth is $K + M/p$, and income is $Y + \mathrm{d}(M/p)/\mathrm{d}t$, both measured in units of goods. Suppose the proportion of wealth that individuals wish to hold in real cash balances is a function of $(r + \pi)$ alone. Then so is the desired ratio of holdings of the two assets, and the condition for equilibrium in asset-holding becomes

$$M/(p \cdot K) = \Lambda(r + \pi), \qquad (8.1)$$

where Λ is a decreasing function.

Next suppose that individuals plan to save a fraction s of income, i.e. to consume a fraction $(1 - s)$. In equilibrium, capital accumulation must equal real output minus consumption. This gives

$$\begin{aligned}\dot{K} &= Y - (1 - s) \cdot \{Y + \mathrm{d}(M/p)/\mathrm{d}t\} \\ &= s \cdot Y - (1 - s) \cdot (M/p) \cdot (\mu - \pi). \qquad (8.2)\end{aligned}$$

At each instant, M, K, and L are all fixed and so is the equilibrium output, $Y = F(K, L)$. Taking p as given, we can regard the two equations as determining $\dot{K}$ and π, or equivalently $\dot{K}$ and $\dot{p}$. Thus, as in the two-asset models of Chapter 6, any initial value of p is compatible with equilibrium over a short horizon provided $\dot{p}$ adjusts suitably. We can then trace the path of K and p. This is in fact most easily done in terms of the transformed variables $x = M/(p \cdot K)$ and $k = K/L$. We find a saddle-point in the phase diagram.[11] Thus a smooth demand function for money as in (8.1) does not help us avoid the basic problem of the Hahn instability with multiple assets. If the initial value of p is too high in relation to the stable paths into the saddle-point, it means that the supply of real cash balances is too low. The real rental or interest rate being fixed by the equilibrium condition $r = F_K(K, L)$, the only way to maintain (8.1) is to have a higher π, thus reducing the demand for real cash balances. But then p grows faster, and the process continues. Conversely, we can think of the phenomenon as one where high inflationary expectations reduce the demand for real cash balances, and the price level rises to reduce the supply, in the process just fulfilling the expectations. This is exactly the problem we found in Chapter 6.

One interesting outcome of such models is that money in them is not neutral — the choice of the level, and more particularly the growth rate, of the stock of money affects real magnitudes. First, the very presence of money lowers the ratio of investment to real output below s, which is what it would be in a similar economy without money. This is of course due to the fact that disposable income as seen by individuals now exceeds real output, and hence their consumption out of real output exceeds $(1 - s) \cdot Y$. Then the steady state levels of capital and output per man will be below those obtained from $s \cdot f(k) = n \cdot k$ in the corresponding economy without money. However, this is a once-and-for-all effect, and is independent of the actual level of the stock of money. The latter affects only the absolute price level. The rate of growth of money supply has further effects. Consider a steady state where x and k are constant. Thus K grows at the rate n, and then $\mu = \pi + n$ in order to keep x constant. Then the steady state is defined by

$$x = \Lambda(f'(k) + \mu - n),$$
$$n = s \cdot f(k)/k - (1 - s) \cdot n \cdot x. \tag{8.3}$$

Differentiating these totally with respect to μ, we find that $dk/d\mu$ is positive. Thus a higher rate of growth of the money supply produces a steady state with a higher capital/labour ratio, although of course it is never as high as it would be in the corresponding real economy.

More complicated models of this kind can produce different results. Cases where real cash balances are an argument in the utility functions of consumers or in the production function can lead to different comparative static results. If the monetary authorities supply money in exchange for capital, the non-neutrality can be avoided altogether.[12]

Let us now consider various modifications of the equilibrium model. The simplest change is to allow the possibility that inflation is imperfectly forecast. Let π now denote the *expected* rate of inflation; this of course entails the heroic assumption that all individuals have the same expectations, and hold them with subjective certainty. Now we interpret (8.1) and (8.2) in a different way. At any instant, π is given, and the equilibrium conditions determine $\dot{K}$ and p. Differentiating, we find an expression for the actual $\dot{p}/p$. Now suppose the expectations are adaptive, i.e. that they are moved towards the latest observation. Thus

$$\dot{\pi} = \lambda \cdot (\dot{p}/p - \pi), \qquad (8.4)$$

where λ is a positive constant, indicating the speed of adjustment of expectations. Now we can reduce (8.1), (8.2) and (8.4) to a pair of differential equations in k and π, and study them in a phase diagram. This yields a stable steady state if λ is smaller than a critical value, and a saddle-point otherwise. Thus the Hahn instability can be countered by sluggishly changing expectations. A disturbance in the current rate of inflation causes only a small change in the expected rate if expectations adapt slowly. Then there is only a small change in the demand for money, and only a small equilibrating adjustment in the actual rate is necessary. Thus an initial disturbance can be dampened. However, there are other examples where the Hahn instability arises even with static expectations.[13]

Next consider the possibility of disequilibrium in the commodity or labour markets. Models which allow this begin by postulating a function for the demand for investment goods, and then follow one of two approaches. The Wicksellian approach assumes full employment of labour. However, the supply of output is allowed to differ from the sum of demands for consumption and investment. A rationing rule is specified to determine the actual allocations, and the rate of inflation is made a function of the excess demand for commodities. This affects the rate of interest, and the story of growth depends on the relation between this rate and the natural rate related to the marginal product of capital. In more sophisticated models, it is the difference between the actual and the expected rate of inflation that depends on the excess demand for commodities. This yields a model that is compatible with a long run equilibrium, but displays different behaviour out of equilibrium.[14]

Keynesian models suppose that the output market equilibrates through an adjustment of the real output. This determines employment, and then the price level or the wage rate change in response to the disequilibrium in the labour market, as in a Phillips curve.[15]

In all these models, stability depends on the speeds of adjustment. Generally, rapid adjustment of expectations to the most recent observation is destabilizing, while rapid adjustment of prices in response to disequilibria is stabilizing. With suitably non-linear functions, cycles can also result.

Such models have also been applied to study the effectiveness of monetary and fiscal policies.[16] The conclusions at a simple level merely confirm the intuition based on the IS-LM apparatus. However, this indicates that the models are suitable for further development, and for investigating questions that are not amenable to simple thinking. This seems a fruitful area for further research.

3. Temporary equilibrium

In the first two sections we met several models involving disequilibrium. Usually, each went its own way, and it was difficult to relate them to each other or to see them as parts of an overall theoretical framework for analyzing disequilibrium. The first, and in my view still the most promising, attempt to provide such a framework is the temporary equilibrium approach of Hicks.[17] In this section I shall outline it briefly.

Consider an economy going through a succession of periods. Fix attention on any one date, say 0. At this date, agents in the economy have expectations concerning future prices. Each agent is assumed to hold his expectations with subjective certainty, i.e. for each price that needs to be guessed, he associates just one value. These values depend on past experience, and also on the current market prices. Of course, different agents may have different expectations.

Each agent, based on his expectations, and constrained by his past decisions and current opportunities, forms a plan for current and future actions. Of these plans, only those concerning supply and demand in markets that are currently open are coordinated by the price mechanism. Thus prices in these markets adjust to equate supply and demand. The outcome is called a *temporary equilibrium* at date 0.

The range of markets that are open at date 0 can be quite varied. At one extreme, there may be only spot markets, i.e. markets for immediate delivery of commodities, and even some of these may fail for the usual reasons. At the other extreme, there may be complete futures markets, i.e. for promised delivery of each commodity at each date. Typically, there will exist all spot markets and a limited set of futures markets, e.g. markets for loans of various durations in one commodity. The relative prices in these futures markets then define the interest rates for these durations in terms of the commodity in question. This commodity may be money.

When the next date, labelled 1, arrives, its own set of markets will open and its own temporary equilibrium will be established. Typically, agents will find that the prices in these markets will differ from what they had expected them to be when making their decisions at date 0. This can of course arise when different agents have different expectations, and most or even all of them must turn out to be wrong. It can also arise because, given their expectations at date 0, the plans the agents had formed for actions at date 1 were such that the total planned supply of some commodities did not equal the total planned demand for them. If the appropriate futures markets do not exist at date 0, the temporary equilibrium at that date provides no check on this. However, even if such markets exist, agents may wish to revise the plans when date 1 arrives, because they have acquired new information in the meantime.[18] In our earlier setting of perfect foresight, there was no new information and no reason to alter the plans made at the outset. Thus, even when all futures markets exist, temporary equilibrium is a more general and realistic setting than equilibrium with perfect foresight.

The most important innovation of the temporary equilibrium approach is that it allows price expectations to depend on current prices. Thus, for any particular good, let p_0 be the price for current delivery at date 0, and let pe_1 be the price that is expected to prevail for current delivery in markets at date 1. Then pe_1 is a function of p_0, and the elasticity of this functional dependence, $(p_0/pe_1) \cdot \mathrm{d}pe_1/\mathrm{d}p_0$, is called the elasticity of expectation for the good and the date in question. For example, suppose it is believed that the price that prevailed at some date in the past is the normal price to which p_1 will revert, any departure of p_0 from the normal price being a temporary aberration, then pe_1 is independent of p_0 and the elasticity of the expectation is zero. If, on the other hand, it is believed that p_0 immediately becomes the new normal value which will persist, then $pe_1 = p_0$ and the elasticity is 1. In many cases, we suppose the elasticity of an expectation to lie between 0 and 1, although values outside this range are possible if expectations are over-regressive or extrapolative.

Now the supply and demand at date 0 depend on the current price p_0 as well as the expected price at the later date, pe_1, and hence on the elasticity of the expectation. Therefore the market-clearing value of p_0 depends on the elasticity of the expectation. Thus the approach allows expectations to be important determinants of current prices, and this is clearly a vital step in understanding disequilibrium.

After studying the temporary equilibrium at one date, we can go on to examine the evolution of an economy through temporary equilibria at a succession of dates. This needs a mechanism for revising expectations, and the method so far has been relatively weak in this respect. We would expect that the functional form which links the expected price pe_2 to the current price p_1 at date 1 will itself depend on whether the expectation pe_1 was falsified by experience and in what way. Further, as expectations are repeatedly shown to be wrong, it becomes harder to believe that agents go on holding them with subjective certainty. Some progress can be made using ad hoc arguments and judgements, but a rigorous theory is lacking.

Hicks used this approach to discuss several questions, notably trade cycles and some aspects of capital accumulation. Since then the method was neglected for a while, but it has recently been revived and extended. Two important advances have been made. The first allows temporary equilibrium to be achieved by quantity adjustments in some markets. This allows a better treatment of Keynesian unemployment. The second allows expectations to be held with subjective uncertainty. For each variable to be guessed, each agent forms a subjective probability distribution, and the parameters of this distribution depend on current prices. Once again, the theory of revision of such distributions in the light of experience is relatively weak. These developments have been carried out at a relatively abstract level, with emphasis on proofs of existence of the relevant equilibria. But they have advanced our understanding of Keynesian issues significantly,[19] and seem to hold some promise for fruitful applications to problems of growth.

4. Scale economies and monopoly

It is often asserted that economies of scale are an extremely important feature of growth. The idea can be traced back to Adam Smith, and its strongest supporters have been Young and Kaldor.[20]

The main problem posed by economies of scale for the method of the earlier chapters is that they threaten the very existence of a competitive equilibrium, and introduce some element of monopoly. This must be qualified in several ways. First, if economies of scale are small in relation to the size of the market, then a competitive equilibrium can be a good approximation.[21] Next, if these economies are not noticed by individuals, then a competitive equilibrium will be possible. Of course the scale economies will appear as externalities, and the equilibrium will be inefficient. Learning by doing provided an example of this in Chapter 4.

Empirical evidence concerning economies of scale is conflicting. There seems to be clear proof that many individual industries have potential scale economies, but these often go unexploited for various reasons. At an aggregate level, the evidence is, to say the least, inconclusive.[22] One explanation of this may lie in considerations of space. Industrial production may have economies of scale, but the transport activity for delivering the output to consumers may have diseconomies owing to congestion etc. Then aggregate output will expand through an increase in the number of plants, and this will show approximately constant returns to scale. However, local monopoly power will remain significant.[23] Thus, although the case for scale economies at an aggregate level is weak, this does not automatically justify the neglect of monopoly.

Monopoly can also be associated with technological change, with or without economies of scale. This is a Schumpeterian view of growth. Innovations generate temporary monopoly, or at least quasi-rents due to temporary cost advantages. These profits stimulate further innovations.[24]

Finally, recent research points to another important cause of monopoly. Disequilibrium by itself and of necessity introduces some monopoly, at least in the short run. The point is that in disequilibrium all prices need not be known to all transactors, and searching for the best price is a costly activity with an uncertain outcome. In such a situation, a seller charging a price slightly above that of other sellers would not expect to lose all his customers at once. In other words, he will face a downward sloping demand curve, and hence be able to exert some monopoly power. Disequilibrium dynamics must therefore involve a shifting situation of monopoly. This important idea originated with Arrow, and has been the subject of a great deal of recent research.[25]

We have here a strong case for making serious attempts to allow monopoly into growth theory. The best-known existing attempt to do so is that of Kalecki.[26] Although a brief summary is bound to do injustice to some of his ideas, a simple outline can be given. National product Y is divided into wages W, material costs M, and profits P. Pricing in industry involves a mark-up over prime costs, the extent of the mark-up depending on the degree of monopoly possessed by the representative firm. Thus we can write $P = \theta \cdot (W + M)$, where θ is the average mark-up. This yields $P/Y = \theta/(1 + \theta)$. Now suppose that all wage income is consumed, and that a fraction sp of profits is saved and invested. Then it is easy to calculate that the warranted growth rate is

$$g = \frac{\theta}{1 + \theta} \cdot \frac{sp}{v} \tag{8.5}$$

For all its attractive simplicity, this theory suffers from several drawbacks. Most importantly, the underlying theory of pricing is microeconomic, but the way in which its macroeconomic implications are derived is unclear. This is particularly important because the products of the different monopolistic firms must have finite cross-elasticities, and therefore output aggregation is a serious problem. Next, the role of fixed capital is not clear. We wonder whether the monopolists will come to recognize 'normal' profits, i.e. interest costs, as parts of unit costs, and apply the mark-up to these as well. Then we have the question of determination of the interest rate. The conclusion I would draw is that a successful attempt to handle monopoly must begin by paying much more careful attention to the microeconomics of equilibrium (or disequilibrium with imperfect information) under monopoly.[27]

More definite answers can be given to questions of centralized planning in an economy with increasing returns. This involves difficult mathematics, but the conclusions can be stated simply.[28] The idea is that output comes from discrete 'plants', and increases more than proportionately with the size of the plant. Saving is then accumulated in an inventory, and when this reaches the right size, another plant is built. The problem is to determine the optimum policy for saving and for the size and timing of plants.

The optimum saving rules are very similar to those of Chapter 5, but the investment rules involve interesting new aspects. Two simple cases emerge. If the degree of increasing returns is fixed, so that a plant embodying investment I produces an output flow of I^v with $v > 1$, then the size of successive plants should increase in geometric progression. If there is a fixed cost of building a plant and a constant marginal cost of running it, i.e. if a plant of size I produces output $(a \cdot I - b)$ for $I \geqslant b/a$, then the optimum plant size in the long run increases as the square root of aggregate output. This has obvious parallels in other problems involving inventories, e.g. the transactions demand for money.[29]

5. Managerial and behavioural theories

An assumption I have maintained so far is that firms maximize profits, in the appropriate intertemporal sense of discounted present values. This was obvious in the marginal conditions under competition, and it also motivated the idea of a price determined by a mark-up over prime costs in monopoly. However, the assumption has been challenged as being unsuitable in the presence of monopoly and disequilibrium. While the implications of this for growth theory largely remain to be worked out, it is worth pointing out some features of the research in progress.

The challenge to profit-maximization comes from two different approaches, the managerial and the behavioural. The managerial critique[30] points out that most industrial production occurs in corporate enterprises, and that the running of most corporations involves a considerable divorce of control from ownership. While the shareholders fare best under a profit-maximizing strategy, the managers have other objectives, and the shareholders have only imperfect control over them. Of managerial objectives, growth is usually taken to be the most prominent. If the growth rate chosen by the managers is not what the shareholders would most desire, this lowers the market value of the equity of the firm. The valuation ratio, i.e. the ratio of the value of the shares to that of the assets of the firm, can then fall short of unity. Under perfect competition this could not persist, since it allows a pure

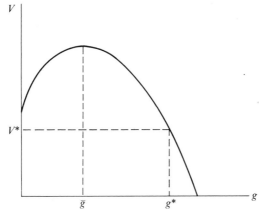

FIG. 8.2

profit to be made by buying up the firm and using its assets for profit-maximization. However, given some barriers to entry, there is some room for the valuation ratio to fall below 1 before such a take-over threatens the existing management. It is supposed that the managers then maximize the growth rate while maintaining the valuation ratio above this critical value V^*. This is shown in Fig. 8.2. The valuation ratio V regarded as a function of the growth rate g has a parabolic form under some assumptions concerning stock market behaviour. The growth rate $\bar{g}$ maximizes V, and under perfect competition the corresponding value $\bar{V}$ would equal 1. However, given their limited freedom from control by shareholders, the managers choose the higher growth rate g^* and the corresponding valuation ratio is the critical value V^*. They do this, of course, by retaining more profits and paying out less dividends than the shareholders would like.

An exercise of building a growth model based on such a view of the representative firm is presented by Marris.[31] The basic idea is that as in the models of Kaldor and Pasinetti, it is possible to obtain a relation $g = sp \cdot r$, where g is the warranted growth rate, r is the profit rate, and sp is now the ratio of profits retained for investment by the firms. However, this retention ratio is chosen according to the mechanism just described. It is therefore an endogenous variable and not a parameter. The complete model must be more complicated, as I warned when discussing the significance of Kaldor's saving assumptions in Chapter 3. To proceed further, Marris assumes that the critical valuation ratio is a function of r, and of a variable β representing the stock market conditions, e.g. attitudes to risk. Then we have $V = V^*(r, \beta)$, and from the analysis of Figure 8.2, $g = g^*(r, \beta)$. Next we must reconcile the valuation ratio with the demand side, considering the total valuation of equities in relation to the consumers' accumulated savings. Including this, we have three equations for V, g, r, and β. We can then proceed in one of two ways. We can take r to be determined elsewhere, e.g. from considerations of monopoly, and then allow β to adjust. Or we can begin with β and determine r. We can also try to reconcile g with the natural growth rate. Next, if the firms' policies for growth include research and development, and this affects the rate of technological progress, we can make the natural rate also an endogenous variable. Finally, having completed the model, we can calculate the implied retention ratio, and also i, the rate of interest available to individual savers, which need not equal the profit rate.

Critics of the behavioural persuasion go further in a sense by challenging the very idea of maximization of any kind. They claim that in a changing and uncertain environment, where information is limited and computation is costly, optimizing behaviour becomes almost inconceivable. They offer the alternative hypothesis that firms operate according to set decision rules, i.e. rules which specify actions as functions of relevant variables exogenous to the firm. These rules are fixed in the short run, but they are monitored for performance. If the performance falls short of a desired standard, the rules are modified by deliberate search for new rules, and this search is motivated by goals of which profit is a prominent one. It hardly needs to be said that a theory of the firm built along these lines has to pay much more attention to the details of the internal organization in decision-making than is the case with a profit-maximization theory.

Many of these ideas originate from the work of Simon, but their ablest recent exponent has been Winter.[32] At one time, the common reply to the behavioural arguments would have been that in a competitive environment only those firms will survive whose decision rules happen to be consistent with profit-maximization, and therefore we may as well assume the latter directly. Winter has taken much of the force out of this response by finding the very restrictive assumptions of stationarity that are necessary for this to be rigorously valid. He has also pointed out that in tracing the dynamic response of a firm to a change in the environment it is hardly legitimate to assume that a rule which happened to be consistent with profit-maximization in the old environment will remain so in the new one. Finally, he has constructed a model where firms set their capacity and mark-up according to fixed rules, and modify these rules if profitability is unsatisfactory. He shows that if the environment happens to be stationary, this process will converge to a competitive equilibrium, thus producing an example of a behavioural model that is compatible with a stationary equilibrium model but shows differences in the disequilibrium path.

Thus Winter's behavioural arguments should be taken seriously. They acquire even more force in the context of growth, since they enable a more realistic treatment of technological progress, viewing it as an active process of search in an uncertain environment. Work on behavioural growth models is only in its infancy, but Nelson and Winter have developed a model to illustrate the possibilities of the approach.[33] They postulate an economy consisting of firms which operate according to rules concerning output and cost-reduction, and modify these rules in the light of market experience. The resulting growth path is simulated. The results compare not unfavourably with those of an equilibrium path fitted using a production function. There is scope for further development of this approach, but also need for much further work before it can compete on equal terms with the prevailing methods.

6. Concluding comments

In this chapter I have sketched some recent developments that show promise for providing a systematic approach to disequilibrium growth. It is to be hoped that further work along some of these lines will enable us to avoid the two-stage approach via a setting of equilibrium that now prevails in growth economics, and will ultimately provide an integrated analysis of growth in and out of equilibrium.

Notes

1. Arrow and Kurz (1970), Foley and Sidrauski (1971) and Hall (1969) are just a few examples of the large literature on this subject.

2. See Caves and Jones (1973, chs. 25, 26) for an elementary geometric exposition, and Kemp (1969, chs. 10, 11) for a more advanced algebraic one.
3. See Brock and Mirman (1972), Mirrlees (1974). A proper treatment of this subject needs some knowledge of the mathematical theory of stochastic processes.
4. See Sen (ed.) (1970, pp. 10–14), Hahn and Matthews (1965, pp. 27–31) and Wan (1971, pp. 12–24).
5. See Encarnacion (1965).
6. See Harrod (1939, §16).
7. Note the implied theory of the upper turning point in trade cycles. As usual, the lower turning point cannot be treated symmetrically.
8. See Kahn (1959), Robinson (1962b), and a discussion of these models in Bliss (1975a, chs. 6, 11).
9. See Sen (1963).
10. See Solow and Stiglitz (1968).
11. See Burmeister and Dobell (1970, ch. 6).
12. See Levhari and Patinkin (1968), Hahn (1969).
13. See Sidrauski (1967), Wan (1971, ch. 8 §2), Hahn (1973).
14. See Stein (1969), Fischer (1972).
15. See Rose (1967), (1973), Uzawa (1973), Nagatani (1969).
16. See Blinder and Solow (1973), Buiter and Tobin (1974).
17. See Hicks (1946, Parts III and IV), (1965, ch. VI).
18. For the precise definition of 'information' that is important here, see Radner (1968).
19. See Arrow and Hahn (1971, ch. 6 §3, ch. 14), Grandmont (1970), Grandmont and Laroque (1974) and Benassy (1975) for recent developments in the theory and use of the temporary equilibrium approach. For an exposition and examination of Keynesian unemployment, see Bliss (1975b).
20. See Young (1928), Kaldor (1973).
21. See Farrell (1959), Starr (1969), Arrow and Hahn (1971, ch. 7).
22. See Pratten (1971), Silberston (1972), Rowthorn (1975).
23. See Starrett (1974).
24. See Schumpeter (1934), particularly chapters II and IV, and also the models along these lines by Shell (1973).
25. See Arrow (1959), and the excellent survey of recent research by Rothschild (1973).
26. See Kalecki (1965) and the exposition by Kregel (1971, ch. 7).
27. See Arrow and Hahn (1971, ch. 6 §4).
28. See Dixit, Mirrlees and Stern (1975), and earlier work by Manne et al. (1967), Weitzman (1970).
29. See Baumol (1972, pp. 5–10) for the simple inventory model.
30. What follows is a very brief and selective summary of a long and

complex theme in the literature. For more details, see Archibald (ed.) (1971), Marris and Wood (eds.) (1971).
31. See Marris (1972).
32. See Simon (1959), Winter (1964), (1971).
33. See Nelson and Winter (1974).

Bibliography

ALLEN, R. G. D. (1967) *Macro-economic Theory*, Macmillan, London.
ARCHIBALD, G. C. (ed.) (1971) *The Theory of the Firm*, Penguin Books, Harmondsworth, Middx.
ARROW, K. J. (1959) 'Toward a theory of price adjustment', in M. Abramovitz *et al. The Allocation of Economic Resources*, Stanford University Press, Stanford, Cal.
——— (1962) 'The economic implications of learning by doing', *Review of Economic Studies,* 29(3), 155–73.
——— (1973) 'Rawls' principle of just saving', *Swedish Journal of Economics,* 75(4), 323–35.
——— and F. H. HAHN (1971) *General Competitive Analysis*, Holden-Day, San Francisco and Oliver & Boyd, Edinburgh.
——— and M. KURZ (1970) *Public Investment, the Rate of Return and Optimal Fiscal Policy*, Johns Hopkins Press, Baltimore, Md.
ATKINSON, A. B. (1969) 'The time-scale of economic models: How long is the long run?', *Review of Economic Studies,* 36(2), 137–52.
——— (1970a) 'On the measurement of inequality', *Journal of Economic Theory,* 2(3), 244–63, reprinted with addition in A. B. Atkinson (ed.) *Wealth, Income and Inequality*, Penguin Books, Harmondsworth, Middx.
——— (1970b) 'On embodiment and savings', *Quarterly Journal of Economics,* 84(1), 126–33.
——— (1971) 'Capital taxes, the redistribution of wealth, and individual savings', *Review of Economic Studies,* 38(2), 209–27.
BAILEY, M. J. (1971) *National Income and the Price Level*, 2nd ed., McGraw-Hill, New York.
BARDHAN, P. K. (1969) 'Equilibrium growth in a model with economic obsolescence of machines', *Quarterly Journal of Economics,* 83(2), 312–23.
——— (1973) 'More on putty-clay', *International Economic Review,* 14(1), 211–22.
BAUMOL, W. J. (1972) *Economic Theory and Operations Analysis*, 3rd ed., Prentice-Hall, Englewood Cliffs, N.J.
BENASSY, J-P. (1975) 'Neo-Keynesian disequilibrium theory in a monetary economy', *Review of Economic Studies,* 42(4), 503–23.
BIRKHOFF, G. and G-C. ROTA (1969) *Ordinary Differential Equations*, 2nd ed., Blaisdell, Waltham, Mass.
BLACK, J. (1962) 'Optimum savings reconsidered, or Ramsey without tears', *Economic Journal,* 72(2), 360–6.
BLINDER, A. S. and R. M. SOLOW (1973) 'Does fiscal policy matter?', *Journal of Public Economics,* 2(3), 319–37.
BLISS, C. J. (1968) 'On putty-clay', *Review of Economic Studies,* 35(2), 105–32.
——— (1975a) *Capital Theory and the Distribution of Income*, North-Holland, Amsterdam.
——— (1975b) 'The reappraisal of Keynes' economics: an appraisal', in J. M. Parkin and A. R. Nobay (eds.) *Current Problems in Economics*, Cambridge University Press.

BOSE, S. (1968) 'Optimal growth and investment allocation', *Review of Economic Studies,* **35**(4), 465–80.

———— (1970) 'Optimal growth in a nonshiftable capital model', *Econometrica,* **38**(1), 128–52.

BRITTO, R. (1969) 'On putty-clay: a comment', *Review of Economic Studies,* **36**(3), 395–8.

BROCK, W. A. and L. J. MIRMAN (1972) 'Optimal economic growth and uncertainty', *Journal of Economic Theory,* **4**(3), 479–513.

———— and J. A. SCHEINKMAN (1975) 'Global asymptotic stability of optimal control systems with applications to the theory of economic growth', *Journal of Economic Theory,* forthcoming.

BUITER, W. H. and J. TOBIN (1974) 'Long run effects of fiscal and monetary policy on aggregate demand', Cowles Foundation Discussion Paper No. 384, New Haven, Conn.

BURMEISTER, E. and A. R. DOBELL (1970) *Mathematical Theories of Economic Growth,* Macmillan, New York.

CASS, D. (1965) 'Optimum growth in an aggregative model of capital accumulation', *Review of Economic Studies,* **32**(3), 233–40.

———— (1972) 'On capital overaccumulation in the aggregative neo-classical model: a complete characterization', *Journal of Economic Theory,* **4**(2), 200–23.

———— and K. SHELL (1975) 'The structure and stability of competitive dynamical systems', *Journal of Economic Theory,* forthcoming.

———— and J. E. STIGLITZ (1969) 'The implications of alternative saving and expectations hypotheses for choices of technique and patterns of growth', *Journal of Political Economy,* **77**(4, part II), 586–627.

———— and M. YAARI (1967) 'Individual saving, aggregate capital and efficient growth', in Shell (ed.) (1967).

CATON, C. and K. SHELL (1971) 'An exercise in the theory of heterogeneous capital accumulation', *Review of Economic Studies,* **38**(1), 13–22.

CAVES, R. E. and R. W. JONES (1973) *World Trade and Payments,* Little, Brown & Co., Boston.

CONLISK, J. and R. RAMANATHAN (1970) 'Expedient choice of transforms in phase diagrams', *Review of Economic Studies,* **37**(3), 441–5.

DASGUPTA, P. S. (1969) 'Optimum growth when capital is non-transferable', *Review of Economic Studies,* **36**(1), 77–88.

———— and G. M. HEAL (1974) 'The optimal depletion of exhaustible resources', *Review of Economic Studies,* **41**, symposium, 3–28.

DENISON, E. F. (1967) *Why Growth Rates Differ,* Brookings Institution, Washington, D.C.

———— (1969) 'Some major issues in productivity analysis', *U.S. Survey of Current Business,* May, supplement.

DIAMOND, P. A. (1965a) 'Disembodied technical change in a two-sector model', *Review of Economic Studies,* **32**(2), 161–8.

———— (1965b) 'National debt in a neoclassical growth model', *American Economic Review,* **55**(5), 1126–50.

———— and D. L. McFADDEN (1965) 'Identification of the elasticity of substitution and the bias of technical change: an impossibility theorem', working paper, University of California, Berkeley, Cal.

DIEWERT, W. E. (1974) 'Applications of duality theory', in M. D. Intriligator and D. A. Kendrick (eds.) *Frontiers of Quantitative Economics*, Vol. II, North-Holland, Amsterdam.

DIXIT, A. K. (1973a) 'Models of dual economies', in J. A. Mirrlees and N. H. Stern (eds.) (1973).

———— (1973b) 'Comparative dynamics from the point of view of the dual', in M. Parkin (ed.) *Essays in Modern Economics*, Longmans, London.

———— (1976) *Optimization in Economic Theory*, Oxford University Press.

————, J. A. MIRRLEES and N. H. STERN (1975) 'Optimum saving with economies of scale', *Review of Economic Studies*, 42(3), 303–25.

DOMAR, E. (1946) 'Capital expansion, rate of growth and unemployment', *Econometrica*, 14(2), 137–47, reprinted in Sen (ed.) (1970), 65–77.

DORFMAN, R., P. A. SAMUELSON and R. M. SOLOW (1958) *Linear Programming and Economic Analysis*, McGraw-Hill, New York.

DRANDAKIS, E. M. (1963) 'Factor substitution in the two-sector growth model', *Review of Economic Studies*, 30(2), 217–28.

ELTIS, W. A. (1973) *Growth and Distribution*, Macmillan, London.

ENCARNACION, J. (1965) 'On instability in the sense of Harrod', *Economica*, 32(3), 330–7.

FARRELL, M. J. (1959) 'The convexity assumption in the theory of competitive markets', *Journal of Political Economy*, 67(4), 377–91.

FISCHER, S. (1972) 'Keynes-Wicksell and neo-classical models of money and growth', *American Economic Review*, 62(5), 880–90.

FOLEY, D. K. and M. SIDRAUSKI (1971) *Monetary and Fiscal Policy in a Growing Economy*, Macmillan, New York.

FRIEDMAN, M. (1966) *Price Theory*, rev. ed., Aldine, Chicago.

GALE, D. (1960) *The Theory of Linear Economic Models*, McGraw-Hill, New York.

GRANDMONT, J-M. (1970) *On the Temporary Competitive Equilibrium*, Ph. D. Thesis, University of California, Berkeley, Cal.

———— and G. LAROQUE (1974) 'On temporary Keynesian equilibria', working paper, CEPREMAP, Paris, to appear in *Review of Economic Studies*.

HAHN, F. H. (1965) 'On two-sector growth models', *Review of Economic Studies*, 32(4), 339–46, reprinted in Sen (ed.) (1970), 281–92.

———— (1966) 'Equilibrium dynamics with heterogeneous capital goods', *Quarterly Journal of Economics*, 80(4), 633–46.

———— (1969) 'On money and growth', *Journal of Money, Credit and Banking*, 1(2), 172–87.

———— (1973) 'On some equilibrium paths', in Mirrlees and Stern (ed.) (1973).

———— and R. C. O. MATTHEWS (1965) 'The theory of economic growth: a survey', in *Surveys of Economic Theory*, Vol. II, Macmillan, London.

HALL, R. E. (1967) 'Speculation in assets which last for ever', working paper, M.I.T., Cambridge, Mass.

———— (1968) 'Technical change and capital from the point of view of the dual', *Review of Economic Studies*, 35(1), 35–46.

———— (1969) 'Consumption taxes versus income taxes: implications for economic growth', *Proceedings of the Sixty-First National Tax Conference*, National Tax Association, Columbus, Ohio.

———— (1973) 'The specification of technology with several kinds of output', *Journal of Political Economy*, 81(4), 878–92.

HAMMOND, P. J. and J. A. MIRRLEES (1973) 'Agreeable plans', in Mirrlees and Stern (eds.) (1973).

HARCOURT, G. C. (1969) 'Some Cambridge controversies in the theory of capital', *Journal of Economic Literature,* 7(2), 369–405.

——— and N. F. LAING (eds.) (1971) *Capital and Growth*, Penguin Books, Harmondsworth, Middx.

HARROD, R. F. (1939) 'An essay in dynamic theory', *Economic Journal,* 49(1), 14–33, reprinted in Sen (ed.) (1970), 43–64.

HATTA, T. (1975) 'The paradox in capital theory and complementarity of inputs', *Review of Economic Studies*, forthcoming.

HEAL, G. M. (1973) *The Theory of Economic Planning*, North-Holland, Amsterdam.

——— (1975) 'The depletion of exhaustible resources', in M. Parkin and R. Nobay (eds.) *Contemporary Issues in Economics*, Manchester University Press.

HENDERSON, J. M. and R. E. QUANDT (1971) *Microeconomic Theory*, 2nd ed., McGraw-Hill, New York.

HICKS, J. R. (1946) *Value and Capital*, 2nd ed., Clarendon Press, Oxford.

——— (1965) *Capital and Growth*, Clarendon Press, Oxford.

——— (1969) *A Theory of Economic History*, Oxford University Press.

HOLMES, O. W. (1857–8) 'The deacon's masterpiece', reprinted in *The oxford Book of American Verse*, Oxford University Press, pp. 194–7.

HOTELLING, H. (1925) 'A general mathematical theory of depreciation', *Journal of the American Statistical Association,* 20, 340–53, reprinted in Parker and Harcourt (eds.) (1969).

——— (1931) 'The economics of exhaustible resources', *Journal of Political Economy,* 39(2), 137–75.

INGHAM, A. and P. SIMMONS (1975) 'Natural resources and growing population', *Review of Economic Studies,* 42(2), 191–206.

JONES, R. W. (1965) 'The structure of simple general equilibrium models', *Journal of Political Economy,* 73(4), 557–72.

JORGENSON, D. W. (1963) 'Capital theory and investment behaviour', *American Economic Review,* 53, Papers and Proceedings, 247–59.

——— (1966) 'The embodiment hypothesis', *Journal of Political Economy,* 74(1), 1–17.

——— (1971) 'Econometric studies of investment behaviour', *Journal of Economic Literature,* 9(4), 1111–47.

——— and Z. GRILICHES (1967) 'The explanation of productivity change', *Review of Economic Studies,* 34(3), 249–83, reprinted with Denison (1969), and in Sen (ed.) (1970), 420–73.

KAHN, R. F. (1959) 'Exercises in the analysis of growth', *Oxford Economic Papers,* 11(2), 143–56, reprinted in Sen (ed.) (1970), 141–57.

KALDOR, N. (1955) 'Alternative theories of distribution', *Review of Economic Studies,* 23(2), 83–100, part reprinted with some changes in Sen (ed.) (1970), 81–91.

——— (1972) 'The irrelevance of equilibrium economics', *Economic Journal,* 82(4), 1237–55.

——— and J. A. MIRRLEES (1962) 'A new model of economic growth', *Review of Economic Studies,* 29(3), 174–92, reprinted in Sen (ed.) (1970), 343–66.

KALECKI, M. (1965) *Theory of Economic Dynamics*, 2nd ed., Allen and Unwin, London.

KAY, J. A. and J. A. MIRRLEES (1975) 'The desirability of resource depletion', in D. Pearce (ed.) *Economics of Natural Resource Depletion*, Macmillan, London.

KEMP, M. C. (1969) *The Pure Theory of International Trade and Investment*, Prentice-Hall, Englewood Cliffs, N.J.

KENNEDY, C. (1964) 'Induced bias in innovation and the theory of distribution', *Economic Journal*, 74(3), 541–7.

———— and A. P. THIRLWALL (1973) 'Technical progress', in *Surveys of Applied Economics*, Vol. I, Macmillan, London.

KOOPMANS, T. C. (1967) 'Objectives, constraints and outcomes in optimal growth', *Econometrica*, 35(1), 1–15.

KREGEL, J. A. (1971) *Rate of Profit, Distribution and Growth*, Macmillan, London.

LANCASTER, K. J. (1969) *Introduction to Modern Microeconomics*, Rand McNally, Chicago.

LEIJONHUFVUD, A. (1968) *On Keynesian Economics and the Economics of Keynes*, Oxford University Press.

LEVHARI, D. and D. PATINKIN (1968) 'The role of money in a simple growth model', *American Economic Review*, 58(4), 713–53.

———— and E. SHESHINSKI (1967) 'On the sensitivity of the level of output to savings', *Quarterly Journal of Economics*, 81(3), 524–8.

LITTLE, I. M. D. and J. A. MIRRLEES (1974) *Project Appraisal and Planning for Developing Countries*, Heinemann, London.

LUTZ, F. A. and D. C. HAGUE (eds.) (1961) *The Theory of Capital*, Macmillan, London.

McFADDEN, D. L. (1973) 'On the existence of optimal development programmes in infinite horizon economies', in Mirrlees and Stern (eds.) (1973).

MALINVAUD, E. (1953) 'Capital accumulation and the efficient allocation of resources', *Econometrica*, 21(3), 233–68, reprinted with correction in K. J. Arrow and T. Scitovsky (eds.) *Readings in Welfare Economics*, Irwin, Chicago.

———— (1960) 'The analogy between atemporal and intertemporal theories of resource allocation', *Review of Economic Studies*, 28(2), 143–60.

———— (1972) *Lectures on Microeconomic Theory*, North-Holland, Amsterdam.

MANNE, A. S. (1974) 'Waiting for the breeder', *Review of Economic Studies*, 41, symposium, 47–65.

———— et al. (1967) *Investment for Capacity Expansion*, M.I.T. Press, Cambridge, Mass.

MARRIS, R. L. (1972) 'Why economics needs a theory of the firm', *Economic Journal*, 82, special issue, 321–52.

———— and A. WOOD (eds.) (1971) *The Corporate Economy*, Macmillan, London.

MATTHEWS, R. C. O. (1964a) 'Some aspects of postwar growth in the British economy in relation to historical experience', reprinted in R. Floud (ed.) *Essays in Quantitative Economic History*, Clarendon Press, Oxford, 1974.

———— (1964b) 'The new view of investment: comment', *Quarterly Journal of Economics*, 78(1), 164–72.

MEADE, J. E. (1962) *A Neo-classical Theory of Economic Growth*, Allen and Unwin, London.

———— (1966a) 'The outcome of the Pasinetti process', *Economic Journal,*
76(1), 161–5, reprinted in Harcourt and Laing (eds.) (1971), 289–94.
———— (1966b) 'Life-cycle savings, inheritance and economic growth', *Review
of Economic Studies,* 33(1), 61–78.
MEADOWS, D. H. *et al.* (1972) *The Limits to Growth,* Universe Books, New
York.
MIRRLEES, J. A. (1967) 'Optimum growth when technology is changing',
Review of Economic Studies, 34(1), 95–124.
———— (1974) 'Optimum accumulation under uncertainty', in J. H. Dreze (ed.)
Allocation Under Uncertainty, Macmillan, London.
———— (1975) 'Indeterminate growth theory', working paper, Nuffield College,
Oxford.
———— and N. H. STERN (eds.) (1973) *Models of Economic Growth,*
Macmillan, London.
NAGATANI, K. (1969) 'A monetary growth model with variable employment',
Journal of Money, Credit and Banking, 1(2), 188–206.
NELSON, R. R. and S. G. WINTER, Jr. (1974) 'Neoclassical vs. evolutionary
theories of the firm', *Economic Journal,* 84(4), 886–905.
NERLOVE, M. (1967) 'Recent empirical studies of the C.E.S. and related
production functions', in M. Brown (ed.) *The Theory and Empirical Analysis
of Production,* National Bureau of Economic Research, New York.
NORDHAUS, W. D. (1969) *Invention, Growth and Welfare,* M.I.T. Press,
Cambridge, Mass.
———— (1973a) 'World dynamics: measurement without data', *Economic
Journal,* 83(4), 1156–83.
———— (1973b) 'The allocation of energy resources', *Brookings Papers on
Economic Activity,* 1973(3), 529–70.
———— and J. TOBIN (1972) 'Is growth obsolete?' in *Economic Research:
Retrospect and Prospect: V,* National Bureau of Economic Research, New
York.
PARKER, R. H. and G. C. HARCOURT (eds.) (1969) *Readings in the Concept
and Measurement of Income,* Cambridge University Press.
PASINETTI, L. L. (1962) 'Rate of profit and income distribution in relation to
the rate of economic growth', *Review of Economic Studies,* 29(4), 267–79,
reprinted in Sen (ed.) (1970), 92–111.
PHELPS, E. S. (1961) 'The Golden Rule of accumulation: a fable for growthmen',
American Economic Review, 51(4), 638–43, reprinted in Sen (ed.) (1970),
193–200.
———— (1962) 'The new view of investment', *Quarterly Journal of Economics,*
76(4), 548–67.
———— (1963) 'Substitution, fixed proportions, growth and distribution',
International Economic Review, 4(3), 265–88.
———— *et al.* (1970) *Microeconomic Foundations of Employment and Inflation
Theory,* Norton, New York.
PITCHFORD, J. D. (1974) *Population in Economic Growth,* North-Holland,
Amsterdam.
PRATTEN, C. F. (1971) *Economies of Scale in Manufacturing Industry,*
Cambridge University Press.
RADNER, R. (1968) 'Competitive equilibrium under uncertainty', *Econometrica,*
36(1), 31–58.

RAMANATHAN, R. (1973) 'Adjustment time in the two-sector model with fixed coefficients', *Economic Journal*, 83(4), 1236–44.

RAMSEY, F. P. (1928) 'A mathematical theory of saving', *Economic Journal*, 38(4), 543–59, reprinted in Sen (ed.) (1970), 477–95.

RAU, N. (1975) 'Two-class neo-classical growth', *Quarterly Journal of Economics*, 89(2), 344–5.

RAWLS, J. (1971) *A Theory of Justice*, Harvard University Press, Cambridge, Mass.

ROBINSON, J. V. (1962a) 'A neo-classical theorem', *Review of Economic Studies*, 29(3), 219–26.

———— (1962b) *Essays in the Theory of Economic Growth*, Macmillan, London.

———— (1965) *The Accumulation of Capital*, 2nd ed., Macmillan, London.

ROSE, H. (1967) 'On the non-linear theory of the employment cycle', *Review of Economic Studies*, 34(2), 153–73.

———— (1973) 'Effective demand in the long run', in Mirrlees and Stern (eds.) (1973).

ROTHSCHILD, M. (1973) 'Models of market organization with imperfect information', *Journal of Political Economy*, 81(6), 1283–1308.

ROWTHORN, R. (1975) 'What remains of Kaldor's law?', *Economic Journal*, 85(1), 10–19.

RYDER, H. (1969) 'Optimal accumulation in a two-sector neo-classical economy with non-shiftable capital', *Journal of Political Economy*, 77(4, part II), 665–83.

SAMUELSON, P. A. (1937) 'Some aspects of the pure theory of capital', *Quarterly Journal of Economics*, 50(3), 469–96.

———— (1947) *Foundations of Economic Analysis*, Harvard University Press, Cambridge, Mass.

———— (1958) 'An exact consumption loan model of interest with or without the social contrivance of money', *Journal of Political Economy*, 66(6), 467–82.

———— (1962) 'Parable and realism in capital theory: the surrogate production function', *Review of Economic Studies*, 29(3), 193–206, reprinted in Harcourt and Laing (eds.) (1971), 213–32.

———— (1965) 'A theory of induced innovation along Kennedy-Weizsäcker lines', *Review of Economics and Statistics*, 47(4), 343–56.

———— (1973) *Economics*, 9th ed., McGraw-Hill, New York.

SATO, K. (1966) 'On the adjustment time in neo-classical growth models', *Review of Economic Studies*, 33(3), 263–8.

SATO, R. (1963) 'Fiscal policy in a neo-classical growth model: an analysis of time required for equilibrating adjustment', *Review of Economic Studies*, 30(1), 16–23.

SCHUMPETER, J. A. (1934) *The Theory of Economic Development*, Harvard University Press, Cambridge, Mass.

SEN, A. K. (1962) 'On the usefulness of used machines', *Review of Economics and Statistics*, 44(3), 346–8.

———— (1963) 'Neo-classical and neo-Keynesian theories of distribution', *Economic Record*, 39(1), 53–64.

———— (ed.) (1970) *Growth Economics*, Penguin Books, Harmondsworth, Middx.

SHELL, K. (1967) 'Optimal programs of capital accumulation for an economy in which there is exogenous technical change', in K. Shell (ed.) (1967).

——— (ed.) (1967) *Essays on the Theory of Optimal Economic Growth*, M.I.T. Press, Cambridge, Mass.

——— (1971) 'Notes on the economics of infinity', *Journal of Political Economy*, 79(5), 1002–11.

——— (1973) 'Inventive activity, industrial organization and economic growth', in Mirrlees and Stern (eds.) (1973).

——— and J. E. STIGLITZ (1967) 'The allocation of investment in a dynamic economy', *Quarterly Journal of Economics*, 81(4), 592–609.

SIDRAUSKI, M. (1967) 'Inflation and economic growth', *Journal of Political Economy*, 75(6), 796–810.

SILBERSTON, A. (1972) 'Economies of scale in theory and practice', *Economic Journal*, 82, special issue, 369–91.

SIMON, H. A. (1959) 'Theories of decision-making in economics', *American Economic Review*, 49(3), 253–83.

SOLOW, R. M. (1955) 'The production function and the theory of capital', *Review of Economic Studies*, 23(2), 101–8.

——— (1956) 'A contribution to the theory of economic growth', *Quarterly Journal of Economics*, 70(1), 65–94, reprinted in Sen (ed.) (1970), 161–92.

——— (1962) 'Comment', *Review of Economic Studies*, 29(3), 255–7.

——— (1970) *Growth Theory: An Exposition*, Clarendon Press, Oxford.

——— (1974a) 'The economics of resources, or the resources of economics', *American Economic Review*, 64, Papers and Proceedings, 1–14.

——— (1974b) 'Intergenerational equity and exhaustible resources', *Review of Economic Studies*, 41, Symposium, 29–45.

——— and J. E. STIGLITZ (1968) 'Output, employment and wages in the short run', *Quarterly Journal of Economics*, 82(4), 537–60.

———, J. TOBIN, C. C. von WEIZSÄCKER and M. YAARI (1967) 'Neo-classical growth with fixed factor proportions', *Review of Economic Studies*, 33(2), 79–115.

STAR, S. (1974) 'Accounting for the growth of output', *American Economic Review*, 64(1), 123–35.

STARR, R. (1969) 'Quasi-equilibria in markets with non-convex preferences', *Econometrica*, 37(1), 25–38.

STARRETT, D. A. (1969) 'Switching and reswitching in a general model of production', *Quarterly Journal of Economics*, 83(4), 673–87.

——— (1970a) 'The efficiency of competitive programs', *Econometrica*, 38(5), 704–11.

——— (1970b) 'On some efficiency characteristics of a general production model', *International Economic Review*, 11(3), 506–20.

——— (1974) 'Principles of optimal location in a large homogeneous area', *Journal of Economic Theory*, 9(4), 418–48.

STEIN, J. (1969) 'Neo-classical and Keynes-Wicksell monetary growth models', *Journal of Money, Credit and Banking*, 1(2), 153–71.

STIGLITZ, J. E. (1967) 'A two-sector two-class model of economic growth', *Review of Economic Studies*, 34(2), 227–38.

——— (1970) 'Non-substitution theorems with durable capital goods', *Review of Economic Studies*, 37(4), 543–53.

————— (1974) 'Growth with exhaustible resources: I and II', *Review of Economic Studies*, 41, symposium, 123–52.

SWAN, T. W. (1956) 'Economic growth and capital accumulation', *Economic Record*, 32(2), 334–61, appendix reprinted in Harcourt and Laing (eds.) (1971), 101–24.

TOBIN, J. (1967) 'Life-cycle saving and balanced growth', in W. Fellner *et al. Ten Economic Studies in the Tradition of Irving Fisher*, Wiley, New York, 1967.

UZAWA, H. (1961a) 'Neutral inventions and the stability of growth equilibrium', *Review of Economic Studies*, 28(2), 117–24.

————— (1961b) 'On a two-sector model of economic growth', *Review of Economic Studies*, 29(1), 40–7.

————— (1963) 'On a two-sector model of economic growth: II', *Review of Economic Studies*, 30(2), 105–18.

————— (1964) 'Optimal growth in a two-sector model of capital accumulation', *Review of Economic Studies*, 31(1), 1–24.

————— (1973) 'Towards a Keynesian model of monetary growth', in Mirrlees and Stern (eds.) (1973).

von WEIZSÄCKER, C. C. (1965) 'Existence of optimal programs of accumulation for an infinite time horizon', *Review of Economic Studies*, 32(2), 85–104.

————— (1971) *Steady State Capital Theory*, Springer-Verlag, Berlin and Heidelberg.

WAN, H. Y. Jr. (1971) *Economic Growth*, Harcourt Brace Jovanovitch, New York.

WEITZMAN, M. L. (1970) 'Optimum growth with scale economies in the creation of overhead capital', *Review of Economic Studies*, 37(4), 555–70.

WINTER, S. G. Jr. (1964) 'Economic "natural selection" and the theory of the firm', *Yale Economic Essays*, 4(2), 225–72.

————— (1971) 'Satisficing, selection and the innovating remnant', *Quarterly Journal of Economics*, 85(2), 237–61.

YOUNG, A. H. (1928) 'Increasing returns and economic progress', *Economic Journal*, 38(4), 527–42.

Index

Accelerator, 175
Aggregation, 84, 93, 126
Asset demand, 118
Asset price, 16, 37

Behavioural theories, 190
Budget constraint, 117

Cambridge model, 4, 60–4, 177
Capital
  accumulation, 47, 50, 156
  deepening, 95
  heterogeneous, 142
  non-shiftable, 145
Capital gains, 38, 138
Capital intensity conditions, 126
Constant returns to scale, 17, 21
Consumption
  in steady states, 58, 136, 161
  optimum paths, 105–10, 166–71
Cost function, 19, 33–5

Depreciation, 38, 69
  due to obsolescence, 71
  one-hoss-shay, 69
  radioactive, 67
Discount factor, 41
Discounted present value, 40, 117, 188
Disequilibrium, 9, 61, 173, 186
Divisia Index, 83

Economic life of machines, 87–97
Economies of scale, 79–82, 186
Efficiency, intertemporal, 10, 59, 162
Efficiency units, 30–2, 74–7
Elasticity of expectations, 184
Elasticity of substitution, 19, 23, 76, 129, 150, 158
Envelope Theorem, 92, 95
Equation of yield, 39
Equilibrium, 2
  growth, 9, 46–8, 52–4, 130–3 163–5

intertemporal, 7
temporary, 9, 183–5
Euler's Theorem, 22
Exhaustible resources
  depletion plans, 152–71
  shadow prices, 153
Extensive margin, 86

Factor-price curve, 23
Factor shares, 22, 31
Factor substitution, 19
Fixed coefficients, 17

Golden Rule, 58, 110, 118, 136, 152
Growth rate
  actual, 175
  natural, 176, 177, 190
  warranted, 175, 177, 189

Hahn instability, 144, 180, 182
Harrod-Domar model, 46

Impatience, 102
Imputed prices, 11, 22
Income distribution, 22, 31, 60, 90
Increasing returns to scale, 79, 186
Inflation, 180
  expected, 182
Innovation frontier, 78
Intensive margin, 86, 92
Interest rate, 37, 101
  nominal, 177
  real, 177
Investment, 13, 40, 175–9
  with economies of scale, 188
Isoquant, 17, 19

Kaldor's stylized facts, 8
Keynes-Ramsey formula, 101
Keynesian unemployment, 61, 175, 185
Knife-edge problem, 175

Labour, 17, 19

Land, 149
Learning by doing, 79, 81
Local optimality, 103

Magnification effect, 126–7
Managerial theories, 188
Marginal productivity theory, 26
Markets, futures, 8, 101, 184
  spot, 183
  simulated, 11
Money, 177, 179–83
Monopoly, 186–7
Multiplier, 175
Multi-sector models, 146

Neo-classical approach, 10, 50
Non-identification theorem, 83
Non-substitution property, 134

Objective function, 104, 113
One-sector models, 44–66
Optimum policies
  existence of, 109, 156
  of capital accumulation, 99–112,
    141, 156–60, 166–71
  of resource depletion, 152–60,
    166–71
Own rate of return, 38, 102

Perfect foresight, 8, 101, 141, 155
  short-run, 39
Perfect futures markets, 8, 101
Period analysis, 12
Phase diagrams, 76, 105, 139, 143, 163
Production function, 25, 34
  Cobb-Douglas, 29, 53, 64, 74, 92,
    151, 160
  C.E.S., 29, 53, 159

Quasi-rents, 87, 186

Rawlsian justice, 115, 171
Rent
  economic, 85, 154
  for capital services, 16, 37, 85
Returns to scale
  constant, 17, 21
  decreasing, 149
  increasing, 79, 186
Revenue function, 36
Ricardian rent theory, 85

Rolling plans, 109
Rybczynski's Theorem, 128, 130

Saddle point, 107, 141, 143–4, 163,
  166
Saving, from capital gains, 138
  life-cycle, 116
  optimum, 111, 169, 188
  propensities, 45, 60, 65, 69, 122, 128
Shadow prices, 11
Solow-Swan model, 49
Speculative boom, 42, 121, 143, 155
Stability, 3, 9
Steady states, 7, 46, 52, 61, 63, 74, 88,
    132, 160
  comparisons between, 55, 64, 90, 96,
    133, 169
  degenerate, 53, 78, 132
  inefficient, 59, 119

Technical progress function, 79, 81–2
Technique, 30
Technology, 30
Technological change, 30
  disembodied, 73
  embodied, 73, 85
    clay-clay, 88
    putty-clay, 94
    putty-putty, 91
  endogenous, 78–82
  factor-augmenting, 30
    capital, 30, 93
    labour (Harrod-neutral), 30, 74
    land, 149
    resource, 162
  output-augmenting (Hicks-neutral),
    31
Turnpike theorems, 108
Two-sector models, 124–46

Unemployment, 48
Utility, 100

Valuation ratio, 188
Vintage, 85

Wage rate, 17
Wage-interest curve, 24, 96, 134
Walras' Law, 35
Warranted path, 175
Wicksell Effect, 136